INSIDE US SPY SATELLITES

COVER IMAGE *Andrey Armyagov/Shutterstock.com*

Dedication

Ut totus intelligence muneris
preteritus quod tendo.

This edition published in 2019 by:
The Rosen Publishing Group, Inc.
29 East 21st Street
New York, NY 10010

Cataloging-in-Publication Data

Names: Baker, David.
Title: Inside US spy satellites / David Baker.
Description: New York : Rosen YA, 2019. | Series: The geek's guide to espionage and warfare | Includes abbreviations and glossary.
Identifiers: ISBN 9781508186175 (pbk.) | ISBN 9781508186182 (library bound)
Subjects: LCSH: Space surveillance—Juvenile literature. | Aerial reconnaissance, American—Juvenile literature. | Aerial reconnaissance—Juvenile literature.
Classification: LCC UG1520.B35 2019 | DDC 358'.88—dc23

Manufactured in the United States of America

Originally published in English by Haynes Publishing under the title: US Spy Satellites manual © David Baker 2016.

THE GEEK'S GUIDE TO ESPIONAGE AND WARFARE

INSIDE US SPY SATELLITES

DAVID BAKER

Rosen YA
New York

Contents

LEFT The requirement for heavier spacecraft has forced the development of more powerful rockets. Here a Delta IV-Heavy launches an early warning satellite. *(ULA)*

RIGHT A KH-9 HEXAGON spacecraft on display at the National Air & Space Museum in Washington, DC. *(Dwayne Day)*

Chapter One

Introduction

We live in a violent world in which threats from extreme political, religious and ideological beliefs collide with the democratic rule of law, as well as the suppression of aggression on a personal or national level. Modern technology has provided numerous tools and devices to alert good people to the destructive violence of disruptive groups, intent on upending the rule of law and the lives of ordinary citizens.

OPPOSITE Destruction caused by the attacks on New York on September 11, 2001, will forever serve as a reminder that terrorists and those with malicious intent must be prevented from prosecuting their violent extremism. *(US Navy)*

ABOVE All branches of the US armed forces and its allies benefit from timely and accurate intelligence, vital for security and for maintaining a deterrent against aggression. *(US Navy)*

Spy satellites are a vital tool in the continuing fight against terrorism, against the machinations of potential enemies, in the fight against illegal escalation in the deployment of nuclear weapons and in the arms control efforts of major states to limit the spread of weapons of mass destruction.

It can be argued that they have contributed more to peace and stability than any other single technology, for they are an enabling tool in the bag of covert and overt security endeavors to neutralize the efforts of violent extremists – be they individuals devoid of any other power, or rogue states intent upon militarily aggressive policies against other countries.

It can also be said that spy satellites have done more than any other instrument of modern technology to support the doctrine of minimum force, as they characterize the nature of the threat, be it tactical or strategic, and allow proportionate use of military force rather than the indiscriminate employment of weapons and all the consequences of unacceptable collateral damage or overkill.

It is not the purpose of this book to analyze the many ways in which these separate uses and applications have been demonstrated throughout the last 60 years. Nevertheless, a few brief real-world examples scattered throughout this book will serve to illustrate the way this technology has played its part in helping to achieve, and greatly exceed, the expectations of individuals who played key roles in establishing a comprehensive net of spy and surveillance satellites.

Notes for the reader

The motivation for this book has been a desire to provide a history of US photo-reconnaissance satellites, including programs which failed to succeed, as an example of the effort made by those kept secret for several decades. The work of scientists, engineers, technicians and rocket scientists to build an infrastructure of factual information about the capabilities of foreign powers was unprecedented. It was prompted by a threat so real that it mobilized a generation of men and women to serve the cause of freedom and democracy in a way rarely seen in peacetime.

The efforts of these pioneers in space technology created a bulwark against aggression and a shield against propaganda and disinformation from potential enemies intent on mischievous deeds. Only now is it possible to string together the separate projects and programs to provide a coherent story of the technical and political challenges which faced these architects, defining new ways of gathering information about potential threats.

Today, in the 21st century, the challenges are no less great but the axis has rotated, and polarized groups of terrorists and dysfunctional states threaten free people everywhere in unique and unparalleled ways, alien to the generation who created the modern intelligence infrastructure after the Second World War. Their work today is no less important and in several ways more demanding than it was in the Cold War era. It rises above partisan politics and it serves the greater protection of the public at large; it is every bit as necessary as the much publicized armies, navies and air forces of the Western powers.

It is for these people that this book is written in the hope that they, who cannot speak for themselves, will be seen by honest and responsible citizens as essential safeguarders of constitutional democracy, freedom and liberty. For the story of the photo-reconnaissance and imaging satellites is the story of the "other half" of the national space effort, one which by necessity and definition has been shrouded in secrecy. As such it is a vital element in fully understanding the way the United States developed a world lead in space technology and engineering.

The book has retained original code names and program designations to preserve the context in which they were generated and it provides the reader with a contemporary political context for specific projects. In particular, it allows the reader to select specific periods and categories to track the progressive evolution of unmanned photo-reconnaissance satellites. It also embraces the major effort to place astronauts aboard orbiting stations in space – the Manned Orbiting Laboratory and the DORIAN program. This was a seminal turning point in Air Force attitudes to manned versus unmanned platforms and had a significant influence on the path of future developments.

By definition, the very latest imaging satellites are highly classified and very little information populates the public domain. Nevertheless, they are included to demonstrate the levels of sophistication and the magnitude of the effort under way today to keep alive the aspirations of those who founded the photo-reconnaissance satellite program more than 60 years ago.

David Baker

BELOW In an age where increasing numbers of countries are acquiring nuclear weapons, the need to know the intentions of potential adversaries has never been more important to prevent their ultimate use. *(Roberts Space Industries)*

Chapter Two

Steps to satellites

Spying is said to be the second-oldest profession and has always employed the latest and most effective tools to supplement the ability of humans to physically observe, from a distance or through infiltration, the activities of others. Human intelligence gathering (humint) is key to many aspects of intelligence, and today people are essential for data gathering, analysis and interpretation by whatever means is employed to gain the information in the first instance. But where intelligence-gathering tools are employed, humans will have fashioned them for the specific purpose of obtaining information.

OPPOSITE During the First World War balloons were used to lift baskets carrying army personnel with binoculars and radio-telephone equipment for directing artillery and reporting on the effectiveness of gunfire. *(David Baker)*

Over the last 150 years technology has allowed a dramatic expansion in those activities. In that period, and in order of introduction, intelligence gathering for reasons of national security and defense planning has been supplemented by the balloon, the camera, the airship, the airplane, radar, the rocket and the artificial satellite. Each has had its part to play in the maturation of humint towards space-based reconnaissance and surveillance, and science has played a vital role using technology to develop enabling tools.

The first example of this was the use of balloons by the *Corps d'Aérostiers*, set up by the French Committee of Public Safety in 1794, which went into action during the battles of Charleroi and Fleurus that year when France was at war against the coalition forces of Britain, Hannover, the Netherlands and the Habsburg monarchy. Their use was urged by Guyton de Morveau, supported by Jean Marie Joseph Coutelle and Nicolas Jacques Conté in developing a hydrogen balloon for this purpose. The first, *L'Entreprenant*, had a capacity of 10,950 cubic feet (310 m³).

Balloons were used in the American Civil War of 1861–65 for the purpose of spying on enemy positions. In fact, two British Army balloonists attached themselves to the Federal Army in 1862 in an attempt to persuade the British government that balloons could play a pivotal role in warfare. The American Thaddeus Lowe demonstrated the practical application of hydrogen balloons as they grew in size and capability. The *Union* and the *Intrepid* each had a capacity of 32,000 cubic feet (905.6 m³) and were capable of lifting five men aloft.

The British were greatly impressed by the

BELOW The first active use of balloons came during the Franco-Prussian War of 1870–71 when the leading figures trapped during the siege of Paris used them as a means of escape. Unfortunately for the occupants, the wind blew them straight into the ranks of the encircling army! *(David Baker)*

historic importance of intelligence gathered before and during a battle and quoted the example of Napoleon Bonaparte's disastrous decision to disband the *Aérostiers* in 1799. Had he not done so his forces would have had three hours' warning of Bülow's approaching Prussian Corps at the battle of Waterloo in 1815, significantly altering the odds in favor of a French success! The French would not resume the use of balloons for intelligence gathering until the Franco-Prussian war of 1870–71.

While both Union and Confederate forces in the American Civil War of 1861–65 employed hydrogen balloons for spying and gun-laying, like the French, the British were slow to take up aerial spying. Not until the Sudanese War of 1885 did the British take balloons to war. But progress had meanwhile been made in uniting the balloon with the camera. In 1883 an automatic camera was taken aloft by Major H. Elsdale of the Royal Engineers in tests in Nova Scotia, successfully obtaining photographs of the fort from the air.

Despite reluctance from disinterested officialdom in London, the Royal Engineers invested in balloons and deployed them during the Boer War, first at the battle of Magersfontein in December 1899 and later at a variety of locations. When the war ended in 1902 the establishment was fixed at five sections, but total strength was never sufficient to mount more than three balloons. Only gradually would interest in Britain transfer to the airship and the aircraft while in America its value had already been foreseen.

The first use of balloons in the American Civil War had been for map-making under the authority of the Union Army Corps of Topographical Engineers. Innovation and the pressures of war forced development of the first aircraft carrier, the USS *George Washington Parke Custis*, which was a converted coal barge adapted for carrying mooring balloons up the Potomac River. But the Confederates had their equivalent, the CSS *Teaser*, for the Confederate Balloon Corps, although their scarce resources resulted in few successful deployments compared to the Federal forces.

The next step was to liberate the balloon from the vagaries of the wind and to un-tether the lighter-than-air envelope from the ground and provide it with motive power to fly in any direction at any height, under the full control of a pilot. Fascinated by the emerging technologies of the American Civil War, Count Ferdinand von Zeppelin had been inspired by the balloons employed in gathering intelligence and returned to his native Germany emboldened by the possibilities – thus was the airship born.

Zeppelin's first airship, the *LZ 1*, took to the air on July 2, 1900, and French and British copies followed quickly but none were very successful. The first American airship flew in 1908, acquired by the Signal Corps, which would become the home of nascent aviation in the United States. While Count von Zeppelin inaugurated the world's first commercial air

ABOVE Balloons were used for spying and for providing intelligence information to the French at the battle of Fleurus in 1794, their first recorded use to support an army at war. *(David Baker)*

ABOVE A basket equipped for reconnaissance during the 1914–18 war, precursors to aircraft in the age-old craft of intelligence gathering, to which was added a new dimension by allowing spotters to see over the next hill. *(Nigel Foster)*

BELOW Represented here by the passenger carrying Zeppelin *LZ 27*, airships were used extensively for reconnaissance both before and during the 1914–18 war. Their eventual use for dropping bombs opened a new era in strategic warfare. *(David Baker)*

service and carried several thousand people before the outbreak of war in 1914, the military applications were not lost on this entrepreneur of flight. Salesmen toured foreign countries boasting of the reconnaissance spying capabilities they afforded, an application not lost on Britain and France.

In an age involved in an all-out arms race for bigger, faster and more powerful warships, control of the seas and oceans was crucial to the Imperial aspirations of Britain and Germany. As the world adjusted to the awesome technology of a new century, it was first through naval considerations that the battle fleets of the belligerent powers would arm themselves with the intelligence gathering capabilities of airships and airplanes. Just as the camera had provided balloons with eyes, new platforms in the form of winged aircraft would come to dominate the battlefields of the future, providing reconnaissance and gun-spotting intelligence.

After the first flight of the Wright brothers' Flyer in December 1903 the aircraft was slow in being adopted for military purposes, but the first fixed-wing aircraft were soon employed in the supporting role of "eyes and ears" for field armies. The world's first military aircraft was inducted to the US Army on August 2, 1909, as the Wright A. By 1912 military aviation had also emerged in Germany, France, Russia and Britain, with strong emphasis on naval support for the seafaring nations. Reconnaissance and observation of ships "over the horizon" were primary roles for seaplanes, flying boats and airships of the period.

It was in Germany, however, that the first signs of an integrated proto-intelligence gathering capability emerged. In May 1904 the German scientist Christian Hülsmeyer had demonstrated the principle of radar when his *Telemobilscope* was able to detect metal objects across a distance of 1.2 miles (2 km) through the applied physics of James Clerk-Maxwell. Hülsmeyer's device could not provide a measurement of distance between the detected object and the device transmitting the radio wave, but it was clearly the forerunner of an operational radar defense system developed by the British 30 years later.

On October 1, 1908, the German General Staff formed a Technical Section, which examined the relationship and interconnectivity between wireless telegraphy, reciprocating engines, airships and aircraft. Had Hülsmeyer's *Telemobilscope* been developed it would have given the German military a capability far ahead of its time, an integration of devices that would later form the pillars of an intelligence-gathering capability. Ironically, the diode was also invented in 1904 and the triode three years later, elements essential to the development of radio and radar. At the time nobody saw the full potential in these devices.

When war broke out in Europe in August 1914 it spurred development of photographic reconnaissance from the air, army cooperation being the first application of the land-based airplane while maritime reconnaissance was conducted from early development of the aircraft carrier and from seaplanes carried on ships. In numerous examples of their efficacy, aircraft proved their worth in gathering information that would underpin military action in this and the Second World War of 1939–45.

Air power came to have a special significance during the latter conflict and popular history has emphasised the role of the fighter, the ground-attack aircraft and the bomber. But crucial information vital to the prosecution of the war was attributable to aerial reconnaissance, sometimes prompted by humint and sometimes by previous aerial photographs. Intelligence about the development of German super-weapons such as the rocket programs underway at Peenemunde on the Baltic was crucial to slowing the pace of development. Likewise, absence of adequate information about the location of the Japanese Navy in December 1941 resulted in the pre-emptive attack on the US naval base at Pearl Harbor.

When peace broke out in 1945 the essential elements of the modern intelligence-gathering apparatus had been developed, the rocket being the last piece in the jigsaw of technologies which together would form the capability realized through the spy satellite. While an American, Robert H. Goddard, had conducted the world's first flight of a liquid-propellant rocket in 1926, it was the Russians and the Germans who did most to advance the state of the art with rocketry and missile technology. It was the German V-2 ballistic missile, adapted post-war into a tool for scientific research, which would take the first pictures of the Earth from space. Only one other element was necessary to provide a global surveillance capability: orbital flight.

ABOVE The epitome of fast photographic reconnaissance aircraft in the Second World War, a Supermarine Spitfire PR XIX powered by a powerful Griffon 61 series engine and displaying under-fuselage camera ports. *(David Baker)*

Before the advent of space-based assets, the value of reconnaissance and surveillance had become clear during the early years of the Cold War, when capitalist and communist countries sat on opposing sides of an ideological divide. The development of atomic, and later thermonuclear, weapons posed a threat to each side from potential aggressors. The need to identify potential targets well in advance of a possible conflict became crucial to the form of deterrence that emerged as each side squared up to the other through a series of proxy wars.

During the 1950s, sophisticated techniques employed revolutionary technologies to acquire airborne spy and surveillance capabilities. These led to dedicated aircraft, such as the Martin RB-57, a development of the English Electric Canberra that was first flown in 1949 and became Britain's first jet bomber. Employed on clandestine missions along the Soviet border, and sometimes into Russian airspace, the RB-57 ran the gauntlet of Soviet defense radars and fast jet interceptors. Other aircraft, such as the massive ten-engine Convair RB-36, made deep penetration flights over Soviet territory, flying far higher than contemporary air defenses could reach.

Prompted by these incursions, it was the widespread deployment of surface-to-air missile (SAM) batteries along the periphery of the USSR that led to development of the unique high-altitude Lockheed U-2, designed by Clarence L. "Kelly" Johnson to fly above the threat. First deployed on clandestine overflights of the Soviet Union in June 1956, the photographs these took helped to debunk (but only at the highest levels of security clearance) the bomber-gap myth that had the Russians in possession of vast bomber fleets ready at will to drop atom bombs on America and its allies.

Yet even before the U-2 made its first flight in 1955, the US intelligence community was planning to develop a series of spy satellites

BELOW A Martin RB-57D flew numerous reconnaissance sorties during the early years of the Cold War. A variant of the English Electric Canberra, it had a specially designed wing that is very distinctive from the B-57 seen in formation behind. *(USAF)*

that would overfly the territory of any country on Earth and avoid the political and military consequences to which the U-2 and its like were exposed. Such things appeared very advanced but they had been studied for several years, and now, with the development of large ballistic missiles that could be converted into satellite launchers, they appeared feasible.

When satellites became possible and the Space Age was born with the launch of Russia's Sputnik 1 on October 4, 1957, the camera and the application of radar technology would underpin a rapidly expanding capability for observing the Earth through various windows in the electromagnetic spectrum. None of this would be easy and the development path for spy satellites would be long and costly. But their value has repaid the investment many times over.

There is an adjunct to the story of intelligence gathering in the 20th century: the detection of signals and electronic communication, which would come to form a vital addition to optical and radar surveillance, creating the triad of technical capabilities upon which 21st-century satellite-based intelligence gathering stands.

ABOVE Designed to carry cameras high above the threat of anti-aircraft defenses, the Lockheed U-2 introduced this aircraft manufacturer to the black world of spying and its commitment to several decades of building America's spy satellites. *(USAF)*

LEFT Clarence "Kelly" Johnson (left) added the U-2 to his design portfolio of outstanding aircraft that propelled him to the pinnacle of aeronautical design achievements. He is seen here in conversation with Francis Gary Powers, shot down in a U-2 in 1960. *(Lockheed)*

Chapter Three

WS-117L

As the various technologies stimulated by six years of war, and a preceding period of modernization and scientific development, stimulated new concepts in science and engineering, novel methods came together in the aftermath of conflict to provide tools for intelligence personnel and their agencies totally unknown a decade previously.

OPPOSITE Launch Complex 14, used for the first three Atlas launches from Cape Canaveral and many subsequent flights, with the dome-shaped blockhouse beyond. *(NASA)*

RIGHT When the Second World War was coming to an end in Europe, and the conflict with Japan was working toward its inevitable conclusion, at Yalta in February 1945 deals were struck between Churchill (left), Roosevelt (center) and Stalin (right) that would seal the fate of Eastern Europe for the next 45 years. The Cold War was defined by mistrust and fear that fuelled a new arms race and the development of exotic air- and space-based reconnaissance and surveillance programs. *(USIS)*

The extraordinary advancements made in Germany between 1933 and 1945 bequeathed to the victors in war a rich harvest of science, technology and engineering that began to turn science fiction into reality. The very existence of the ballistic missile in the form of the V-2 made it in every sense a "wonder weapon," transforming the way military scientists and engineers viewed the future. As a wide range of new design concepts married to the jet engine provided aerodynamicists with blueprints for a new age of fast, unstoppable aircraft, the atomic bomb itself rendered past ways of deterring war largely redundant.

With the emergence of the Cold War, however, military chiefs in the United States looked with increasing concern at developments, known and suspected, in the Soviet Union. Plans began to emerge for space vehicles and satellite concepts capable of spying on the communist world and its vast war machine. It worried many military personnel that while politicians disarmed the West, communist Russia maintained a vast standing army only a few hundred kilometers from Western Europe. There was a determination to gain as much knowledge as possible about the USSR by gathering detailed information on what for outsiders was a closed country.

German and Austrian scientists captured at the close of the Second World War provided details about highly advanced aeronautical studies suggesting the possibility of supersonic and even hypersonic (above Mach 5) flight and rockets capable of delivering atomic weapons across intercontinental distances. Much of this was a total surprise to American military chiefs, who became intoxicated with the rush of possibilities laid before them. For many it was a steep learning curve, but for some it was the next logical step in warfare.

Nevertheless, the new research made available to British, French and American

RIGHT Offered employment with the Army in the United States, one of Germany's leading rocket exponents, Dr. Wernher von Braun, fuelled a euphoria over what was possible in missile and space exploration, encouraging the development of orbital systems for military purposes. *(NASA)*

scientists was fraught with technical challenges. While the theory of hypersonic flight, ballistic missile propulsion and orbiting satellites was well known the engineering principles required to transform them into reality was not, and the material required to fabricate them was as yet unavailable. Yet several German and Austrian research projects had already begun to open a window of opportunity.

While the achievements of the German rocket teams were well known, what had not been realized was how far advanced were the studies into projectiles capable of bombing America from Continental Europe and even to placing satellites in orbit. A key exponent of the possible, the V-2 scientist Wernher von Braun went to the US with a quiet assumption that all these things would become reality if only the necessary resources were made available.

When von Braun had first been interrogated in May 1945 he laid out a sequence of developments that would become possible given sufficient material and political support. The information he disclosed about existing plans fired the imagination of personnel at the US Navy. On March 7, 1946, it proposed a joint Navy-Army program to develop plans for satellite reconnaissance and surveillance. The Navy had long had a deep commitment to intelligence gathering and this fed right into their wired-up thinking. The offer of cooperation with the Army was not through altruism, but rather as a way of circumventing severe budget cuts.

In 1946 the Navy was challenging the Army for funds to develop the next step in strategic war-fighting capability, pitching its proposed super-carrier against the Air Force Convair B-36 hemispheric bomber. But with plans to bring the separate armed services closer together in a unified Department of Defense (DoD), cooperation was politically desirable. When presented with the satellite proposal the Joint Army-Navy Aeronautical Board of Research and Development met on April 9 and decided to consult Major General Curtis E. LeMay before reconvening on May 14.

LeMay was one of the new generation of aerial strategists who seized the radical weapons of strategic warfare and demonstrated their uncompromising use in devastating mass air raids on Japanese cities. Creating fire storms and conflagration incurring a greater number of casualties in a single raid than either of the two atom bombs dropped on Hiroshima and Nagasaki, the potential of the atomic age was not lost on LeMay who, very shortly, would head up Strategic Air Command and the largest bombing force in history.

LeMay wanted detailed information about Russian towns and cities, about the industrial heartland of the USSR and about the precise location of marshalling yards, power stations, train stations, airfields, arms dumps and depots. LeMay turned to Douglas Aircraft Company's RAND (Research and Development) department to get a briefing on the possibilities of assembling a space program.

Delivered to Air Materiel Command at Wright

BELOW The V-2 set the design trend for a generation of rockets and missiles that would come to underpin the space launch capabilities sought by the military in the 1950s, rockets that would build on the outstanding achievements made by the German rocket teams during the 1930s. *(David Baker)*

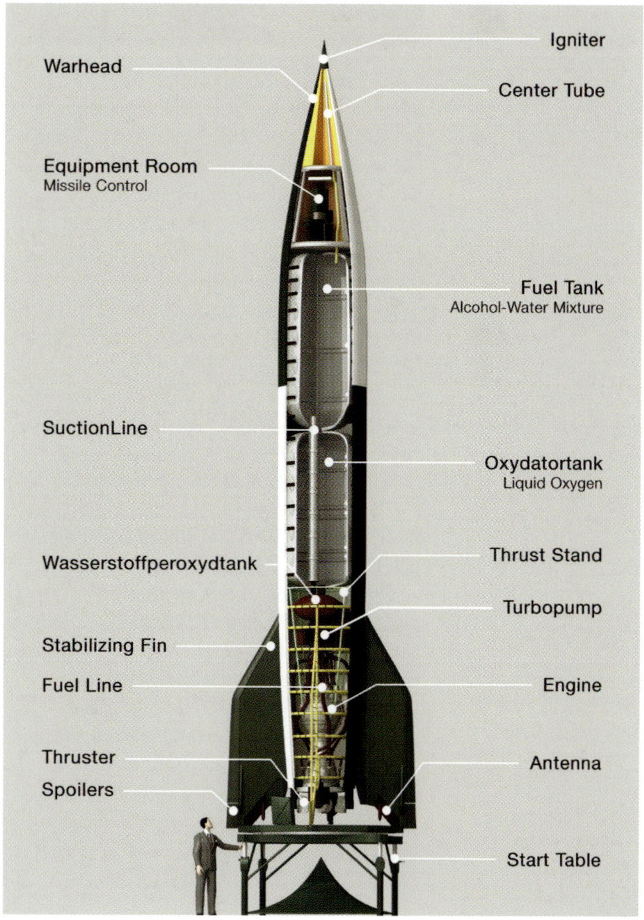

RIGHT **The V-2 comprised a cylindrical projectile propelled by the reaction of combusted liquid oxygen and alcohol fuels in a rocket motor with a thrust of 249 kN (56,000 lb) that provided sufficient energy to throw a 2,205-pound (1,000 kg) projectile 200 miles (322 km). This cutaway motor is in the Deutsches Museum, Munich.** *(David Baker)*

Field, Dayton, Ohio, on May 12, RAND's report, the "Preliminary Design of an Experimental World-Circling Spaceship" defined the problem, explained the necessary requirements to make it possible and summarized the functions such a satellite might possess. In addition to reconnaissance these included weather observations, communications relay between distant military units, missile guidance and their use as orbital weapons platforms. Mindful of its recipient, enthusiastic for all the many possibilities, it fired the imagination and concluded that: "We can see no more clearly all the utility and implications of spaceships than the Wright brothers could see fleets of B-29s bombing Japan...a satellite development program should be put in motion at the earliest possible time."

The initial RAND report sparked such interest that a second report was ordered in June 1946, titled "World-Circling Space Ship," with the aim of readying specifications and requirements so that selected contractors could prepare proposals. This study was managed by James E. Lipp, head of RAND's missile division. On February 1, 1947, it published seven papers in a multi-volume work on possible designs and functions, describing a television system combined with a Schmidt telescope.

Developed by the Estonian optician Bernhard Schmidt in the 1930s, this type of instrument is defined as a catadioptric astrophotographic telescope with a wide field of view (fov) and reduced aberration. As such it is ideal for observing and photographing wide areas with only minimal distortion, appropriate for the type of image and the required coverage, as envisaged in the mid-1940s. In astronomy the Schmidt was really coming into its own, and it had a proven record in all-sky surveys.

The report also described the different types of orbit that would determine the rate at which a satellite could complete full coverage of the Earth's surface, postulating a scan in a swathe 200 miles (320 km) wide on each 90-minute orbit. Since the planet would have rotated 1,500 miles (2,400 km) in the time it took the satellite to go once round the Earth, complete coverage would be accomplished in a week. RAND suggested that the satellite should be switched off when orbiting uninteresting areas, to conserve power.

This was a time of great convulsion in the US defense establishment, as the Navy and the War Department were preparing to be subsumed into the Department of Defense, with an independent US Air Force intent on achieving pre-eminence in the budget allocations. The National Security Act that formalized these events became law on July 26, 1947, and was enacted on September 17, 1947, the Pentagon at first being known as the National Military Establishment.

At this date no long-range ballistic missiles had been authorized and a decision was pending as to which of the armed services would get the job: the Navy saw it as their role to conduct strategic defense of the United States, citing their outstanding achievements in carrier-based strike forces as giving them priority; the new Air Force saw long-range bombing as the ultimate strategic deterrent. Both saw nuclear weapons as part of their respective arsenals. Satellites required large rockets to put them in orbit, and without even a long-range missile satellites would never get off the ground. Because of this, the RAND proposals ground to a halt and service interest evaporated.

But it did not die out completely. The formal assessment of the RAND reports did not take place until September 25, 1947, several days after the Department of Defense replaced the War Department. Three months later, in response to favorable recommendations, the Air Materiel Command agreed that a satellite was feasible but concluded that it was premature. A meeting of the Joint Army-Navy Aeronautical Board, which had survived the administrative shuffle, decided on December 19 that the Air Force should take up responsibility for satellite studies and the Navy withdrew from all further work on the concept.

By March 1948 the Research and Development Board encouraged the services to continue studying the concept but resisted the urge to assign specific responsibility to any organization. Further to this, RAND was given contracts to examine other aspects of satellites, and in early 1949 held a classified conference studying the psychological impact such a program might have on the USSR. By this date deep divisions had opened up between East and West and the Berlin airlift (June 1948–May 1949), which broke a transport blockade by land and river routes, was a mere foretaste of a bitter chill in the Cold War.

Nevertheless, in a rather unlikely scenario the satellite was viewed by the psychoanalysts as a potential tool for unseating the Soviet regime, by periodically disclosing information thus gained about the country to destabilize public enthusiasm for the closed system, drip-feeding disillusionment among the Russian people that, it was said, could bring about recrimination and possible purges in their political system. It is remarkable that the psychological reaction of a people to a potential enemy placing a satellite in orbit first was discussed at all – very telling, and quite ironic, since, as time would disclose, it was the Americans and not the Russians who were shocked into criticizing their leadership after the launch of Sputnik 1 on October 4, 1957!

Separate studies by elements within the military, and by RAND itself, led to press leaks and a flurry of reports appearing in public, fuelled by uninformed speculation and an over-excessive imagination. The fact that this work was veiled by a security blanket appeared to the public to give it credibility; surely if it was implausible it would not be hidden behind a security screen, opined the newspaper and TV news reporters. Speculation was encouraged further by a bland and noncommittal phrase in the 1948 First Annual Report of the Secretary

ABOVE Several V-2 rockets were sent from Germany to the United States where initial flights were launched from White Sands Test Range, New Mexico, as here on March 10, 1946, with the rocket raised vertically from its carrier-transporter. *(US Army)*

BELOW Designated Bumper-WAC, this V-2 rocket launched July 24, 1950, carried a WAC Corporal upper stage on top, essentially a battlefield missile adapted for carrying out high-altitude atmospheric experiments. *(US Army)*

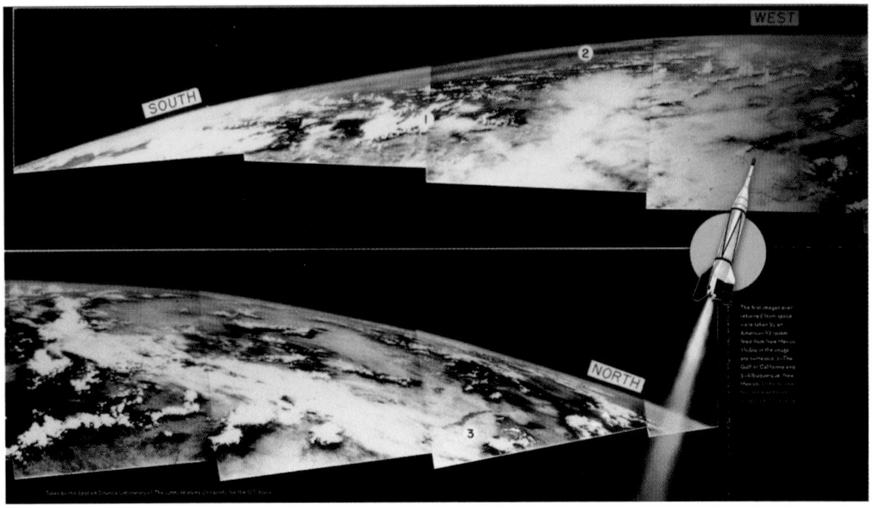

RIGHT Photographs from an altitude of 100 miles (160 km) for the first time during a Bumper-WAC flight on March 7, 1947, gave little indication of how eagerly the first pictures of the Earth from an orbiting satellite would be sought. *(US Army)*

of Defense in 1948 commenting on an Earth Satellite Vehicle Program.

Ever watchful for exciting leaks, Stewart Alsop wrote in the *Washington Post* on August 13, 1950, "all this is no mere fantasy…and is not to be treated as 'science fiction'…In the end President Truman will order work on this fantastic project if only for an old familiar reason – if we don't the Russians will!" The general public were incredulous that such possibilities might exist, or be thought feasible, and despite an increasing fascination with science fiction, and the ambitious concepts envisioning vast fleets of Mars-bound spaceships espoused by Wernher von Braun, few could accept these ideas as plausible.

The negative view held by most Americans forced the Air Force to put a cap on open discussion of satellites, spaceships and long-range rockets. Only a modest effort had been made, and that shortly after the war, to test possible developments of the basic V-2 rockets for extended capabilities and there was very little enthusiasm for pressing the Pentagon for

BELOW While space projects languished and awaited the development of new technology and improvements in rocket propulsion and orbiting satellites, conventional aircraft such as the Convair B-36 were used to routinely penetrate Soviet airspace on reconnaissance missions, photographing the ground below. *(USAF)*

approval to study them further. Instead, the Air Force focused on vast fleets of strategic bombers with atomic weapons, backed by cruise missiles such as Mace and Matador, leaving intercontinental rockets for a future push-button age.

The technology for very long-range rockets did not exist in 1950 and the Army, with von Braun guiding and influencing some of its thinking, pressed ahead with development of battlefield rockets, missiles that explored enabling technologies with better designs of rocket motor, new alloys, smarter guidance packages and increased reliability. Some of these designs would mature into the first-generation missiles employed by the Army and the Air Force, and during this nascent period in rocket development lessons were learned the hard way, with many failures and few successes. In any event, the Army and the Air Force were each left without a binding role, as each service conducted its own research pertinent to its own responsibilities and without a specific mandate.

Some stabilization of effort finally came with the announcement on March 21, 1950, by the Secretary of Defense, Louis Johnson, that on the recommendation of the Joint Chiefs of Staff the US Air Force would have responsibility for long-range missiles. At last, with a defined role to fill, the Air Force had a clear path forward for developing both the technologies required for long-range rocketry, ensuring the capability to mount a space program, and the satellite it had sought since 1946. But the desires of the Air Force were far removed from those of the Department of Defense, for there was still considered to be a wall of technical obstacles to both an intercontinental ballistic missile and a satellite capability.

Many studies conducted in those four years had established the viability of what was informally known as a Satellite Intelligence System. The Advanced Reconnaissance System (ARS) that emerged from the RAND studies concluded that a reconnaissance satellite was feasible but that its use as a weapons carrier was not. The mission was now more focused and the objective a lot clearer – the Air Force could pursue advanced studies in long-range rocketry and begin to define a workable satellite program.

In 1950 the Research and Development Board tasked the Air Force with examining the possibility of developing an artificial Earth-orbiting satellite for such a purpose.

LEFT General Curtis LeMay brought his experience from bombing raids on Japan during 1944 and 1945 to bear on the challenges posed by a nuclear-armed enemy during the Cold War, shaping the USAF Strategic Air Command into a finely tuned force in constant readiness. Sceptical at first, his eventual support for space projects would be key to their development. *(USAF)*

BELOW As the Cold War set in, Russia raised the threat level when it closed access to West Berlin to ground and water (canal) transportation, hoping to starve the West Berliners into pressurising the Allies for concessions. The only route into the former capital of a now-divided Germany was by air. *(David Baker)*

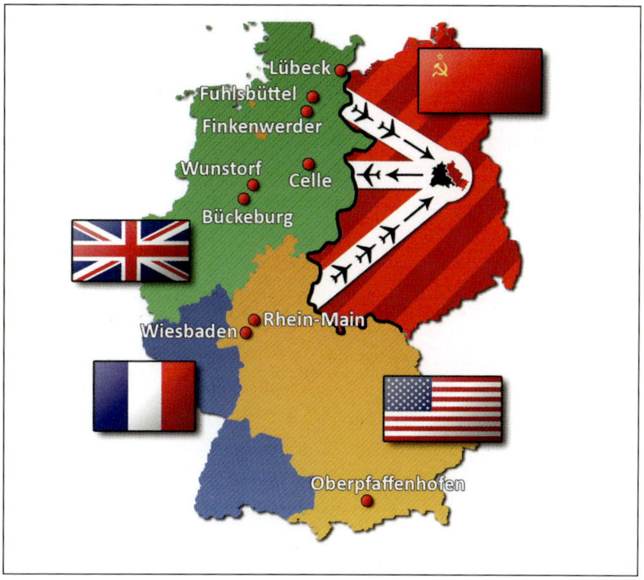

ABOVE **The Berlin airlift lasted 11 months from June 1948 but it broke the blockade imposed by the Russians and stiffened a resolve to intensify intelligence-gathering capabilities from the air. Here, C-47 cargo planes offload supplies at Tempelhof Airport.** *(David Baker)*

BELOW **A year after the Berlin blockade, communist forces assisted by Russia invaded South Korea, and the United Nations asked the US and its allies to send military forces to liberate the country. The need for surveillance and detailed intelligence about enemy forces had never been more acute.** *(NATO)*

Acting upon this, the Air Staff issued a formal report (RAND-217) in April 1951 and study contracts were awarded to RCA (for examining the feasibility of a television system), North American Aviation (for attitude control systems), Bendix Aviation, Frederick Flader, Allis-Chalmers and Virto Corporation for research into possible nuclear power sources.

Based on extensive experience with operating photographic reconnaissance units during the Second World War, the Air Force had made great progress with the science of imaging technology and this served as a benchmark for defining the requirements of a space-based system. What was not known were the challenges ahead in designing a system to accommodate the very high speed of the satellite and the fixed targets on the surface of the Earth. However, basic principles of resolution and target discrimination remained firmly within the realm of physics and the technology of optical systems.

Defining intelligence

Several discriminating levels of intelligence call for sequentially increased levels of resolution, including detection, general identification, precise identification, description, and technical intelligence.

The degree of resolution required to fill each of these levels differs according to the target. *Detection* requires determination of a general type or class of object, while *general identification* requires the analyst to be able to decide on the type of target observed. *Precise identification* allows identification of "known" targets within a matrix of other "known" types, and *description* provides detail for determining the dimensions of a target, proportionality of shape and the general layout or configuration of a building or a surface feature. *Technical intelligence* would provide a resolution sufficient to identify specific types of weapon and equipment or to identify specific military units, even the identifying features of unit markings on individual vehicles, ships or aircraft.

Most early studies conducted by RAND approached the problem with a required resolution base necessary to justify a space-based system. In military terms, a resolution of 100 feet (30 m) would allow the detection of ports and harbors, coasts and beach landing zones, urban areas discriminated from rural zones and the observation of surfaced submarines. But for general identification purposes only urban versus rural and terrain types would be achieved at this level. RAND believed it would be possible to get the resolution down to at least 20 feet (6.1 m), enabling precise identification of ports and harbors, railroad yards and workshops.

Several events conspired to put in place the stepping stones to both an intercontinental ballistic missile (ICBM) and a military space program. On June 24, 1950, North Korean troops invaded South Korea and began the first major proxy conflict of the Cold War. The desire for intelligence information, not only on the Chinese communist activities but those of the Soviet Union too, accelerated the pace of development for intrusive overflights to evaluate the level of military build-up and to increase the scale and direction of internal activity.

Just before the start of the Korean War a bizarre programme began involving camera-carrying balloons released in northern latitudes during winter months when the high-altitude westerlies would blow them across the USSR, a distance of 5,000–10,000 miles (8,000–16,000 km) in eight to ten days for recovery in the north-west Pacific Ocean. An ambitious plan to launch an estimated 2,500 balloons was set down under a program given the code name GENETRIX. By 1952, after faltering performance, the program was reorganized, given better funding and formally identified as WS-119L.

Operating under the cover story that it was part of a worldwide effort to study weather patterns, not until January 10, 1956, was the first operational balloon launched, but the program ground to a halt on February 6 as a result of formal protests from the Soviet Union. Nevertheless, of the 512 balloons released, the Americans recovered 54 payloads from which they obtained photographs covering 1,116,449 square miles (2,891,603 km^2) of Sino-Soviet territory. GENETRIX and the U-2 spy-plane (CIA code-named AQUATONE), which appeared in 1956, stimulated attempts to develop a truly invincible, and certainly more

ABOVE Aircraft attack a train with rocket projectiles during the Korean War. President Harry Truman handed the keys to the White House to Dwight Eisenhower in January 1953, the new incumbent pledging to end the conflict but resolving to never again be unprepared for a surprise attack. These elements in his presidency would invigorate a determination to broaden the intelligence-gathering base. *(NATO)*

BELOW In 1956 the Hungarian uprising hit the streets of Prague when ordinary citizens revolted against oppressive communist rule. The deployment of tanks in urban areas and evacuation by people fleeing persecution further hardened Western attitudes against the Soviet Union. *(USIS)*

RIGHT The communist revolution in China intensified as its rulers imposed draconian laws bringing death to millions of people and adding another threat to Western democracies as the Red influence spread across South-East Asia. *(USIS)*

sustainable, method for obtaining detailed photographic intelligence.

Right about the time GENETRIX was starting up, in 1950 the Air Force authorized further study of a satellite system and in April 1951 RAND delivered two studies, one of which advocated the use of a television system for broadcasting images to the ground. At this early date the concept of taking wet film images and returning them to Earth in recoverable capsules was pure science fiction. The second report focused on the use of satellites for weather pictures, which, it was said, could assist the military. At this date photographs taken from very high-altitude rocket flights using German V-2 rockets mated with a second stage known as the WAC Corporal gave reason to believe that this was a plausible proposition.

When presentations were made to the Air Force, what was confidently proclaimed as a viable resolution of 200 feet (61 m) from a satellite was totally unacceptable to photo-interpreters already working with very high-resolution cameras from high-flying aircraft. Ironically, in setting up a test experiment with coarse-grain film and a small lens flown at 30,000 feet (10,000 m) to debunk the idea, the detractors became ardent converts when, under simulated conditions, they were readily able to identify runways, bridges and buildings!

Based on these two reports the Air Force contracted RAND to study the various technical issues regarding reconnaissance satellites and to make recommendations on how to proceed in a research effort known as Project Feed Back. In March 1952 RAND pulled in the aircraft manufacturer North American Aviation to study guidance problems and three months later sought help from RCA to look at a variety of television systems, radiation sensors and various forms of delivery and projected reliability.

As said above, with the knowledge available at the time the basic Feed Back satellite was believed to have a life of at least one month and that alone dispensed with the wire-photo concept familiar to the news industry whereby film is exposed, developed and scanned, with the image then transmitted by electrical signal – in the case of the satellite, broadcast to the ground. The sheer weight of the film alone (1,500 lb/680 kg) was prohibitive. There was some discussion of a film return capsule using technology developed for ballistic missiles but the weight of the copper heat shield was also too great. Thus a pure television system was preferred.

But while some elements in the RAND/Air Force satellite study groups were highly supportive, others questioned the whole idea. The Air Force wanted reconnaissance for strategic strike purposes and were too obsessed with manned photo-reconnaissance aircraft to envision a future where satellites would do most of the imaging. For their part, the CIA – relatively new and formed out of the Office of Strategic Services – thought in terms of spies, secret agents and humint, not of technical wizardry with information flowing in electrons rather than secret messages smuggled out of dark places.

But there were a further two steps toward a clear path for satellite development, the first being the inauguration of President Dwight D. Eisenhower in January 1953, entering the White House on a promise to end the Korean War and to operate a more fiscally prudent economy. Part of that was to use science and technology to bolster Western defense capabilities by working smarter and less expensively on a range of clandestine assets, many of which were veiled in secrecy for decades after.

The second step was taken by nuclear

scientists in early 1953 when they made breakthroughs in the development of lightweight thermonuclear warheads for ballistic missiles, reducing their mass to such an extent that it became feasible to think of developing an ICBM capable of throwing nuclear warheads to targets in Russia or China. Trevor Gardner, Assistant Secretary of the Air Force, took heed of reports that the Russians were already developing long-range rockets and set up the Strategic Missiles Evaluation Committee (SMEC) in late 1953.

Chaired by Dr. John von Neumann, it held its first meeting in November that year and forwarded its recommendation in early 1954 that the US accelerate development of long-range ballistic missiles and increase its effort to produce an ICBM. At Gardner's request the Air Force set up the Western Development Division (WDD), located at Inglewood, California, commanded by Brigadier General Bernard A. Schriever. This would develop what became known as the Atlas ICBM, the first US missile capable of throwing a nuclear warhead from the United States to Soviet Russia.

On July 26, 1954, Eisenhower asked Dr. James R. Killian Jr. to head up a Technological Capabilities Panel (TCP) to determine whether there was a real and present threat to the United States from Soviet missile developments, one which might pre-empt completion of the Atlas ICBM and its deployment. Under Killian, in February 1955 the TCP concluded that there probably was and recommended that the Air Force fast-track development of an intermediate-range ballistic missile (IRBM) with a range of 1,750 miles (2,820 km). Named Thor, this was given to the WDD under Schriever – who was reluctant at first to take on another project, as they had already started work on a second ICBM called Titan as a hedge against problems delaying Atlas.

As it turned out, while starting late and albeit with a less challenging technology, the first flight of the Thor IRBM was only a few months behind Atlas but it would come to play a key role in the spy satellite program, would be deployed to the UK on the front line of the Cold War and would have an enduring life as a civilian satellite launcher, growing in size and capability to the present day.

LEFT Under the chairmanship of Dr. John von Neumann, in 1954 the Strategic Missiles Evaluation Committee recommended a major development program for strategic ballistic missiles to counter impending threats from the communist world. In this single move the United States began a surge in research that would revitalize flagging rocket programs. From this would emerge the satellite proposals underpinning a generation of spy satellites. *(LANL)*

LEFT General Bernard Schriever played a pivotal role in mobilizing a highly efficient program for the development of long-range and intercontinental ballistic missiles such as Atlas and Titan, with Thor brought along as a rocket that would be adaptable for launching satellites. *(USAF)*

Meanwhile, on May 22, 1953, the Air Research and Development Command was ordered to re-energize Project Feed Back. The ensuing report was submitted on September 8, 1953 and James E. Lipp, head of RAND's missile studies division, forwarded it to ARDC. It proposed full-scale development of a military spy satellite, and Project 409-40 was instituted by the ARDC in December 1953 for what was known as a "Satellite Component Study."

RAND continued to refine the feasibility of such a satellite and a final report (RAND-262) forwarded in February 1954 and dated March 1 endorsed its earlier conclusions. ARDC was directed in May 1954 to take charge of the effort and the Air Force issued a System Requirement (SR-5) on November 27, 1954. But there were still dissident voices, not least at the Department of Defense, where Secretary Charles E. Wilson was cool about the idea, reciting reports of a possible Soviet satellite with the comment "I wouldn't care if they did!" As described below, this was a very real threat to American prestige, although almost no one recognized the propaganda value of launching the world's first satellite.

Eyes in space

Because of opposition in high places at the Pentagon, not until March 1955, did the DoD issue its "General Operational Requirement for a Reconnaissance Satellite Weapon System," GOR-80. As then projected, the satellite would have a radio-TV broadcast system and a signals intelligence (SIGINT) instrument for intercepting Soviet radio communications, with operational readiness of an initial precursor system set for mid-1960 with a fully developed and operational capability by 1965.

In the spring of 1955 design study proposals were sought from selected contractors. In wishing to maintain maximum security only four companies were approached. Lockheed Aircraft Company, RCA and Glenn L. Martin Company agreed to submit proposals but Bell Telephone Laboratories declined.

The three contractors began their work in June 1955 and submitted results in March 1956, each presenting a distinctly unique approach to the requirement, with Lockheed being favored as the most attractive concept. Air Research & Development Command issued a system development directive, War (later Weapon) System-117L (WS-117L), on August 17, 1956, with Lockheed being awarded a contract on October 29.

At the same time, the Massachusetts Institute of Technology (MIT) received a contract for the guidance and orbit attitude control system and the Air Force Ballistic Missile Division (AFBMD) was given executive management of the project. Between January 1956 and October 1957 it established a development program and plan for the ARS with an office under Colonel Otto Glasser and Commander Robert Truax. WS-117L had been assigned a priority of 1-A and a precedence of 1-6 in August 1955.

While enthusiasm ran high, outside the tight confines of program development there was a wider world within which to set the general effort, and within the tight fiscal constraints imposed by the Eisenhower Administration, Deputy Defense Secretary Donald A. Quarles was reluctant to give the go-ahead while other activities were also drawing down funds; the work slowed considerably. A new first-flight date was set for no earlier than January 1960 with an expectation that the development of WS-117L should be continued "along conventional lines." But how would the Russians react to this sudden peeling back of the veil that shrouded so much of their activity?

In 1955 another program came along that would do much to legitimize the "overflight"

BELOW Known at first as the Visual Reconnaissance Model, this Lockheed proposal for WS-117L based an orbiting observation system on a rocket stage powered by a motor from the Convair B-58 Hustler. Eventually known as Agena, this stage would be the basic platform on which generations of spy satellites would fly. *(Lockheed)*

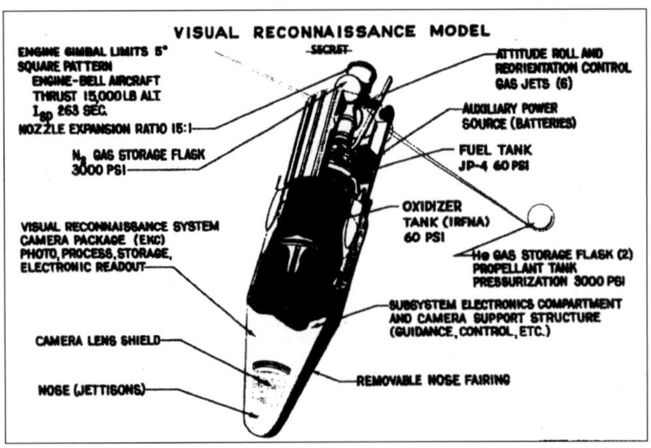

RIGHT A poor-quality reproduction from the then-classified proposal for an Agena rocket motor which adopted inhibited red fuming nitric acid (IRFNA) as oxidiser and JP-4 as fuel, which would comprise the propellant for the first Agena A. *(Lockheed)*

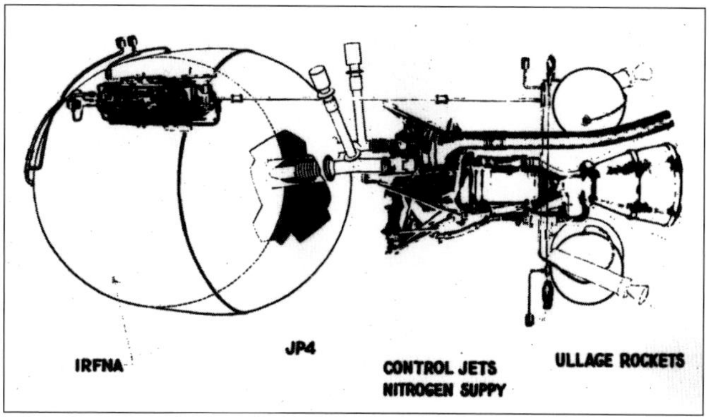

concept that had bothered the Russians for so long – plans for the International Geophysical Year (IGY) of 1957–58. On July 21, 1955, President Eisenhower had presented his "Open Skies" proposal at a Geneva summit also attended by Britain, France and Russia. In this, all nations would permit free access to overflights of their territory as a means of verifying levels of armaments, a step toward maintaining a verifiable balance of forces, the lack of which could trigger a conflict due to uncertainty as to force levels and mobilization.

As expected, the Russians refused to consider Eisenhower's proposal but he had achieved his objective in exposing the USSR, as he saw it, as a closed society disinterested in arms control. But this did nothing to crack open the shell of misinformation and obfuscation that left the West in the dark as to Russia's real military research and development program and just how advanced they were in rocketry, ballistic missiles and nuclear weapons development.

Ever the cautious military leader and consummate politician, even Eisenhower was unsure as to how the Russians would take the overflight of a military satellite; they had been routinely shooting down aircraft patrolling their borders and some aircraft on deep penetration reconnaissance missions had disappeared without trace. It would be several decades before the full scale of the spy flights became known, far in excess of the few flights made by the U-2 – missions which gave Eisenhower, by his own admission, several sleepless nights. He feared that while the Soviets would not be able to shoot down a satellite in space, it would so anger them that the repercussions might unleash hostile action on Earth.

There was good reason for the Russians not to want full disclosure of the real situation regarding their mediocre bomber fleets and flagging rocket programs, knowledge of which would only emerge over the next several years.

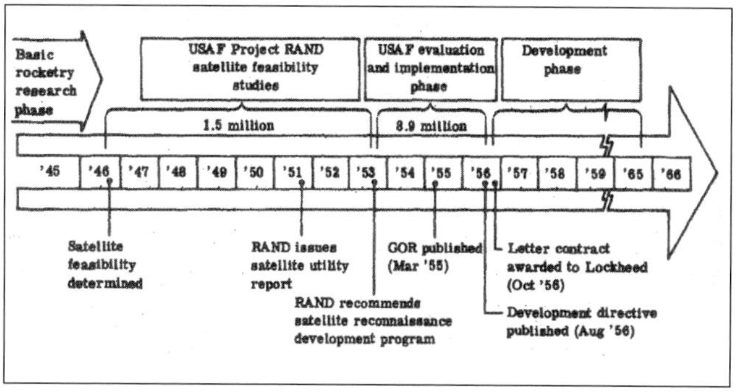

ABOVE Endorsed in April 1956, this full-scale development plan for WS-117L for an Advanced Reconnaissance System (ARS) assumed a protracted development period with fully operational flights not commencing before 1966. *(Lockheed)*

BELOW Proposals for spy satellites were linked closely to placing humans in orbit, using the newly developed Atlas launch vehicle. This proposal was linked to spy satellite capabilities, with the ARS planned to fly on this system. *(Lockheed)*

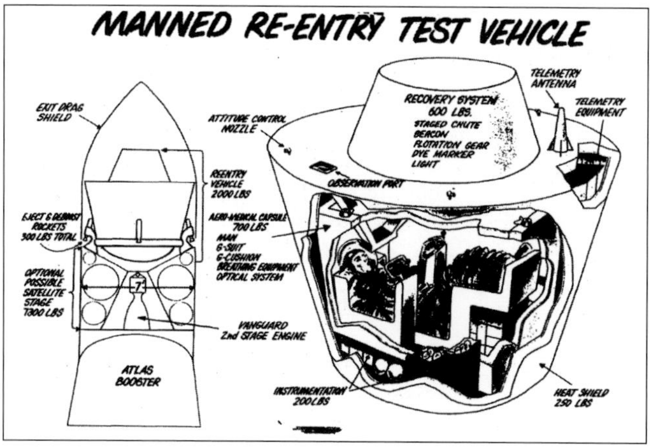

RIGHT Dwight D. Eisenhower publicly approved the plan to launch a scientific satellite for the 1957–1958 International Geophysical Year (IGY) while supporting a classified spy satellite programme to achieve a reconnaissance capability to better assess developments in Russia and China. *(White House)*

Much of their rhetorical bombast was not substantiated by the real situation hidden from foreign prying, although intelligence officials in America were still hotly debating whether the boasts were justified or not; they simply did not know – which is why there was such a drive to fly spy satellites.

But there was a way to ease Eisenhower's concern about the sudden shock of American overflights of Soviet territory by what the Russians would always interpret as a hostile act shrouded in espionage and intelligence gathering: making use of the International Geophysical Year. It was the Russians who, in 1954, first suggested that they would launch an artificial satellite in 1957–1958 and in January 1955 Radio Moscow intimated as much.

The Americans followed suit with plans for their own satellite, approved in an announcement issued on July 29, 1955. But the decision by Eisenhower to separate military rockets from those for purely scientific and peaceful purposes delayed the launch while new technology was adapted for a completely new satellite launcher called Vanguard. In effect a considerably modified Viking sounding rocket (one capable of "sounding" the upper atmosphere by sending a package of science instruments on a ballistic trajectory), Vanguard utilized a modified Viking for its first stage with a liquid propellant second stage and a solid propellant upper stage. The entire launcher was capable of placing a small satellite with a weight of 19.9 pounds (9 kg) in low Earth orbit.

Although a civilian project it was managed by the Naval Research Laboratory (NRL) despite protests from the Army, which was all ready to use its Redstone rocket to place a satellite in orbit. Redstone was a battlefield surface-to-surface missile with a maximum range of 201 miles (323 km). It was America's first indigenously developed military rocket capable

LEFT The Vanguard project was America's answer to claims from the USSR that it would launch an artificial satellite for the IGY. Using an existing Viking research rocket with additional upper stages, Vanguard was a small project with limited capabilities. *(NRL)*

of being used at theatre level. It was already modified to fly warhead re-entry tests as the Jupiter-C, and for this it had been equipped with two solid-propellant upper stages which, if supplemented with a third upper stage, could place a satellite weighing 24 pounds (11 kg) in low Earth orbit.

Developed by the Redstone Arsenal rocket team headed by Wernher von Braun, it would have been capable of launching an American satellite more than a year before the Russians flew Sputnik 1. In fact, on September 20, 1956, a Jupiter-C lifted an equivalent satellite payload to an altitude of 680 miles (1,100 km) and a speed close to that of orbital velocity. But any attempt to place an object in orbit was prohibited – Vanguard was to be the sole launcher for the International Geophysical Year and the White House was firm in its conviction that it must be accomplished using a rocket exclusively built for placing peaceful payloads in space.

As time would tell, this was an almost unique situation. For several years all launchers, Russian or American, were adapted or modified military missiles such as Thor, Atlas, Titan and Jupiter (a different rocket to the Jupiter-C) and certainly the Russian rockets were developed out of their military missile programs, for they never professed any discrimination between military and civilian categories. Not until the first NASA solid-propellant Scout rocket flew in February 1961 would another non-military satellite launcher after Vanguard be used to place a payload in orbit, followed by the Saturn I in January 1964.

But it seemed that the Russians, in leading the way with plans for a satellite during the IGY, had acquiesced to the inevitable and accepted the reality of an impending Space Age, preferring to use it as a demonstration of Russian rocket power that, while very slow to mobilize an operational ICBM, could at least boast equality of technology by being first to reach the cosmos.

None of this, of course, was known to Eisenhower, but as the months rolled by and it became apparent that the Soviets were serious about launching a satellite, fears of a backlash dissipated – for the Americans, their scientific satellite would legitimize the highly secret spy satellite; for the Russians their own satellite would be a spectacular propaganda tool. The National Security Council specifically regarded the decision by the Russians to launch a satellite of their own removed any possible backlash from an American flight.

Pressure to know more about the Soviet Union had been increasing in intensity since the Russians exploded their first atom bomb on August 29, 1949. Then, on August 12, 1953, less than eight months into the Eisenhower administration, the Russians detonated their own hydrogen bomb – a thermonuclear weapon of a type several thousand times more powerful than the bombs dropped by the Americans on Hiroshima and Nagasaki toward the end of World War Two.

This fed directly into concerns expressed by Eisenhower as to the gap between tests and

BELOW Development of military rockets for the Army resulted in the Redstone, designed by the team led by von Braun at the Redstone Arsenal, Huntsville, Alabama. Designed during the Korean War, it was an urgent response to worsening world tension and would itself form the basis for the launcher that would eventually place the first American satellite in orbit. *(DoD)*

ABOVE **The Redstone had a range of 200 miles (320 km), a design hurried through to provide the Army with a theater weapon which would be used in a range of variants for launching satellites and, in separate flights during 1961, of sending the first two American astronauts on suborbital ballistic flights to space and back.** *(DoD)*

operational deployment. As the supreme Allied commander in World War Two for D-Day and the subsequent liberation of Western Europe from Nazi occupation, he was well aware that the time between experimental tests and field-ready weapons was frequently many years. Exacerbated by belligerent statements and a degree of paranoia in US defense and national security circles, imagination filled in the gaps – of which there were many – and the need for definitive intelligence was never more urgent.

It was in this period that penetrative overflights with RB-47 Stratojets were stepped up and concerted efforts were made to develop a unique type of aircraft flying very high, unarmed, and (it was erroneously believed) unstoppable by the known Soviet air defenses of the day. As developments in re-entry technologies for nuclear warheads made great progress toward a family of survivable entry bodies, the science and engineering could be usefully applied to re-entry capsules carrying film. This idea was looked at again in the light of very new capabilities feeding back across from the ICBM program.

By the summer of 1957 RCA had decided that the original camera concept had to change to one in which a film-scanning system would be employed. First it would be exposed and processed automatically on the satellite and a light beam would transform the pictures into electronic signals that would be transmitted when the satellite was over a ground receiver. It was felt to be the best compromise between real-time direct transmission and film-return capsules plucked from the ocean after re-entry. In all of this the Air Force was defining a satellite concept for which there was no precedent and no certainties.

It was about this time that frustration over the languid pace of development with the WS-117L program spurred General Schriever to encourage a more rapid pace of development. Seasoned reconnaissance chief Lieutenant Colonel Richard S. Leghorn had been instrumental in honing acceptance of WS-117L through a mix of technical and engineering capabilities merged with political reality. When Leghorn left the Air Force he joined Eastman Kodak and in 1952 had concluded the Beacon Study examining the possibility of unmanned aerial reconnaissance combined with plausible cover stories about weather observations and scientific study. It was during this work that he caught the attention of General Shriever, at the time the assistant for Air Force development planning.

With fewer than six employees, Leghorn had founded the Itek (Information Technology) corporation from funding provided by Laurence Rockefeller and still had influence with Schriever, so much so that he was instrumental in giving the program the hurry-up when in mid-1957 Schriever tasked Colonel Oder, chief of WS-117L, to examine possible options to get an earlier flight date. All Air Force space-related programs had been tainted with the desire for absolute secrecy, requiring a shuffle among candidate projects to allay suspicion that they were associated with exo-atmospheric flight. Space was considered the futuristic ideal of dreamers and fantasists and even the Dyna-Soar space-plane had been couched in terms of high-speed/high-altitude flight goals.

ABOVE **Launch pads 5 and 6 which were used for many Redstone and Jupiter launches before flight tests with the more powerful Thor, Atlas and Titan.** *(NASA)*

Throughout 1957 General Schriever worked stoically to convince apathetic administrators in the Department of Defense that more money was needed to get the results desperately required to supplement, and eventually replace, U-2 spy-plane overflights with satellites. President Eisenhower was constantly worried that the Russians would shoot down one of these high-flying spy flights, and there was sufficient precedent with conventional aircraft lost while prowling the borders of the Soviet Union to warrant that concern.

The first annual revision of WS-117L was

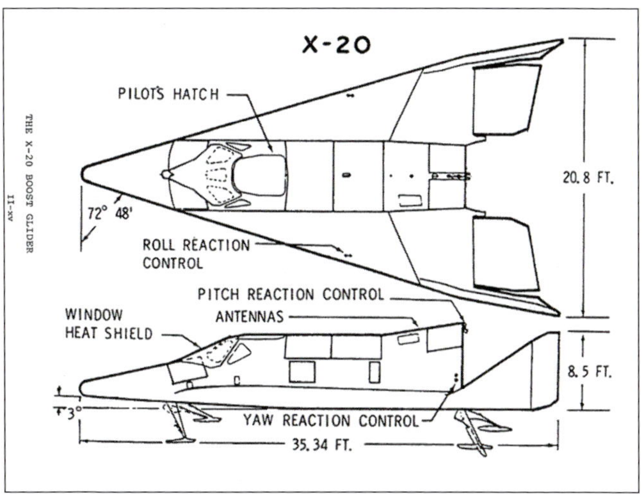

RIGHT **Considered vital for an Air Force presence in space, the Dyna-Soar spaceplane was to have pioneered human space flight for a wide range of military activities in space and the outer atmosphere, but the project was downgraded by the Kennedy administration and abandoned in 1963.** *(Boeing)*

ABOVE Various launchers were considered for the Dyna-Soar/X-20 program but the Titan derivative was eventually selected, a launch vehicle which was also chosen for the Manned Orbiting Laboratory but in a much more advanced configuration. *(USAF)*

conducted during April 1957 and it again became apparent that the budget for the following year would fall far short of the required level to achieve a first flight in 1960 and full operational capability by 1965. In mid-June Schriever met with the President's Board of Consultants on Foreign Intelligence Activities in an attempt to garner required funds. Against an estimated need of $46.9 million for the coming year, he was given a ceiling of $10 million at most, significantly below the level required for an initial flight in 1960.

Matters reached a head when General Schriever worked with Oder to define requirements for a significant change in the program. Within his office, Schriever organized a "Second Story" file constructing a plan to propose cancellation of WS-117L, organization of a "heavyweight" Air Force program to succeed Vanguard and a new spy satellite program under the CIA, technically managed by the Air Force Western Development Division. The WDD was officially formed on July 1, 1954, (at that time the beginning of fiscal year 1955) under Schriever, with headquarters in Inglewood, California, and specific responsibility for developing land-based strategic nuclear missiles. Its role would grow to embrace military satellites and launch vehicles, known today as the Space and Missile Systems Center (SMC) at Los Angeles Air Force Base, California.

When Schriever met with the president's intelligence board in June 1957 he told Lieutenant General D.L. Putt, Deputy Chief of Staff, Development, and Assistant Secretary R.E. Horner of the alternative plan, and Leghorn broached the matter with James R. Killian, the president's science adviser. Schriever took Dr. Edwin H. Land, the founder of Polaroid, to see Richard M. Bissell, assistant to Allen W. Dulles, director of the CIA. Over the next several months interest grew in merging plans with the "Top Story" concept and both WS-117L and a "scientific" Air Force satellite were proposed in parallel when Lockheed was given a notional start on developing the Agena rocket stage.

Meanwhile, the CIA covertly began preparing for participation in the alternative concept and, knowing such a project could not remain covert for long, Oder began working on a "weather satellite" story for public release in due course. Leghorn and Oder put together a plan for cancellation of WS-117L at presidential level followed by robustly secure covert development of a reconnaissance satellite system.

It was generally believed in top circles that the Soviets would probably launch a satellite quite soon, that it would be bigger than the Vanguard satellite but smaller than the WS-117L concept with Agena stage and that the "Top Story" concept would fit neatly into that sequence, maintaining US technological pre-eminence in world opinion while gathering useful data about the Soviet Union. Having experienced the Berlin airlift, the shock of the Korean War, the nuclear muscle of Russian atomic tests and a possible new arms race, prestige and intelligence gathering were hand-in-hand in this global race for loyalty from uncommitted countries.

RIGHT Walt Disney (left) and Wernher von Braun pose beside a model built for a science fiction film. Von Braun's ability to enthral his public did much to encourage public acceptance that space flight was just around the corner, while also inspiring a more serious approach from the conservative military, which frequently saw talk of spy satellites as remote from reality – the reverse was in fact true, military acceptance of this fact being impeded by the highly secret nature of the WS-117L program. *(David Baker)*

Bigger rockets

By early 1957 it was becoming apparent that the Russians were about to test the world's first ICBM, albeit a test rocket and far from an operational system. It was the creative product of a genius by the name of Sergei Korolev, who had been plucked from the gulag several years earlier after being incarcerated on charges of wasting public money by experimenting with rocket devices. A brilliant engineer, he persuaded Khrushchev to support the development of an ICBM, eventually known as the R-7 and then to use it to launch a satellite, hoping to beat the Americans and grab a propaganda coup.

The R-7 was far bigger than anything under development in the West, largely because the Russians did not have low-weight thermonuclear weapons and needed a more powerful rocket to lift their heavier war load. America's Atlas ICBM had a total lift-off thrust of about 1,468 kN (330,000 lb) compared with 4,537 kN (1,019,960 lb) for the R-7. Adapted as a launch vehicle, with the nuclear warhead replaced by a protective aerodynamic fairing enclosing a satellite, the rocket was capable of placing a weight of 1,100 pounds (500 kg) into low Earth orbit, far greater than anything the Americans could lift at the time, as witnessed by the 20-pound (9 kg) capacity of Vanguard.

Design work on the R-7 had begun in 1953 at the behest of Stalin. Russia was surrounded by potential enemies and to reach the United States their bomber force – such as it was – would have to fly right across the North Pole, or across Europe, through unfriendly skies. A ballistic missile could fly with impunity, far above

LEFT Sergei Korolev, imprisoned for wasting government resources on studying rockets for space travel, was released so that he could develop the USSR's first intercontinental ballistic missile, the R-7, and its first generation of satellite launchers. *(Novosti)*

the atmosphere, delivering its nuclear war load to cities across the United States. By 1957 the R-7 ICBM was ready for test launches, the first of which was conducted on May 15, 1957, but was a failure. The second flight occurred on July 12, another failure, but success came with the third attempt on August 21.

When the Russian news agency released information about this first flight of a Soviet ICBM it had little effect in the West and was even received with scepticism by some. Korolev had persuaded Khrushchev that a satellite launch would take the world by storm but the fickle manner in which public opinion, or anxiety, could be induced by a single event strode a very narrow line between disinterest and paranoia. They could only hope that a satellite bleeping overhead would finally galvanize the public into recognizing the USSR as a world leader in advanced technology.

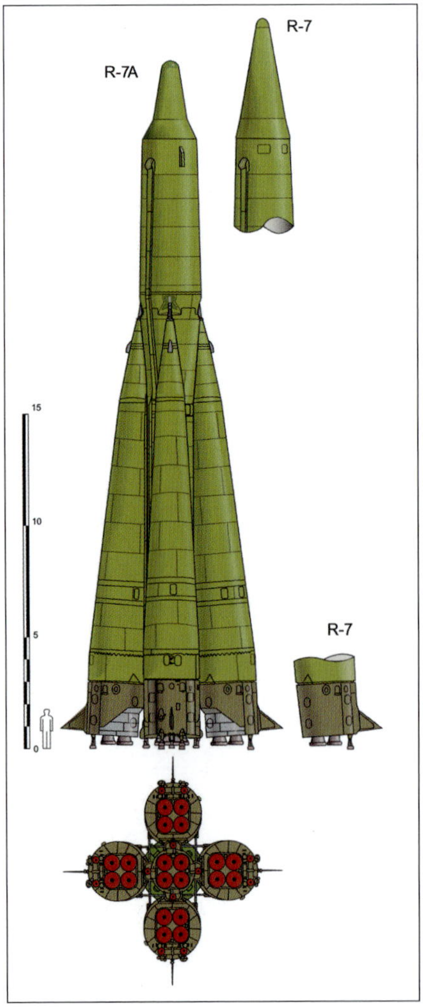

RIGHT The R-7 rocket was an innovative concept that utilized five clusters of four relatively small motors to achieve a high throw-weight for warfare or payload-to-orbit capability as a launch system. With the need to spend several hours preparing it for flight and fuelling it with non-storable liquid oxygen, its demise as a weapon was inevitable. *(Heriberto Arribas Abato)*

Nevertheless, despite the early failures of the R-7, in observing the pace of development with America's equivalent ICBM the Russians would have gained some relief by noting the failure of the first two Atlas flights from Cape Canaveral, on June 11 and September 25. Not until December 17, more than two months after the launch of the first satellite, did the third Atlas launch finally make it successfully. But Atlas was designed to have a central sustainer engine flanked by two booster engines taking propellant from the same tanks. These early Atlas flights were development launches without the central sustainer engine. Not until August 2, 1958, would the full three-engine configuration fly successfully for the first time – the tenth Atlas flight, of which six had been failures.

So it was with some degree of justified self-satisfaction that the Russian rocket engineers and space scientists saw their hopes soar into space with the launch of the world's first artificial satellite. But the Americans knew Atlas would play a critical role in flying their military spy satellites and whatever was happening with "peaceful" satellites for the IGY, they were in reality merely a side-show to the real work going on through the WS-117L program. But the Russian satellite was a shock to most and a very specific inducement to the Americans to accelerate development of the spy satellite.

Following the launch of Sputnik 1 on October 4, 1957, Neil McElroy, Secretary of Defense from October 9, reversed the earlier "business as usual" pace and ordered maximum-rate development with the Air Force's General Operational Requirement (GOR) defining WS-117L as providing "continuous (visual, electronic or other) coverage of the USSR and satellite nations for surveillance purposes." And to do so at "the maximum rate consistent with good management." The earlier decision by Quarles to go slow on development of the military satellite was now dead.

But the president also was concerned at the military possibilities, and potential first-strike opportunity, laid open to the USSR by the achievement of launching the world's first satellite. On November 7, he informed the American public that he had appointed Dr. Killian (head of the Technological Capabilities Panel) to run a new office, that of Special Assistant to the President for Science and Technology, to keep him informed about scientific and technical methods for improving the US defense posture through a small team of highly specialized advisers.

There were many prestigious individuals rushing to advise the president on possible reaction to Sputnik, not least the nuclear physicist Edward Teller, who organized a special committee to look into the matter and come up with a list of recommendations. Included were several satellites and even Moon probes, and a recommendation from the RAND organization to adopt the smaller Thor missile as a launch vehicle for smaller 200–300-pound (91–136 kg) satellites launched at an early date.

In the rush to provide the military with a comprehensive suite of capabilities, WS-117L (at this date named SENTRY by the contractors) embraced not only visual and electronic reconnaissance – and by implication, surveillance – but also infrared reconnaissance of weather systems and communications capabilities for maintaining global support of US forces. Briefing charts of the time include detection of nuclear tests, the use of SENTRY for strategic warning of attack and a watch for launch of enemy ICBMs. But much of this was wishful thinking on the part of Lockheed, keen to push the Agena stage as the basis for an entire family of military satellites with wide-ranging applications.

Grand plans

Amid the contest between WS-117L and the "Top Story" proposals and concepts, these tasks were to be achieved in sequential phases of increased capability, with visual reconnaissance from 1958 on satellites launched by Thor rockets and from 1959 using Atlas missiles, followed in 1961 by advanced visual reconnaissance systems and in 1962 by electronic ferret SIGINT satellites and infrared early-warning capabilities. In effect, a bag of desirable but imaginative assets wrapped up in the one program.

The launch site was to be Cooke Air Force Base at Lompoc, California, later renamed Vandenberg Air Force Base, with tracking facilities across the United States, including Hawaii. Utilizing the standard Atlas rocket, the SENTRY payload was assessed at 9,300 pounds (4,218 kg), including the mass of an upper stage for orbital injection at an altitude of 300 miles (483 km) into polar orbit.

The upper stage itself would provide the structure to which would be attached, at the forward end, the payload specified by the mission requirement, and both would go into orbit as an integral package. At this date solar, battery or radioisotope thermo-electric

BELOW **The launch of Sputnik 1 sent shock waves across America, but to a seemingly apathetic president it was of no great moment, Eisenhower having already authorized a top-secret spy satellite program that would serve the nation well.** *(Novosti)*

THE DENVER POST

HOME EDITION

The Voice of the Rocky Mountain Empire

RUSS 'MOON' CIRCLING EARTH

560 Miles Up at 18,000 MPH

Rockefeller Says Crisis Hurts Arkansas Future

U. S. Scientists Attempting to Chart Course

More Join Rioting in Warsaw

Reds Say 'Moon Next' In Race Into Space

Hoffa Election May Spur Laws

Bright October Days in Store

Vital Facts On Satellite

THE WEATHER

IN TODAY'S POST

Burglar Takes Dollars, Leaves Series Tickets

ABOVE Compared to Russia's R-7, America's Redstone rocket – the only one that would be capable of placing a timely satellite in orbit – was very small. Here a Redstone lies horizontal at the Army Ballistic Missile Agency, Huntsville. *(US Army)*

generators (RTGs) were being considered for electrical power. RTGs would use a small pellet of radioactive material such as plutonium 238 dioxide to produce electrical power from the heat given off by the radiation via a thermocouple.

With the technology of the day, batteries would provide the necessary power for 20–30 days at most while RTGs would provide power for up to 180 days. A small nuclear reactor would extend that to 360 days but solar cell arrays would last several years.

There was one other radical technology – fuel cells. Using the chemical principle of reverse electrolysis, hydrogen and oxygen brought together over a catalyst would produce electrical power and water as a by-product. Because they would have to be kept at cryogenic temperatures, the reactants would be effective for only 10–15 days. In the late 1950s fuel cell technology was sufficiently robust to give promise but there was little confidence that it would be a practicable solution – it was just one more advanced system to add to an ever-larger collection of unknowns stacking up.

Even at this early stage it was accepted that precursor development satellites would have an initial "Pioneer" capability, leaving the more developed "Advanced" system for later. The Pioneer phase was postulated to provide a camera system with a 6-inch (152 mm) focal length and a lens speed of f2.8 within a camera system weighing 300 pounds (136 kg). Lockheed based its analysis on obtaining strips of exposed film covering a section of the Earth's surface 100 miles (160.9 km) in width and 2,000 miles (3,218 km) in length. The mission was expected to last nine days.

The more advanced system would utilize a camera with a focal length of 36 inches (914 mm) at f2.8 covering an area 17 miles (27.3

LEFT Jupiter-C was a Redstone rocket adapted to develop re-entry warhead technology that would underpin America's nuclear deterrent and provide support for theater warfare. Jupiter-C would be further modified as America's first satellite launcher when Vanguard suffered a succession of technical failures. *(US Army)*

km) in width and 360 miles (579 km) in length intermittently. This camera would weigh 400 pounds (181 kg) and operate for 30 days. The wide-area Pioneer system would provide a ground resolution of about 100 feet (300 m), while the advanced close-look system would see objects down to 20 feet (6.1 m). Film used was to be Microfile Eastman F570-6.

Advanced polar-orbiting TV satellites would operate from an orbit of 1,000 miles (1,609 km) with direct readout to ground stations as they passed across the United States. Overall power requirements for the satellite bus were considerably greater than for the camera payload, the 80 square feet (7.4 m^2) of solar array area providing a useful power level of 1.248 kW/day versus the 1.1 kW/day required by the satellite. The total panel output would be 3.796 kW/day, but of that 2.548 kW/day would be lost in degradation, conversion, storage and regulation. Overall efficiency of 30% was normal for the late 1950s.

As defined for the more advanced Phase IIA flights, recovery of a film pod from the satellite would be made on the 18th revolution after little more than a day in orbit, the impact area being off Kaena Point, Hawaii. At this date the pod was to parachute into the Pacific Ocean and be recovered by ship following beacon-tracking by circling aircraft. For all phases of application, SENTRY was to have a length of 24.5 feet (7.47 m), a diameter of 61 inches (1.55 m) and a nose cone with an included angle of 30°.

Briefing charts of the period from Lockheed display a man carried in a recovery capsule adapted from the film/sample retrieval pod, an undisguised bid to show an early man-in-space capability driving right out of an existing program already in development. But this was a clear problem with WS-117L: it was all things to many people and lacked the focused sophistication of a dedicated mission. Above all, it lacked awareness of the enormous technical challenges ahead and there was a naivety about the way it could be swung into action as an operational system. The entire satellite program was expected to be handed over to Strategic Air Command to run, units responsible for strategic bombing and ICBMs. And it was based around the Atlas rocket, still somewhat behind in development.

ABOVE The RAND Corporation had been the first organization to push for a satellite launcher and had proposed development of a spy-satellite system just after the end of the Second World War. It would continue to play a vital role in helping define successive generations of spy satellite. *(RAND)*

The earliest recommendation for use of the Thor rocket was in a RAND report structured by Merton Davies and issued through advance copies released on November 12, 1957. It envisaged abandoning the WS-117L for this interim system, applied as a more permanent

BELOW Topical among scientific discussion of spy satellite requirements was the choice between visible and infrared technology. Initially satellites would use the visible part of the spectrum, using reflected light to record images on exposed film. Later, infrared film would allow observation of crops and agricultural harvests, while radio waves would be used to spy on defensive radars and data would be relayed via other satellites to stations on the ground. *(David Baker)*

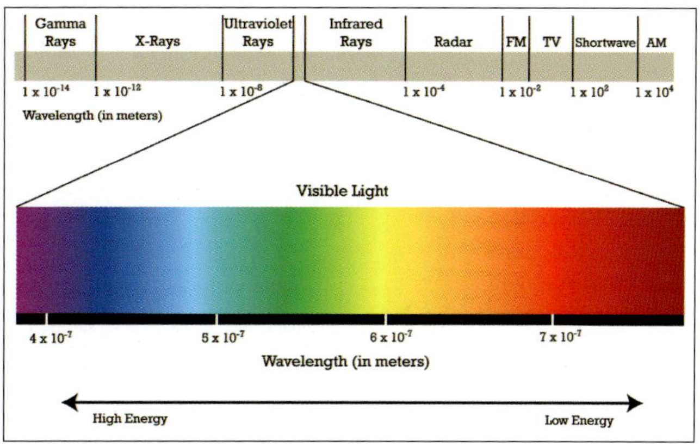

LEFT Many satellite projects, not least those that spilled out of the cancellation of WS-117L, were dependent on the Agena rocket developed by Lockheed – one of the most successful upper stages ever designed. *(Lockheed)*

program that RAND believed could become the core of several sequential developments resulting in a reliable, fully operational system.

Already involved in a range of proto-operational space ideas, General Electric suggested a camera subsystem, a recoverable film-carrying pod, and a camera with an f3.5, 18-inch (45.7 cm) lens and a resolution of 75 feet (23 m). GE's initial idea was to adopt a standard GE re-entry body of the type developed for ballistic missiles, dispatched to an ocean splashdown, whereupon the cone would crack open and allow the film-carrying sphere inside to float and be recovered by ships.

ABOVE Developed versions of the Agena would be employed in a wide range of programs, for which it would not have been available had the reconnaissance satellite program not forced its production. Here, Agena stages are being produced for the manned Gemini program, where they were used as target vehicles fitted with a docking collar. *(Lockheed)*

BELOW The aft end of the Agena, which, when fitted with a suitable adapter, would find application with Thor, Atlas and many variants of the Titan rocket, adapted to a satellite launcher from its primary role as an ICBM. *(Lockheed)*

ABOVE **A generation of propulsion systems for aircraft and for spacecraft emerged from the original design for the V-2, either directly through its indigenous technology or by completely new designs inspired by the leap forward achieved by German rocket engineers during the Second World War. The author remembers how the German rockets were still used in the 1960s for teaching the principles of rocket engineering.** *(David Baker)*

BELOW **Initial WS-117L concepts assumed the availability of the Atlas missile for launching the Advanced Reconnaissance System, a missile that had a central sustainer engine and two booster engines attached to a common structural frame that would be jettisoned on the way up.** *(NASA)*

Responding to a request from General Schriever on December 23, the first definitive proposal for the Thor-launched concept was presented by Lockheed on January 6, 1958, a highly detailed description of an efficient spy satellite system. Lockheed had achieved great success with its U-2 spy-plane and the company was well placed to take a lead on extending the reconnaissance-gathering capacity to space. There were strong links between key players at the CIA, which operated the U-2, and Schriever's office and his coterie of fellow travellers.

The break with WS-117L came on February 28, 1958, when the Director of the Advanced Research Projects Agency (ARPA) sent a memorandum to the Secretary of the Air Force disconnecting this from the Lockheed satellite and adopting Thor boosters for a program which, eventually, would be known as Discoverer, a concealed veil for photographic reconnaissance and biological experiments. It had already been decided the previous month to schedule nine Thor flights for the program and later an additional five flights were authorized for biomedical science.

Edwin Land and Richard Bissell had been central to the reorganization of the spy satellite program and on hearing that McElroy had approved the use of Thor with the WS-117L upper stage for tests of airframe components and a recoverable film capsule, Shriever ordered a series of "black" funding requirements. He put Oder in charge of working the plan with the CIA and transferred contract costs from the Ballistic Missile Division to the CIA.

As a part of President Eisenhower's response to Sputnik, ARPA had been set up on February 7 as the dominant organization for controlling and managing the separate military space concept on offer, and its first director, Roy W. Johnson, issued a direction 21 days later opposing WS-117L and authorizing the Air Force to adopt the Thor and to commence test firings with the Agena second-stage for a series of scientific tests. The cover story was that the program was supporting the development of manned space flight and that a series of such flights would precede piloted launches.

Key to success with the project, as it had been with the U-2, would be a strong and abiding relationship with the CIA, and the Air Force immediately began a series of meetings to develop the idea, review the technology and focus on getting an operational system in place. On March 10, 1958, at one such meeting with Bissell, someone raised the issue of what to call this project. Looking down at his typewriter he read the maker's name – Corona. And so it

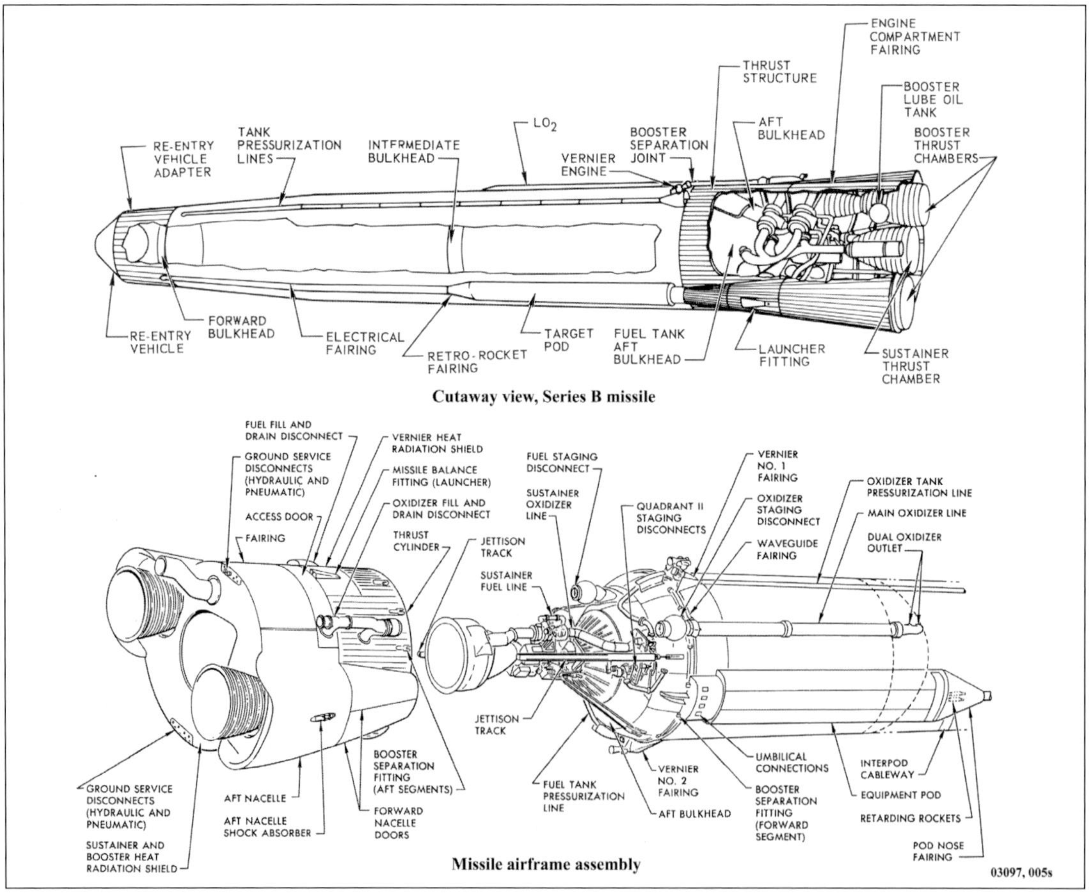

BELOW The layout of the Atlas was unique in that it used a pressurized core stage with booster rockets drawing propellant from the same tanks as the central sustainer. *(General Dynamics)*

was agreed, the spy satellite program would be known as CORONA.

The original 15 WS-117L flights had been authorized on September 4, 1958. On March 24, 1959, ARPA approved a 13-flight Discoverer program and this was increased to a 29-flight manifest by July that year. On December 3, 1959 ARPA transferred the Discoverer program to the Air Force Air Research and Development Command.

ARPA examined closely the SENTRY program and proposed a reorientation of its function in June 1959, removing the mapping and charting capabilities and moving those functions to SAMOS, before moving the reconnaissance satellite to the Air Force on November 17, 1959. The name SAMOS was chosen by the ARPA director, Admiral John Clark, and refers to the Greek island, not "Space and Missile Observation System," which countless writers and historians have assumed ever since.

This was also the date the Air Force took over the MIDAS (Missile Defense Alarm Satellite) program from ARPA. But ARPA's days as a satellite and upper stage management organ were numbered. In September 1959 the DoD switched the technical direction of the Agena military satellite program to the Air Force Ballistic Missile Division (BMD), which left ARPA carrying out research and development.

In effect, WS-117L became three sub-programs: CORONA, MIDAS and SENTRY. By 1959 Discoverer was the public name for the Top Secret CORONA spy satellites. SAMOS represented three separate programs: Project 101A (E2) for constant readout television spy cameras; Project 101B (E5) for film recovery of high-resolution imagery; Program 201 (E6) for film recovery, also high resolution. MIDAS was for an infrared sensor capable of monitoring missile launches by observing their hot exhaust plumes from space.

LEFT An early Atlas ready for launch on a development flight, November 28, 1958. *(USAF)*

RIGHT A dramatic shot of an Atlas just released for flight, flame from one of its two vernier attitude-correction engines bright against the blue sky, the missile topped with a General Electric warhead. *(USAF)*

Chapter Four

CORONA

In some respects CORONA was a "bootstrap" design put together to fast-track a spy satellite capability before the more advanced system could be deployed. Then the follow-on system was cancelled and CORONA endured for more than 14 years, transforming the way Western intelligence saw Russia's military potential and rewriting the text books on reconnaissance and surveillance.

OPPOSITE Obtained by CORONA flight 98, the KH-4A flight launched on August 17, 1965, took this view of Tuczno, Poland, with lakes nearby. *(NRO)*

ABOVE On December 6, 1957, the first attempt to launch America's first satellite, weighing 4 pounds (1.8 kg), failed when the Vanguard rocket collapsed back on to the pad having barely lifted free of its restraints. *(NASA)*

BELOW Weighing 31 pounds (14 kg), Explorer I comprised the terminal stage of the Jupiter-C, which consisted of a solid propellant rocket provided by the Jet Propulsion Laboratory, California, and instrumented for measurements of radiation levels. It discovered the famous Van Allen belts, named after the scientist who devised the instrument. *(JPL)*

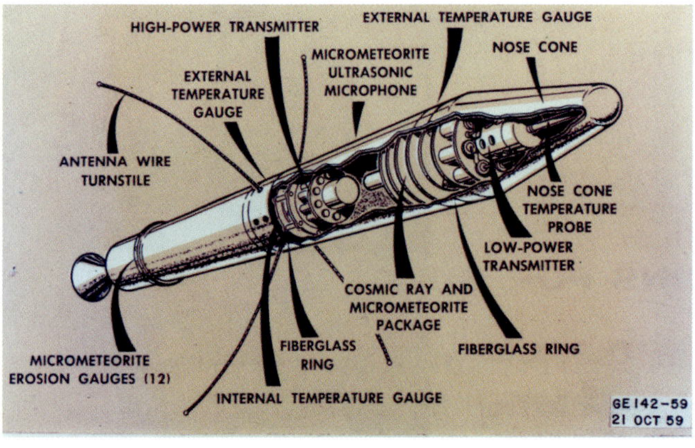

By mid-June 1958 an initial ten-vehicle flight program had been structured together with a misinformation plan to allay suspicions about the program's true intent. The first two flights were assigned to engineering development, flights 3, 4, 6, 8 and 10 were for biological flights, while 5, 7 and 9 were said to be for advanced engineering activities. This was the publicized plan for the Discoverer series of CORONA flights. Unmentioned was the fact that some of the biological and all the advanced engineering flights would carry cameras for spying on the Soviet Union.

The underlying reasons why there was such sensitivity to matters regarding the use of space for military purposes lay in Operation Candor, best defined as a policy on the part of the Eisenhower administration to be open and honest with the American public about the realities of the new technological age but to persuade them that all these developments were benign and that they had nothing to fear from them.

As part of this, when making his "Atoms for Peace" speech on December 8, 1953, Eisenhower spoke of the civilian benefits from nuclear power and helped seed many nuclear power plants in several countries around the world, diluting the association of the atom with destruction. In stressing the "Peaceful Use of Space" theme in approving an ostensibly civilian-led satellite program for the International Geophysical Year, he leaned on the same theses: that rockets are not necessarily things to be feared, but potentially instruments of great benefit.

This helps explain why Eisenhower was casual regarding the potential threat to America of the Soviet ICBM adapted for use as a satellite launcher; the administration was under no illusion that this was a marked step up from US capabilities at the time but he sought to downplay the hysteric response from American citizens that it was a military threat, publicly accepting it as a natural progression on the part of the Russians to share with American scientists the gathering of information about the Earth.

It also explains why Eisenhower was insistent that there should be a clear division between civilian and military space activities – one that has persisted to the present day. In the furore that followed the launch of Sputnik, special Congressional hearings were held in Washington DC, and a parade of specialists and experts were received to testify on the state of space engineering and on the opportunities and prospects for the United States in organizing itself into a space-faring nation.

In the first half of 1958 a series of hard-fought battles developed in the Pentagon and between the Defense Department and the civilian scientists and engineers working on the Vanguard program and other space research programs such as those associated with sounding rockets. A fight was under way to seize control of the nation's space activities, not only between the military and civilian factions but between each of the three armed services. It was during this period that the Air Force, the Army and the Navy fought hard for supremacy, much as they each had done a few years previously when vying for funds to develop the nation's strategic nuclear arsenal.

When the first attempt to launch a satellite in the Vanguard program ended in a launch pad explosion on December 6, 1957, (dubbed "flopnik!" by the press), the Army's von Braun used the Jupiter-C rocket to launch America's first satellite in a unique opportunity that would not last. Instead Congressional action and directives from the president steered the US toward a new civilian agency (NASA) for non-military space research and exploration, assigning the Air Force to provide the technical muscle for a series of military projects which at first were shrouded in secrecy.

On October 1, 1958, the National Advisory Committee for Aeronautics (NACA) metamorphosed into the National Aeronautics and Space Administration and NASA opened for business. Formed on March 3, 1915, NACA had supported the burgeoning growth in US aeronautical prowess for more than 43 years and it had spawned a new and powerful government organization that would absorb all non-military space research and engineering, including the von Braun team at Redstone Arsenal, near Huntsville, Alabama, renamed the Marshall Space Flight Center after it was acquired in October 1959.

The Air Force manned space program (MISS, for Man-In-Space-Soonest) was moved to NASA and renamed Project Mercury, while the Army's plans for Moon bases using von Braun's Saturn rockets (Project Horizon) were shelved. The Saturn designs were moved to NASA and the rockets would underpin a decade and more of Moon exploration using teams of astronauts. But in 1958 two very different space programs emerged – one in the "white," and the other in the "black."

Keeping CORONA a secret within the open nature of the Discoverer program was a completely unprecedented challenge for the CIA and the Air Force. With an overt side to the program, scientists from across the nation were drawn to Discoverer, as they knew the program to be. Between April and October 1958, when most of the technical challenges for CORONA were addressed, there was a compromise between the overt and the covert sides of the same program.

With few civilian programs being developed, attention focused on the Air Force, the natural lead organization for this kind of activity. Before NASA came into being there was little

ABOVE Explorer I sits on top of the Jupiter-C rocket, deployable antenna attached to the upper section, prior to its launch on January 31, 1958, (local time) – a small satellite with a very big place in history as the first US satellite. *(NASA)*

RIGHT Vanguard SLV-4 stands ready for launch from Cape Canaveral in February 1959. Vanguard made several successful flights and contributed to the International Geophysical Year through the series of satellites it launched in support of the global search for information about the upper atmosphere and near-Earth space. *(NASA)*

FAR RIGHT The tiny 3.2-pound (1.45 kg) Vanguard satellite on top of the terminal stage of the rocket provided early experience of putting together packages for space exploration. From this research quickly grew a base of knowledge to build bigger satellites – information that fed across to the military space projects as well. *(NASA)*

else around to attract attention. But, with promise of biological experiments calling for an atmospherically controlled environment, the fact that the re-entry capsule had to be unpressurized and light-tight was difficult to explain, as was the fact that the acceptable flight mode of orientating in a forward attitude ran counter to the requirement for the orientation downward for taking pictures!

Nevertheless, the need for a completely new system of clandestine activity emerged and this would form the basis for an expanding system of secrecy that would grow to embrace many aspects of US intelligence gathering. Between April and July 1958 essential elements of the program were put in place, including the decision on launch schedules in April and the completion of a fabrication and assembly plan involving the Air Force, the CIA, Douglas Aircraft, Lockheed, Itek, General Electric and the Hiller Aircraft Company. Founded by Stanley Hiller Jr. in 1942, in 1944 Hiller Aircraft developed the first helicopter to fly with a co-axial configuration. In 1954 Hiller was doing work for the US government through a contract with the ARDC for a variety of vertical take-off projects.

Hiller had a small facility near Lockheed and it was from them that Lockheed leased a building to assemble the CORONA payloads to go on the Agena stages. Some Hiller people were hired by Lockheed and it was there that the company founded its "Skunk Works," but most were transferred to the new unlisted facility paid for through Hiller, who were told that the work was proprietary and could not be discussed. Moving equipment and delivering materials to the Hiller plant helped displace interest in what was going on. Hiller never did space-related work and it all seemed very normal.

Elsewhere there were greater difficulties, none insurmountable. The CIA developed the rationales for security considerations and established protocols to allow covert liaison with the Department of State and to ensure compatibility between the overt and covert sides of the program, which was unique in intelligence history. But there was a precedent. The CIA had been using civilian

ABOVE The National Advisory Committee for Aeronautics (NACA) was formed on March 3, 1915, as a government organization responsible for conducting basic research into the science of aerodynamics and the study of aeronautics. It was stimulated not least by the emerging role of airplanes in the First World War, and the enormous strides achieved by the aero-engine and airframe companies of the belligerent powers. *(NASA)*

LEFT NACA formed the core body from which the National Aeronautics and Space Administration (NASA) emerged, officially open for business from October 1, 1958, the beginning of fiscal year 1959. It was established to satisfy President Eisenhower's desire for a demarcation between military and non-military space activities. *(NASA)*

aircraft on legitimate commercial flights to carry cameras and other radio devices for gathering information on, for instance, Soviet activities in Eastern Europe. Two halves of a bipolar program. But CORONA was unique in that it was the exclusive purpose of Discoverer but with an overt cover for something that in fact did not exist.

To maintain contact between the organizing and participating partners in CORONA, the CIA set up a special cryptographic teletypewriter that linked together the CIA headquarters, the Ballistic Missile Division and the Lockheed Skunk Works. Bogus mail drops under fictional names helped scatter mischievous trackers of communication links attempting to trace the connections, much of which was in hard copy. In the non-digital world of the late 1950s these things were much easier to achieve than they are today. However, some people knew too much simply because of their background.

One official Air Force officer who had previously been made aware of WS-117L, on hearing of Discoverer tried energetically to persuade the program managers that they should be looking to use the satellite for spy flights from space rather than the scientific investigations publicly declared, without realizing that beneath Discoverer lay CORONA, unseen and on a similar purpose but, technically, on quite a different path. It served its purpose to have him associated with the Discoverer program because those who knew his background could believe that if *he* didn't know about a spy satellite program, it didn't exist!

But the cover stories were not exclusively for individuals with former experience. Even the Department of Defense knew nothing about it, and when the proposal was mooted for deploying all the Thor rockets to operational duty as ballistic rockets and moving Discoverer

BELOW The NACA Special Committee on Space Technology met on November 21, 1957, to discuss and plan potential space activities in the aftermath of the launch of Russia's Sputnik 1 six weeks earlier. *(NASA)*

RIGHT T. Keith Glennan was NASA's first administrator, given the job to run the new space organization on August 19, 1958. He would remain at the helm until January 20, 1961, and constructed an effective working dialogue with the Department of Defense for the exchange of technical information and for planning a national launch vehicle program. *(NASA)*

to the Army's Jupiter missile it took a call to Bissell at the CIA for drastic action. Shifting launch vehicle at this stage could have caused a delay of at least a year and that would have been disastrous.

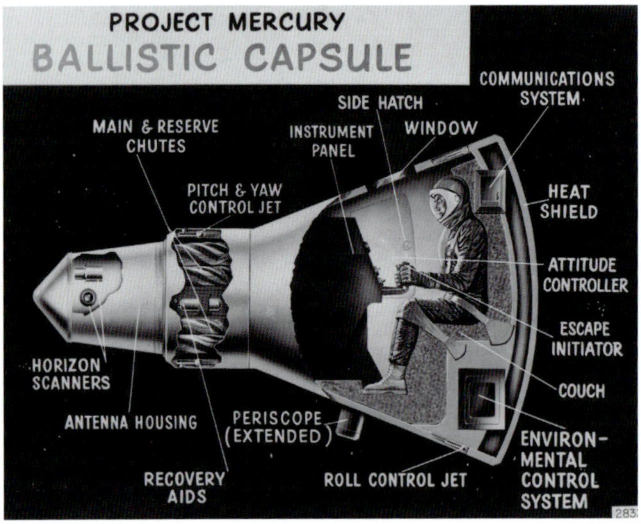

BELOW The Air Force set out plans for a manned space vehicle in a program known as Man-In-Space-Soonest (MISS), but this was taken over by NASA and would be renamed Mercury, denying the military a manned space program. *(NASA)*

The very existence of a Soviet ICBM, now evident by the launch of the Sputnik satellites, made it vital to get detailed information about launch sites, factories and deployments. Photographs obtained during overflights with the U-2 would provide some information for the time being but time was running out on their survivability, and with every passing day the president got increasingly nervous about using them for these vital photo-runs. In fact Eisenhower grounded the U-2 from October 13, 1957, to March 2, 1958; resumption of its activity, with an overflight across the Far Eastern regions of the USSR, brought a formal protest from Khrushchev. Flights were again halted on March 7 and it would be 18 months before they resumed.

The first operational flight of a U-2 had taken place on June 20, 1956, and the Soviet rocket test site at Baikonur had been photographed in August 1957, even the very launch pad from which Sputnik 1 would fly. The Russians designated the site as Tashkent-50 but to the CIA it was Tyuratam, after the nearest railway station. Soon it would fall to an RAF pilot to fly the U-2 from RAF Watton in East Anglia, but it would not be long before Eisenhower's worst fears were realized and a U-2 would be shot down, over central USSR.

The most opportunistic flights originated in Peshawar in Pakistan, taking them up to the Sverdlovsk region before diverting to bases in Iran or other locations in the Middle East. Other flights being planned would take place right across central USSR from Peshawar to Bodo, Norway, a distance of 4,040 miles (6,500 km) and a flight time of more than nine hours. Soviet air defenses were getting better and the international consequences of a downed U-2 were incalculable. There was a new urgency with each overflight.

The proposal to use Thor, rather than Atlas, for the CORONA satellite was fitting, since this Air Force missile, named after the Norse god of thunder, was in a more advanced stage of development. Recommendations to cancel WS-117L and move to a multiple-satellite military space program, rather than wrap all the desired tasks of separate programs into one satellite, had been discussed as early as November 5, 1957, when the Armed Services

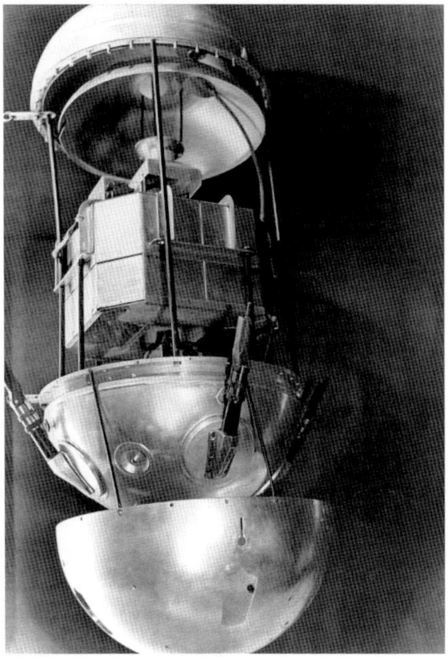

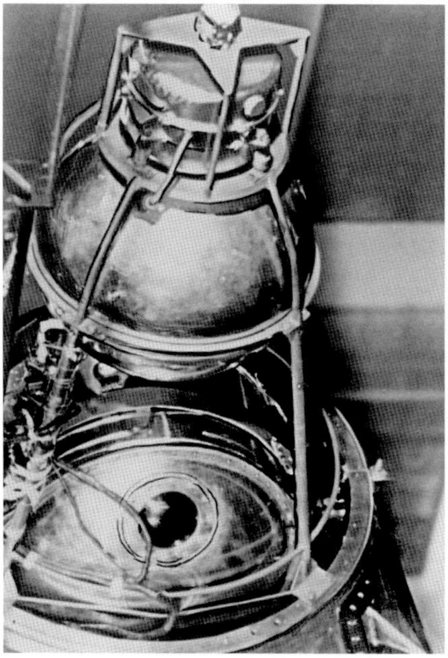

Policy Council heard compelling evidence to support that shift. The first Thor had launched on January 25, 1957, but it was a failure, as were the next three, but a full range successful flight was achieved on September 20.

Early plans to develop an upper stage for the Thor, and applicable also to Atlas, was the XRM-81 rocket motor developed for the B-58 Hustler, a Mach 2.5 bomber, later re-designated XLR81. The Hustler had a separable under-fuselage pod for carrying fuel for the outbound leg and a rocket motor for directing a nuclear weapon to a distant target after jettisoning prior to turning around for home. Developed by Bell, the XRM-81 began as a turbopump liquid propellant rocket motor (Model 117). It burned JP-4 with red fuming nitric acid (RFNA) as oxidizer. As such it was considered at first to be unsuitable for use as an upper stage.

The issue over large two-stage rockets had plagued engineers for many years. Many thought that such a motor would not ignite in the vacuum of space and this uncertainty resulted in the redesign of the Atlas missile to a parallel-burn design, where both the booster rockets and the sustainer motor ignited together on the launch pad rather than sequentially. Dispensing with an upper stage would ensure that as far as Atlas was concerned there was one less technical hurdle to cross. By 1958, however, it was apparent that ignition in a vacuum was indeed possible, as evidenced by several two-stage systems having already proved their worth as launch systems.

FAR LEFT Weighing 184 pounds (83 kg), the Sputnik I spacecraft was a simple satellite equipped with basic instrumentation, but it demonstrated the large throw-weight lifted by the R-7 rocket, from which engineers were able to calculate its ability to deliver an atomic warhead across intercontinental distances. *(Novosti)*

LEFT Launched on November 3, 1957, Sputnik II weighed 1,121 pounds (508 kg) and contained the dog Laika. The world's second satellite, it demonstrated the full lifting potential of the R-7 rocket. The immediate impact within the military was concern at Russia's ability to strike the United States, but nobody knew the size of that force nor how many missiles the Russians had deployed, invigorating the call for intelligence information. *(Novosti)*

LEFT The rocket employed to launch Sputnik II was almost identical to that used for Sputnik I and the same launch pad would be used to send the world's first human to reach orbit into space on April 12, 1961. *(Novosti)*

ABOVE **Built for research into distant radio sources within the universe, the Jodrell Bank radio telescope in Cheshire, England, inadvertently played a role in tracking Russian spacecraft as the Soviets turned to sending spacecraft to and past the Moon. Its director, Sir Bernard Lovell, became an international figure, providing the Americans with much detailed information on the trajectories flown by Soviet spacecraft and on the telemetry they used.** *(David Baker)*

BELOW **In seeking a rocket motor for an upper stage to put a camera in space for military intelligence purposes, Lockheed chose to develop one originally designed for an under-fuselage pod carried by the Convair B-58 Hustler, the prototype of which is seen here taking off on a test flight.** *(Convair)*

Agena variants

While several upper stages had been developed for other rockets, including the Vanguard IGY satellite-launcher itself, the development of what would be known as Agena was unique. Proper materials had to be selected for manufacturing the propellant tanks, and for developing a thermal control system to ensure a relatively benign temperature for the internal systems, with minimum weight always sought. The name Agena was chosen by an ARPA committee some time around mid-1958 and conformed with the Lockheed tradition of naming its products after celestial phenomena, such as their Vega, Sirius, Altair, Constellation, Shooting Star and Saturn aircraft and their Polaris missile. The star Agena, also named Beta Centauri, is the tenth brightest star in the sky, and that seemed appropriate enough.

The first few Agena A stages employed the Bell XLR81-BA-3 (Bell Model 8001) rocket motor before moving to the YLR81-BA-5 version using unsymmetrical dimethylhydrazine (UDMH) fuel and inhibiting red fuming nitric acid (IRFNA) as oxidizer. The first flight model Agena A used JP-4 instead of UDMH. This model, XLR81-BA-5 (Bell 8048), had a gimballed nozzle for pitch and yaw control during ascent and delivered a thrust of 68.9 kN (15,500 lb) for up to 120 seconds. Attitude control gas jets were used for yaw stabilization. The BA-5 had a specific impulse of 277 seconds and a thrust of 69.40 kN (15,600 lb). The Agena A tanks carried a total propellant load of 2,960 kg (6,525 lb).

Considerable gains were made with the technology of rocket stage design through the evolving CORONA program, not least the adoption of a new material, magthorium (magnesium-thorium), adopted for its light weight, strength and high temperature characteristics with creep resistance up to 662°F (350°C). This magnesium alloy was also used in the Bomarc missile and the Lockheed D-21 drone. Magthorium was utilized in structural elements of the Gemini spacecraft but concerns over the radioactivity of thorium resulted in its abandonment as a structural material; those parts of the Gemini spacecraft that contained any being removed before surviving examples went on museum display.

The propellant tanks for the Model 8048 Agena, a considerable improvement on the 8001 Hustler engine, were fabricated from spun aluminium, which also reduced overall weight, and after seven Discoverer flights this technology was applied to the stages used for the MIDAS and SAMOS satellites. Magthorium was used in all areas except the propellant tanks, which were non-integral and had to be shaped in a unique way to deliver short length and width while being very light in weight. After examining stainless steel, titanium and aluminium, it was the last that was finally selected.

At first Lockheed tried to manufacture the tanks in an orange-peel fashion from stainless steel, where a continuous process of spot welding held the layers tight before spinning. This technique had been developed by Lockheed, but it was impossible to maintain a uniform thickness so the company turned to aluminium. This lighter material allowed the use of continuous spot welding while remaining within weight specification. The helium pressurizing sphere was moved out of the original design of a nested configuration that had been proposed for the WS-117L stage and relocated to the aft equipment rack. This was where the attitude control gas tanks were located.

Serious analysis was made of the environment in which the stage was to operate. In the vacuum of space it would be roasting hot on the side facing the Sun and intensely cold in shadow, temperature variations that could easily damage stage systems and payload instruments. Various coatings were tried in simulated environmental conditions and a decision made for an entirely passive thermal control system, whereby all heat or cold transfer took advantage of the lack of convection in weightlessness and was designed around conductivity and thermal radiation. This was the first satellite designed entirely with passive thermal control concepts and as such pioneered several new technological design approaches that would benefit many other space vehicles.

Efforts were made to apply as much of the technology from WS-117L as possible, including the work from Lockheed on the

BELOW Foisted on the Air Force when it was already at near-capacity developing the Atlas and Titan ICBMs, the Thor ballistic missile was intended as a stopgap deployment prior to operational readiness with the intercontinental rockets. The only deployment of Thor was the 60 set up on RAF launch pads in eastern England between 1959 and 1963. *(USAF)*

ABOVE Photographic intelligence from the high-flying Lockheed U-2 reconnaissance aircraft returned the first pictures of the launch pad at Baikonur from where the early Russian satellite flights began. These pictures and others like them began to show that the Russians had yet to mobilize rocket production on the industrial scale already funded in the United States. Unable to access top-secret intelligence information, the general public saw only the dramatic Russian space shots and assumed the worst. *(CIA)*

LEFT U-2 spy flights were committed to several denied areas, including the Soviet submarine depots at Severodvinsk as well as other places on the shores of the White Sea as far round the northern tip of Europe as Murmansk, the home of the Arctic Fleet. *(Arkangelsk.ru)*

power production for CORONA. Design of the spacecraft itself was integral to the Agena because it was based around that propulsion package and decisions involved selection of the lightweight solar arrays and the development of power inverters and regulators. In early flights batteries would be the prime source of electrical power, the solar cells being the recharging element on later flights. Deployed on extendable wings, they were initially applied as direct sources of power, but as missions progressed they could equally be used for power storage and secondary batteries for direct power from the arrays.

In the late 1950s the development of solar cell technology was in its infancy and there was no possibility of using them for direct power. At this date silver-zinc oxide batteries were available, and these required a pressure-sealed case but provided increased capacity over the standard contemporary batteries, a voltage regulator providing conversion of the battery power to regulated DC power with a high efficiency. Silver-zinc batteries were retained throughout the early years of the Agena program.

In 1958 the primitive stage of transistor development moved design engineers to initially select 400-cycle rotary inverters rather than solid-state types. The weight penalty and 22A rest penalty, plus its life of only a few orbits, forced a technology drive to improve transistor design and quality. Lockheed developed the bridge style 2KC inverter as a result of the lack of good transistors.

As it had been with WS-117L, Lockheed analyzed the downstream availability of better power sources by looking to nuclear power, focusing on the SNAP (systems for nuclear auxiliary power) designs, with SNAP-1 and SNAP-2 nuclear drive turbine power plants also working a 2,000-cycle system so that they would be compatible with future SNAP designs. The earliest work to develop isotope power generators began in 1956 with the SNAP-1 design. The objective was to provide a 500 W system capable of supporting a satellite for 60 days. Cerium 144, a beta source with a 290-day half-life was selected as the heat source and a small turbo-electric generator was developed to convert the heat into electricity.

SNAP-2 was the second reactor built for space applications and used uranium-zirconium hydride with a power output of 55 kW and integrated flight control assembly. Tests ran from April 1961 to December 1962 with some limited development on the reactor itself as well as the associated elements and support systems. A variant was used in development of the SNAP-10A reactor that was launched into orbit by an Atlas-Agena D on April 3, 1965. Known as Snapshot 1, the reactor ran until May 20, 1965, producing 600 W of power. It remains in orbit, where it will stay for at least the next 4,000 years.

Meanwhile, in the late 1950s, as research progressed, the reactor concept for CORONA was abandoned when development shifted to the radioisotope thermo-electric generator (RTG) and an entire generation of SNAP systems using thermoelectric conversion with SNAP-3 assembled and tested in January 1959. The unit produced 2.5 W of electrical power from polonium 210 and opened the door to a series of more advanced designs. SNAP-3 was first flown in space on the Transit 4A navigation satellite launched on June 29, 1961, employing plutonium 238 producing 2.7 W.

The development and application of SNAP power systems for satellites and space vehicles is a story in itself. Suffice it to say here that the SNAP-11 RTG was considered as a power backup for the Surveyor series of unmanned Moon landers (1966–68), but not employed. It was, however, employed to power the Apollo lunar surface instruments deployed at five of the six landing sites (Apollos 12–17) and on several planetary probes beginning with Pioneer 10 launched in 1972.

In some respects the application of solar arrays and RTGs was at first a race to see which could promise the best power output compared to life. Rapid improvements to solar cell technology shifted the balance for Earth-orbiting satellites away from SNAP designs for all but very long-lived applications and for

ABOVE At Cape Canaveral work went on around the clock preparing rockets for test and launchers to send satellites into space – activity also mirrored elsewhere, particularly at Vandenberg Air Force Base on the West Coast, where spy satellites would be launched. *(NASA)*

BELOW Concerns about the pace of Soviet space technology were reinforced by the flight of Luna 3 in 1959. Returning on a high-inclination orbit, it transmitted to Earth pictures taken of the far side of the Moon, the first ever taken. These were first picked up by the radio telescope at Jodrell Bank, England. *(Novosti)*

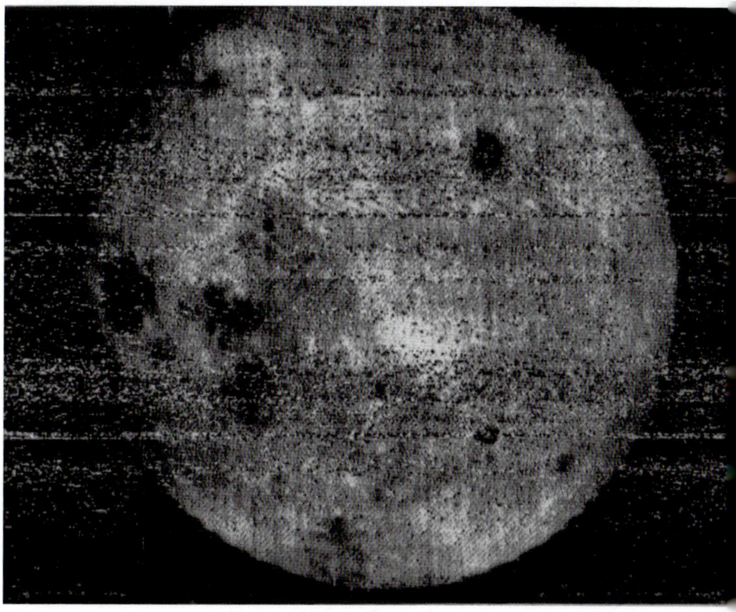

ABOVE The Itek headquarters in California. This company provided research, test and experimentation on high-quality optics, cameras and associated instrumentation for spy satellites. *(NRO)*

places where there was infrequent sunlight. But the stimulus for both came from the early demands for reliable power sources for military satellites. However, not until 1960 would the first Agena fly with solar cell arrays, followed by rotating mechanisms to allow the satellite to point down at the Earth while its arrays tracked the Sun.

A major challenge for Lockheed was the demanding requirement of providing guidance and navigation (G&N), where there was very little space-related previous experience to go on. In this requirement the Discoverer program forged new techniques and designed innovative technologies that would spill out into the broader satellite design field. Several different G&N methods were around: radio guidance, inertial guidance, celestial navigation and radar from the rocket. Stellar and booster infrared concepts were examined and rejected, as were IR horizon sensors which, during tests in 1956, had proven not to be so effective; in the real world of space flight they would prove very useful indeed.

Guidance proposed for the ascent phase of the Agena, taking over from the Atlas rocket to propel itself into orbit, was an open-loop system whereby the Atlas would incorporate a programmed autopilot with radar tracking of the Atlas-Agena combination. From this information the ground would send radio commands to the Agena for ignition (after separation) and on the delta-velocity (ΔV) required for orbit insertion. The Agena would be equipped with three gimballed gyroscopes, a single axial accelerometer and an integrator.

The "interim" system finally selected applied a horizon sensor rather than gimballing the gyroscopes, flight guidance and attitude control coming from a combination of gimballing the main engine and cold-gas attitude jets. Operational experience would show that this "interim" system was more than capable and it was retained throughout the program.

Agena A had a total length of 19.5 feet (5.9 m)

RIGHT The development of the Hustler rocket motor into the Agena upper stage was the core enabling technology allowing a camera to be attached to a payload section that over time would carry a wide range of camera types. *(USAF)*

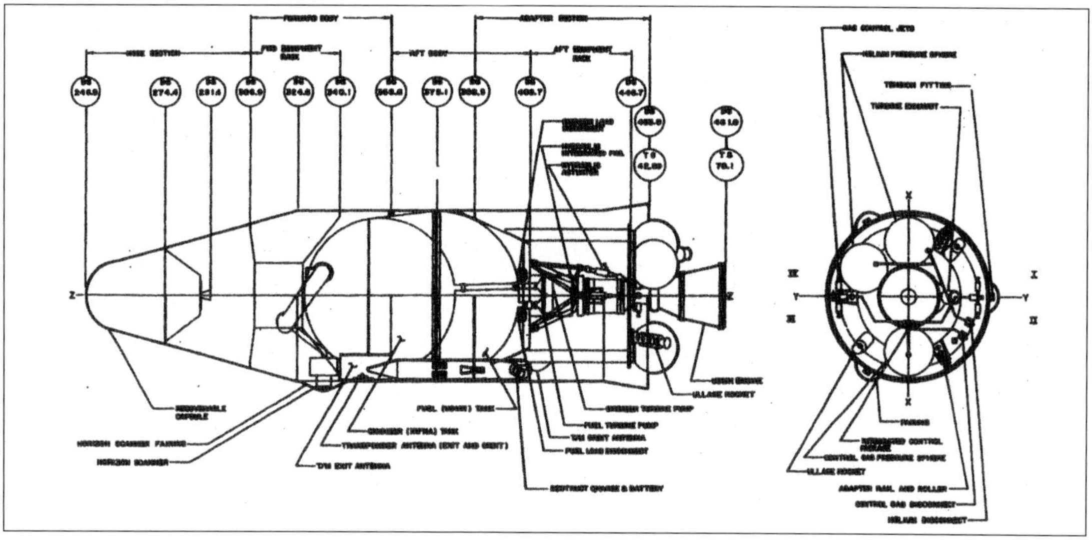

with a diameter of 5 feet (1.5 m) and a total weight of 8,500 pounds (3,850 kg), although some of the later ones pushed up to 8,662 pounds (3,930 kg). In this condition the stage had an inert weight of 1,262 pounds (572.4 kg) and carried a payload of 497 pounds (225 kg). The Thor rocket used for the Agena A (DM-18) had a lift-off thrust of 676.1 kN (152,000 lb) with a stage burn time of 163 seconds.

With longer propellant tanks, Agena B had a length of 24.8 feet (7.56 m) but the same diameter as Agena A and a fuelled weight of 15,800 pounds (7,160 kg). Early examples of the Agena B employed the XLR81-BA-7 rocket motor (Bell 8081) with a burn time of 240 seconds, double that of its predecessor. Later models employed the XLR-81-BA-9 (Bell 8096), which had a slightly higher thrust at 71.1 kN (16,000 lb). Agena B had a dual restart capability and was carried aloft by a Thor DM-21, lighter than earlier versions and with the more powerful Block 2 MB-3 rocket motor delivering a thrust of 751.7 kN (169,000 lb).

There was a proposal to develop an Agena C, with double the capability of Agena B, a modified Bell engine and changes in propellant

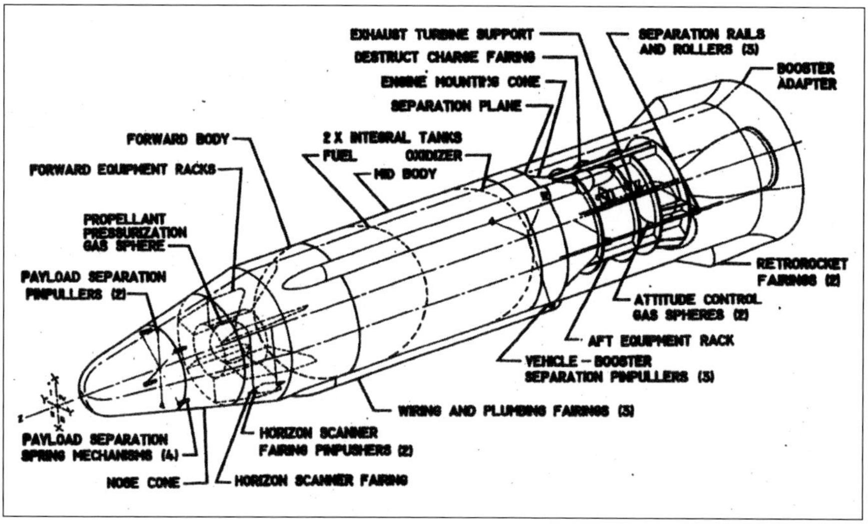

ABOVE A page from a technical report on Lockheed's Agena stage shows the common dividing wall between the spherical propellant tank holding nitric acid and the fuel tank behind it carrying hydrazine. The recoverable capsule is located at the forward end, forming the cone-shaped nose, with its retro-rocket motor attached to its base. The aft view in the diagram at extreme right shows the spherical tanks containing helium pressurizing gas. *(Lockheed)*

LEFT Later versions of Agena carried equipment shelves at the forward end, longer propellant tanks and an optional adapter for attaching the stage to an Atlas rocket. *(Lockheed)*

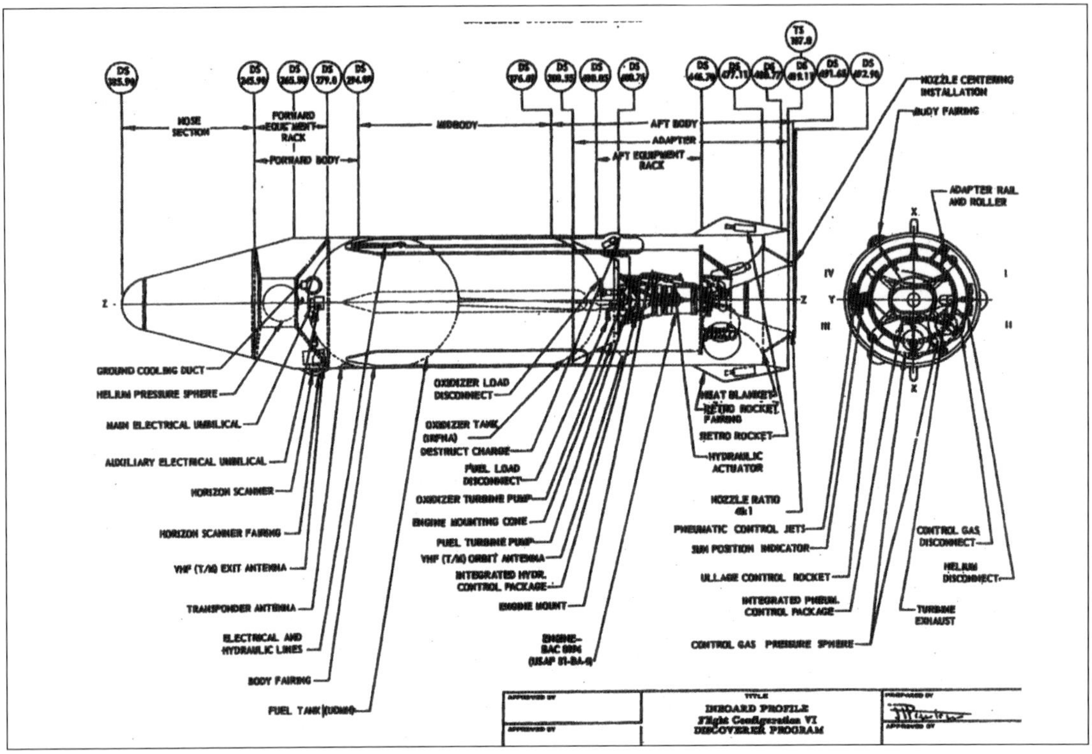

ABOVE With extended propellant tanks, the Agena B and D series had several refinements including longer burn times, restart capability and the provision for a more automated sequencing of events. *(Lockheed)*

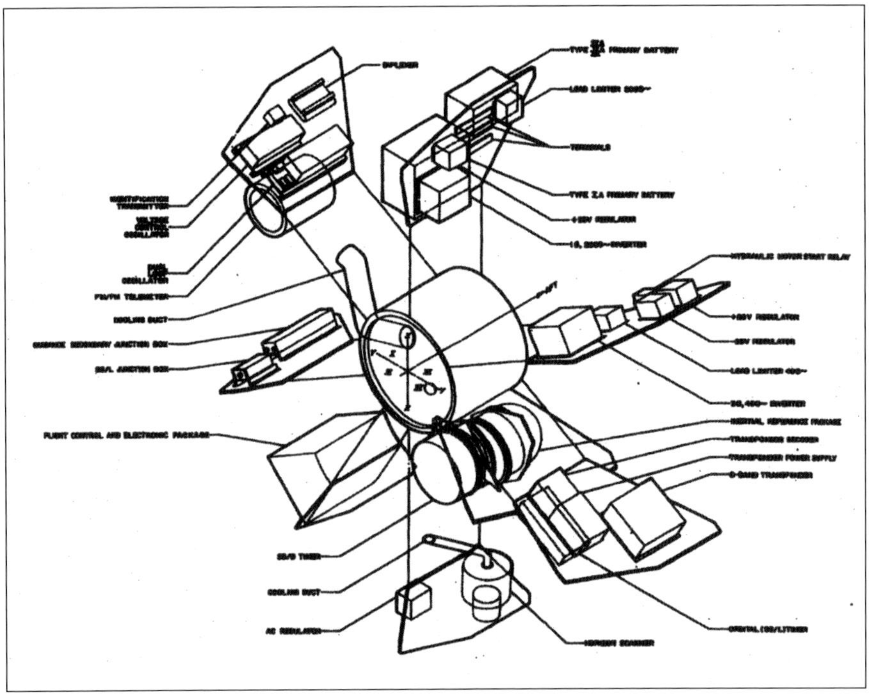

RIGHT The forward section of the Agena was designed to provide separate and dedicated segmented compartments each with their power connectors and with provision for external packages. *(Lockheed)*

RIGHT **To maintain a directed thrust vector during firing, the engine combustion chamber and expansion nozzle were attached to a set of jacks that responded to gyroscopes to maintain the desired thrust vector and pointing angle.** *(Lockheed)*

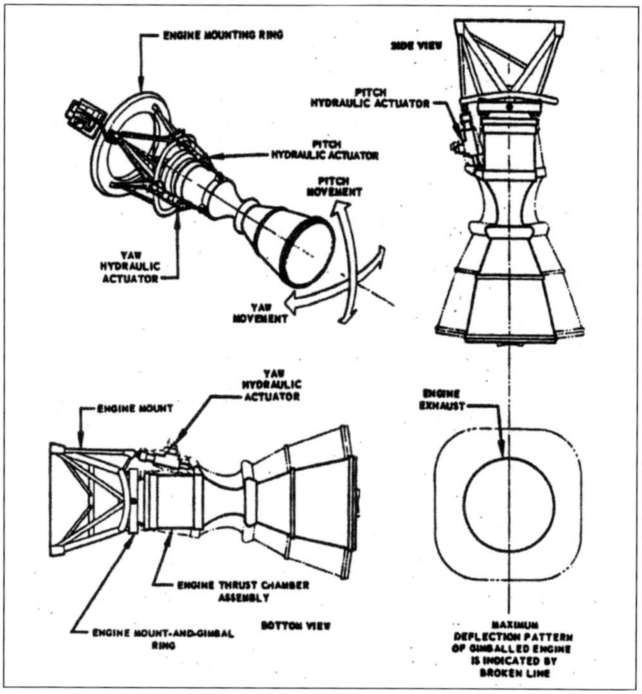

and tank design, but this was turned down. The evolution passed to Agena D. This final Agena derivative was essentially the same as the B but with the ability to roll off a production line in standard configuration and to be capable of mating to either a Thor, Atlas or Titan first stage without modification. It also had provision for a conical payload section in the nose, which greatly assisted payload planners in integrating it with the highly versatile upper stage. NASA would use Agena D for many of its missions and adapted it as the target vehicle for the Gemini flights of 1966, its restartable motor pushing Gemini to record altitudes for Earth-orbiting manned spacecraft that stand to this day.

Standardization was a vital shift in preparing fast-reaction requirements and for lowering costs. A great deal of effort went into this and Lockheed was able to significantly improve the stage reliability record by sealing all stage-related components so that only the payload – already a self-contained package – would be plugged in and operated once it arrived in orbit. In the early years of the Agena program it was apparent that 50% of the failures were attributable to bespoke manufacturing where invasive insertion of payload-related elements created a distinctly new iteration of stage, which had no actuarial record and therefore was similar to starting a new stage design with every flight.

The Agena D configuration was presented to the Air Force and a letter contract awarded on August 25, 1961, authorizing 12 flight "D" versions. Under-secretary of the Air Force Dr. Joseph Charyk set up a committee chaired by

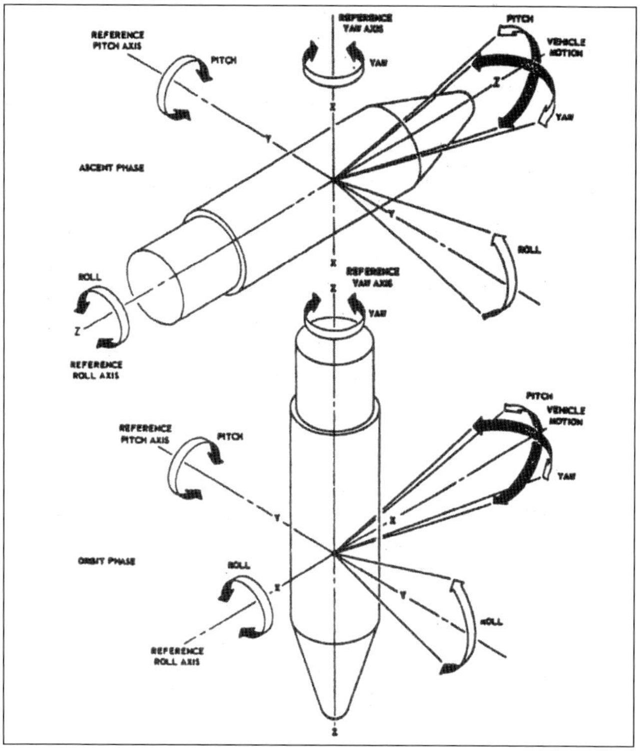

RIGHT **Attitude control of the Agena stage was critical for accurate pointing angles during drifting flight, gas jets providing impulses to maintain the correct orientation in pitch, roll and yaw when referenced to the vehicle's long axis.** *(Lockheed)*

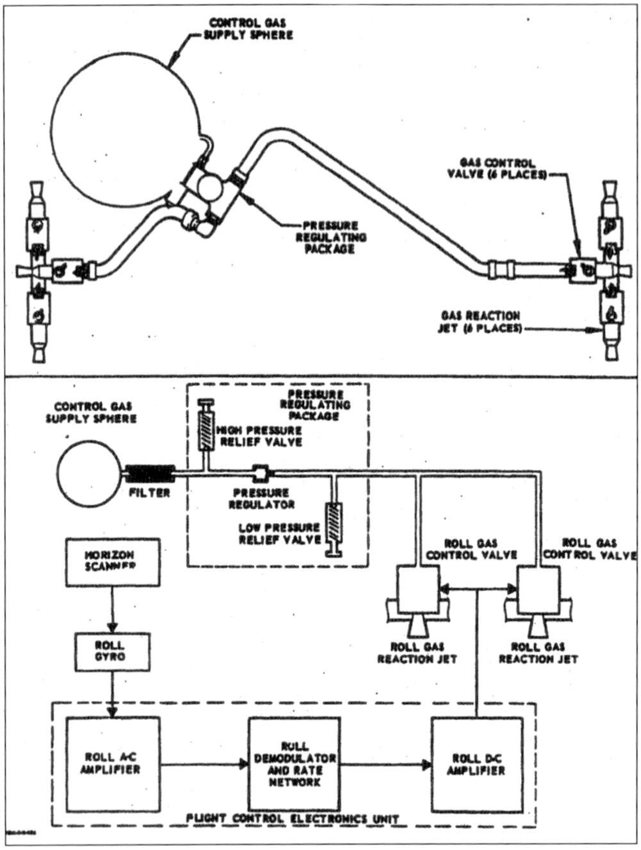

ABOVE The pneumatic system on the Agena showing the connecting pipes between the supply of attitude control gas and the thruster jet orifices. *(Lockheed)*

Clarence "Kelly" Johnson to investigate ways it could be improved further. Several Air Force and national security projects were lining up for which Agena D would be ideally suited, especially the KH-7 GAMBIT spy satellites, and an acceleration was recommended, with go-ahead ordered on November 7, 1961.

So keen was Lockheed to get the Agena D up and running that they formed a special team to focus specifically on this stage. CORONA had only ever been started as an interim system and by 1961 it was apparent that a succession of stage-tailored camera systems would be developed from the Discoverer program and that this more flexible approach to orbital support from multiple restarts and expanded lifetime capabilities would warrant unique attention.

The handpicked team set about reassessing how the basic Agena B model could be adapted to these more advanced and demanding requirements, reintegrating design changes into a standardized manufacturing plan and a cost-effective production line. The initial Agena D was sold to the Air Force on April 16, 1962, and the payload section was installed 11 days later. The first Agena D was launched on June 27, 1962, a mere seven months after the go-ahead.

Following a successful introduction to operations, further improvements were made including replacement of the magthorium skin with beryllium metal door panels and other sections on the cylindrical casing. Since introduction of the Agena A, significant improvements had been made to working in beryllium and that reduced the empty weight of the stage and translated into increased payload capacity. In addition a new secondary propulsion system (SPS) was available as an optional strap-on package in a circular mounting ring attached around the aft section of the stage where the Primary Propulsion System (PPS), or main engine, was installed.

The SPS provided two levels of thrust, 71.2 kN (16 lb) or 890 kN (200 lb) thrust from two separate motors. The SPS served the needs of the more advanced spy satellites that required orbital maneuvering to change the phase of the orbit with selected ground target.

Maneuvering was also key to another application that would be assigned to Agena D: piggyback satellites carried on the external structure and released to independent orbit. For this, Agena D maneuvers were vital to placing dedicated satellites in their own unique orbits, leaving the main payload section on the front end to be positioned in a marginally different orbit for its primary role.

The subsatellite package designed by Lockheed also had its own solid propellant boost motor to carry it further away from the Agena into its own orbit, parameters dictated by the unique nature of its mission. In this way, payload improvements could be shared with additional satellites without the need of a separate launch. The first subsatellite was released from an Agena D in April 1963 and over the following years a wide range of separate packages were launched for a variety of different government military and national security organizations.

Further development of the Agena D allowed

sequential shutdown of selected systems to conserve electrical power and save attitude control propellant. In powered-down mode, the Agena was spin-stabilized about the pitch plane so it tumbled end-over-end at 3°/sec, which provided passive thermal control and reduced the requirement to use active thermal control for sensitive low-temperature equipment. When required, the electrical system activated the G&N system and nulled out the roll rate, using horizon sensors to reorientate the vehicle and establish attitude control once more.

Although Agena D was designed as a standardized rocket stage run off a production line, several separate improvements kept pace with increasing demands from the customer for more power and longer operating life. Over time the battery life increased from 55 W/hrs/lb in 1959 to 100 W/hrs/lb in 1966 and there were schemes to introduce fuel cells to raise this further, to 500 W/hr/lb, but this was never implemented. The requirement to pack cryogenic reactants into the existing stage was too problematical and generally considered to be too ambitious for the job.

Improvements were, however, made to the G&N system, where twin-head horizon sensors with three-axis body-mounted gyroscopes were installed instead of the singe-head sensor. This greatly improved ascent trajectory accuracy and benefitted from the radio guidance package for the Thor booster designed and installed by Bell Telephone Laboratory, which in itself refined the flight path angle and accuracy of the inclination. Yet further refinement was made by the addition of a velocity meter that could command engine shutdown based on the velocity increment achieved.

From 1963, radio guidance on the Agena increased the closed-loop steering of the ascent vehicle and decreased the injection dispersions, reducing the amount of attitude control gas required to establish the precise orbit required. This became increasingly necessary for the multiple uses to which the stage was applied, with frequent orbital changes.

Agena D was fitted with the Bell 8096 (XLR81-BA-11, or YLR81-BA-11) PPS engine that evolved from the Bell 8081 (Agena B) motor but incorporated titanium with molybdenum reinforcements to the nozzle expansion skirt, which raised specific impulse to 280 seconds. Designed by Lockheed's Lawrence Edwards, developed versions could be restarted in space up to 16 times with the Bell 8247 engine.

Agena D had a common configuration with four separate systems modules for guidance, beacon transmissions, electrical power and radio-telemetry. Electrical power was provided by batteries with 19.5 kW/hrs that could be recharged from plug-on solar cell arrays, if required for a specific mission. The forward section had a payload canister that varied according to the customer. It had a basic length of 20.67 feet (6.3 m) and a standard diameter of 4.9 feet (1.5 m).

The Agena used an FM/AM telemetry system operating in P-band (215–260 MHz) with an S-band (2.4 GHz) beacon providing command reception and orbit determination. The telemetry systems had 17 channels of sub-carrier oscillators modulating an FM transmitter

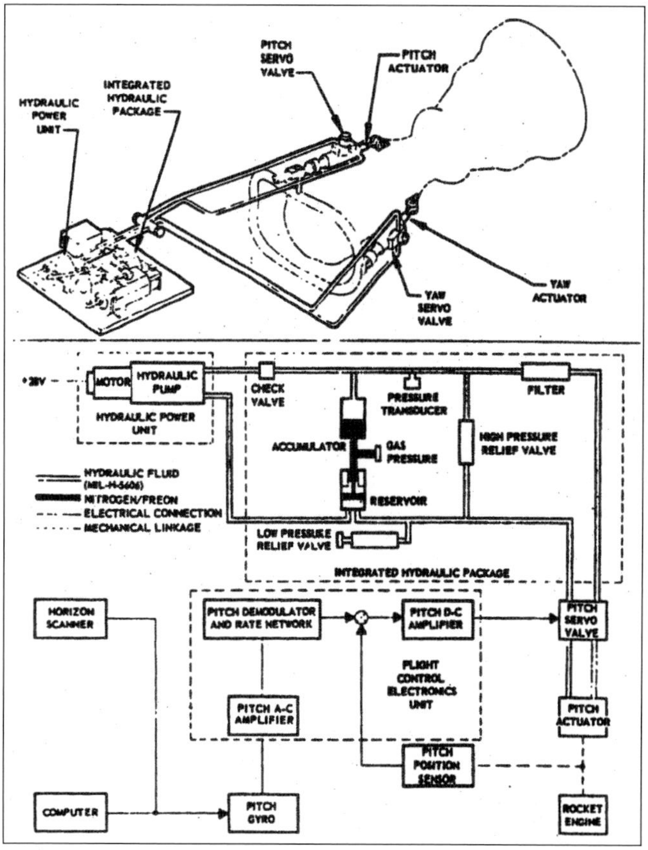

ABOVE The Agena's hydraulic system for the pitch and yaw axes controlled the firing attitude with the rocket motor so as to impart the correct orbit change vector and pointing angle. *(Lockheed)*

with a few oscillators commutated by 60-point motorized switches. Some of these oscillators monitored film motion in the camera and one gave a readout of film quantity. A mechanical sequencer was used for command execution when out of sight of a ground station with two magazines of punched Mylar tape. It could cover all 26 command executions repeatedly for 256 orbits of the Earth, and in addition there was a programmer for 52 pre-programmed commands and a register for 32 commands that could be loaded in for a specific flight. A UHF command system provided backup.

The most commonly used frequency in the early flights was 237.8 MHz and information coming down to the several tracking stations as the satellite came within range was staffed by people quite unaware of what it was actually doing. Many civilians worked at the tracking stations and nobody at these facilities was aware of what the commands they were sending would result in. When command instructions came in to send to the satellite it required the command officer to go and hunt out the appropriate tape from a depository of many held on Sperry Rand computers and send it to the satellite, preserving the "need to know" basis.

Agena was the mainstay of the early space program and a total of 365 stages of all three types was launched into space between February 28, 1959, and February 12, 1987. Of this total, 20 were Agena A, 76 were Agena B and 269 were Agena D (with a 95% success record), some pushing planetary spacecraft to the Moon and the nearest planets. The majority placed in Earth orbit entire generations of early-period military surveillance and signals intelligence satellites, as well as civil weather and communications satellites. In several regards the Agena was a spacecraft "bus" itself, serving as the stabilizing platform providing life support and communications for a host of classified payloads. In its most public role it was the rendezvous and docking target for four NASA Gemini missions in 1966, for which it was equipped with the Bell 8247 engine.

Flight sequences

There were several code names applied to America's first orbiting spy satellite. Using familiar methods of coding, a two-word name implied a secret program with restricted access but an accessible identity while a single word implied a top secret piece of hardware, in this case a specific satellite or a series using effectively the same lineage. Thus it was that the program name can be found identifying CORONA as being within Operation Bootstrap or Project Forecast, while the name of the satellite itself remained constant. For the general public the deliberately evasive name of "Discoverer" purported to embrace scientific, technical and biomedical investigations into the space environment.

In reality, CORONA embraced a separate set of sequentially more capable systems in

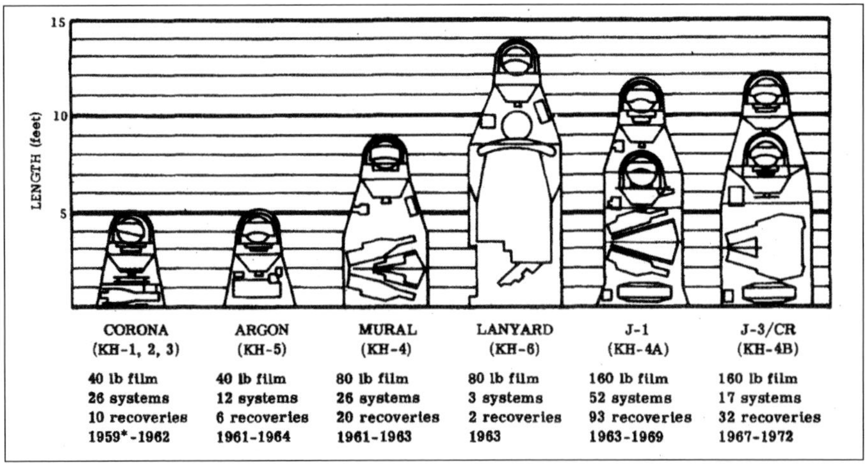

RIGHT **The breadth of CORONA satellite programs throughout the duration of the program embraced by the Discoverer series of publicly announced launches, together with pertinent characteristics of each camera system and launch record.** *(NRO)*

Designator	C (KH-1)	C' (KH-2)	C''' (KH-3)	ARGON (A) (KH-5)	MURAL (M) (KH-4)	LANYARD (L) (KH-6)	JANUS (J-1) (KH-4A)	J-3/CR (KH-4B)
Camera manufacturer	Fairchild	Fairchild	Itek	Fairchild	Itek	Itek	Itek	Itek
Lens manufacturer	Itek	Itek	Itek	Fairchild	Itek	Itek	Itek	Itek
Design type	Tessar, 24 inch, f/5.0	Tessar, 24 inch, f/5.0	Petzval, 24 inch, f/3.5	Terrain, 3 inch; Stellar, 3 inch	Petzval, 24 inch, f/3.5	Hyac, 66 inch, f/5	Petzval, 24 inch, f/3.5	Petzval, 24 inch, f/3.5
Camera type	70° pan, vertical, recipro-cating	70° pan, vertical, recipro-cating	70° pan, vertical, recipro-cating	Frame	70° pan 30° stereo, recipro-cating (2)	90° pan, 30° stereo, (roll joint)	70° pan, 30° stereo, recipro-cating (2)	70° pan, 30° stereo, rotating (2)
Exposure control	Fixed	Fixed	Fixed	Fixed	Fixed	Fixed	Fixed	Slits (4) selectable
Filter control	Fixed	Fixed	Fixed	Fixed	Fixed	Fixed	Fixed	Filters (2) selectable
Primary film (film/base)	1213/ acetate 5.25 mil*	1221/ acetate 2.75 mil	4404/ estar 2.5 mil	3400/ estar 2.5 mil	4404/ estar 2.5 mil	3400/ estar 2.5 mil	3404/ estar 2.5 mil	3404, 3414/ estar 2.5 mil
Recovery vehicles	1	1	1	1	1	1	2	2
Subsystem (stellar/index)	None	None	None	N/A	1 S/I,† 80-mm stellar 38-mm terrain	1 S/I, 80-mm stellar 38-mm terrain	2 S/I's, 80-mm stellar 38-mm terrain	DISIC (Fairchild) 3-inch stellar (2) 3-inch terrain

* Support thickness
† Index only missions 9031-9044

LEFT CORONA camera characteristics and different film types employed. *(NRO)*

three versions carrying two camera packages as selectable payload options. Initial flights would carry a single camera/single recoverable capsule, followed by a dual stereo camera/ single capsule or dual stereo camera/dual capsule design. They would all be embraced by the CORONA program but at times the names changed for each of the three selectable types. Other names attached would be MURAL (triple stereo camera version), ARGON or LANYARD.

MURAL had been the original design configuration for CORONA but it was not the first to fly. It had been assumed – erroneously, as it turned out – that the MURAL system would in fact become a separate program, but that was not to be. While the CORONA concept was heavily biased by the needs of the CIA, it was believed the MURAL configuration might be operated by the Air Force. Before MURAL, however, there were a series of improved camera configurations using the prefix "C" – for CORONA, not for "camera."

The original camera system was known as C with successive, proposed, improvements known as C' (single prime), C'' or C'''. The C'' and C''' designs had been proposed by Fairchild, but Itek put up a preferred concept for the C''' requirement and C'' never appeared. It was here that Fairchild disappears as a CORONA camera contractor. Following MURAL, proposals for a dual-capsule capability were identified as MURAL-J, or M², and this eventually became CORONA-J.

Another variation was ARGON, which can sometimes be found as CORONA-A, but separate from the CORONA program due to its significant difference in specification from the original program. Sponsored by the Army, ARGON was essentially a mapping system and was not designed for photographic reconnaissance in the original sense. Another development was LANYARD, an evolution of the SAMOS E-5 (which see), which was intended as a replacement for CORONA and a backup for GAMBIT, but this was cancelled in 1963 when it could serve neither purpose.

One drawback in announcing the Discoverer

BELOW A close shot of the forward end of a CORONA satellite displaying the forward section of the Agena stage and its protective encapsulating cover that gives scale to the size of the vehicle. *(NRO)*

ABOVE **Technicians remove the front cover of the integrated satellite/ Agena stage during an early phase in the development program when the Advanced Projects Research Agency ran the operation.** *(NRO)*

BELOW **Advanced development of the Agena stage provided momentum wheels for attitude orientation on later stages for specific missions, reducing the amount of propellant required for pointing control.** *(Lockheed)*

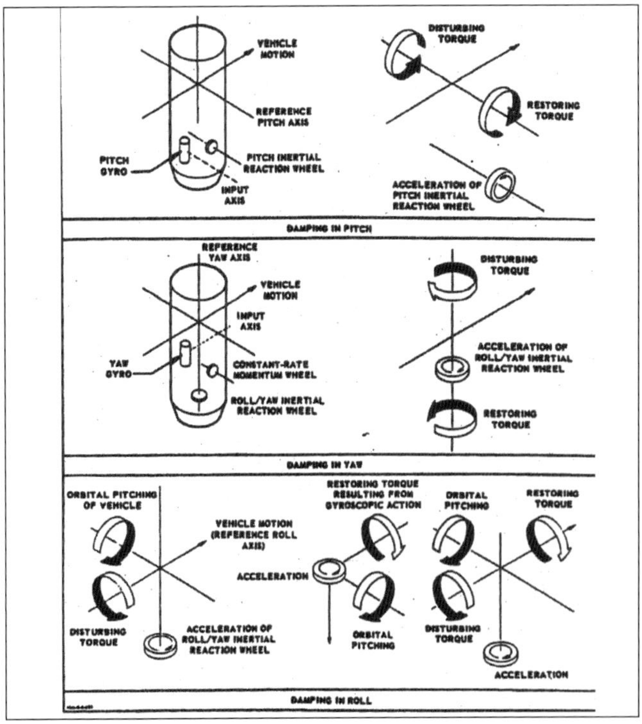

program as a general scientific platform for a variety of experiments was the interest expressed by scientists in seeing the results of these launches and of reading the data on biophysical flights presumably using monkeys. Monkeys and sapiens had been used in earlier ballistic flights, and as NASA's manned Mercury program accelerated they were integrated into the test flights of spacecraft prior to humans. By this time, however, scientists were getting increasingly more satisfying results from NASA satellite flights and this tended to take the pressure off the Air Force.

The "white" designation of the CORONA program under the name Discoverer was abandoned by the Air Force in 1962, although they continued to be used by the media, the technical press and the public at large. However, after Discoverer XXXIX their identification came under a Department of Defense number before the adoption of Program 162, which became the preferred application, although other program numbers such as 12, 75, 241 and 622A were also used – all purely fictitious concoctions.

For security classification purposes another, parallel, coding system was adopted using the two words Key Hole (KH), from the Keyhole Byeman system: KH-1 for C; KH-2 for C', KH-3 for C''' and KH-4 for MURAL systems; KH-4A for CORONA J-1; and KH-4B for CORONA J-3. Further definition of these categories will be described later in this chapter.

Identification is a double-edged sword in intelligence programs, where predictable formality can lead to disclosure through isolated leaks leaving common sense filling in of the blank spaces. Despite that, however, just as with serial numbers for military aircraft and registration numbers for the civil aviation industry, CORONA too had its recognition numbers.

Internally, and only for those with a need to know, four-number designators were attached to each launch, the initial number indicating the type of CORONA variant flown. The initial, basic, CORONA flights were in the 9000 series, with the first (9001) being known openly as Discoverer IV, through 9066A (the A indicating the last ARGON flight). Included in these were the MURAL and all ARGON launches. The dual capsule missions all ran in the 1000 series, the first being 1001, while CORONA-J flights ran from 1101 to 1117 inclusive. The three LANYARD flights were numbered 8001, 8002 and 8003. Initially, of course, all had publicly quoted Discoverer launch numbers up to Discoverer XXXIX, launched on April 17, 1962.

Organizational structures were set up to remain in the "white" as long as possible. For instance, procurement of the Thor launcher from Douglas and the Agena spacecraft from Lockheed went through the normal channels but the payloads for specific satellites were procured in "black" from CIA funds that were routed through complex channels to hide the precise amounts and the source of origin. Only four people at Lockheed knew the full CORONA program, and camera payload packages for the Agena were assembled at a special work area at Menlo Park, California, a facility rented from April 1, 1958.

For some flights the small science packages that were carried piggyback on the Agena were integrated in a way that would not interfere with or comprise the primary function of the satellite. These were procured by the sponsors of the payloads and provided to the integration personnel at the launch site.

With flights out of Vandenberg Air Force Base in a southerly direction, the launch vehicle, upper stage, camera payload and any piggyback packages were delivered separately and mated at the launch pad from the Thor stage up. The tradition in the US has always been to stack the vehicle on the pad in a vertical position, stage by stage, with the payload and its fairing on top, the entire stack usually protected in a weather enclosure. The Russians assemble the entire stack in a horizontal position within a separate building, only rolling it out on rails to the launch site prior to flight.

Because Vandenberg AFB is on the Pacific coast and generally inaccessible, public viewing is almost impossible, except for a long-range view of the ascending rocket. This author remembers the very long and seemingly lonely drive he had to make between the base gatehouse north of Lompoc and the Thor launch complex itself across deserted and flat brush-strewn terrain, the launch pads not as numerous as those at Cape Canaveral but isolated as they stand against

ABOVE Buttoned up and hidden from view, a Thor rocket at SLC-3, Vandenberg Air Force Base, lies within a servicing enclosure from where technicians prepare the vehicle for flight. In reality, the program went to extraordinary lengths to veil the CORONA missions from public view. *(USAF)*

LEFT Discoverer 1 prepares for launch from Vandenberg with "cherry-picker" gantry and mast feed for fluids and electrical power. *(USAF)*

LEFT The launch of the first CORONA satellite on February 28, 1959, from launch pad 75-3-4 at the start of the spy-satellite program. *(USAF)*

the shimmering skyline. Known as Cooke Air Force Base until October 4, 1958, Vandenberg AFB was transferred from the Air Research and Development Command to Strategic Air Command (SAC).

Nevertheless, for all the effort to hide the true purpose of Discoverer (CORONA), it was not difficult for inquisitive news-hounds to put together several publicly sourced pieces of the story and use guesswork to fill in the blanks. In the US, in April 1961 the *San Francisco Examiner* noted that during testimony about a new Mach 3 bomber for the Air Force a comment was made to the effect that "amazing work…by the cameras of the Discoverer satellite" would not invalidate the function of the new project in development.

In the UK, in 1962 the *Daily Mirror* announced to readers that a Discoverer satellite had returned to Earth with photographs of Russia. And in December 1963, the *New York Herald Tribune* published a story by Joseph Alsop claiming that Major General O.J. Ritland was in charge of a satellite photo-reconnaissance program (he was) and that confirmation that there were no operational Soviet ICBMs came as early as August 1960 (it had). But the man who had kept that knowledge secret until he won the presidential election in November 1960 had been assassinated the month before the *Herald* carried the exposure.

One serious area of concern was just what the Russians would make of all this. While the Soviets could not hide their launches, and indeed were quite open about them, countries around the world could pick up the radio signals containing all manner of information from engineering data to radio telemetry and scientific measurements. It was quite impossible to hide the launch of a rocket into space and radio traffic was a certain giveaway that prevented clandestine launches. But the pattern by which countries usually did business in various sectors of engineering as well as the observed practices in the development

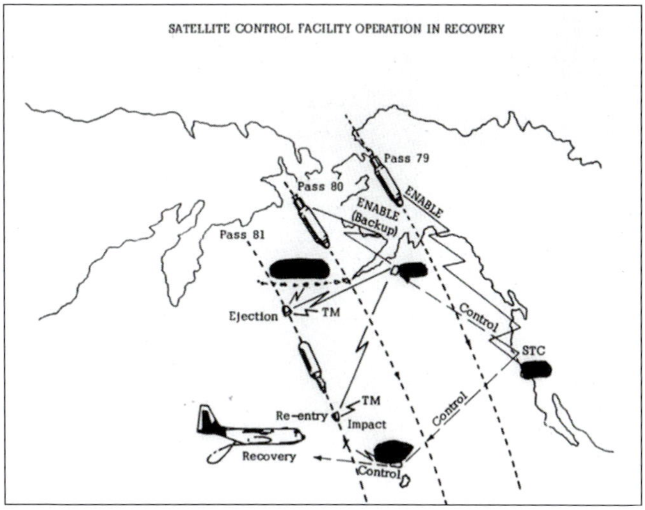

RIGHT Although no recovery vehicle was carried on the first CORONA flight, this orbit track shows the apparent migration of the orbit from east to west, in reality caused by the Earth moving in a counterclockwise motion when viewed from the North Pole. The recovery track lies off the western seaboard of the United States. *(NRO)*

of military systems provided a profile of how projects were put together and, in observing the intensity of effort applied to new endeavors, to gauge their value to the host country.

This "patterning" of government administrative control over national projects worked directly in favor of CORONA. The Russians were not impressed by America's display of halting progress and lack of results from the relatively small-scale Vanguard satellite program set up as a rather lackluster contribution to the International Geophysical Year. They observed with some amusement how officials scurried around to get a German rocket scientist to put together a test missile to shoot up America's first artificial satellite the size of a grapefruit while they, with their mighty R-7 rocket, could put in orbit a satellite weighing as much as a small car.

In this way did the Russians watch as the United States rushed, as if in panic, to hold numerous Congressional hearings before setting up NASA, the civilian space agency; and then watched again while the military, seemingly sidelined in their own endeavors, put up a small satellite launched by a small rocket. Surely nothing could come of this and surely no seriously effective piece of equipment could be orbited by a Thor-Agena launch vehicle, the lift-off thrust of which was less than one-fifth that of their own R-7?

By seeming to characterize the collective behavior of an entire nation and its people, from the apparent simplicity with which the publicly disclosed Discoverer program was announced, the Russians interpreted it as a hastily contrived research program providing a vehicle for exploring separately many aspects of the space environment. In truth, at the end of the 1950s it was the Russians who were already falling seriously behind the United States, although neither side knew it at the time. But it was the way the Soviets interpreted US behavior that was one of the best covers for CORONA, hidden inside the Discoverer program.

With the American predilection for making a loud noise and big news out of major decisions in modernizing the armed forces with new equipment, launching new ships, rolling out new aircraft and mounting big engineering projects, the dry and low-key, matter-of-fact way in which this program was made public as part of the big disinformation campaign effectively diverted suspicion. It seemed completely out of character yet it fit exquisitely within

BELOW A schematic of the KH-1 camera satellite on its Agena A stage with recovery vehicle and its retro-rocket in the nose section colored red. *(Giuseppe de Chiara)*

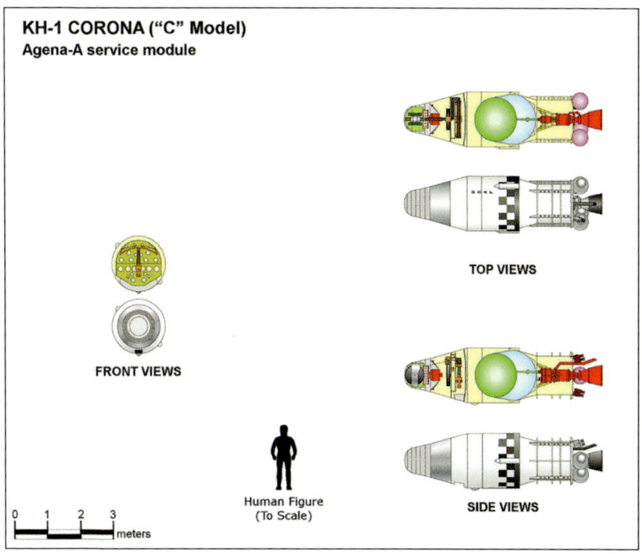

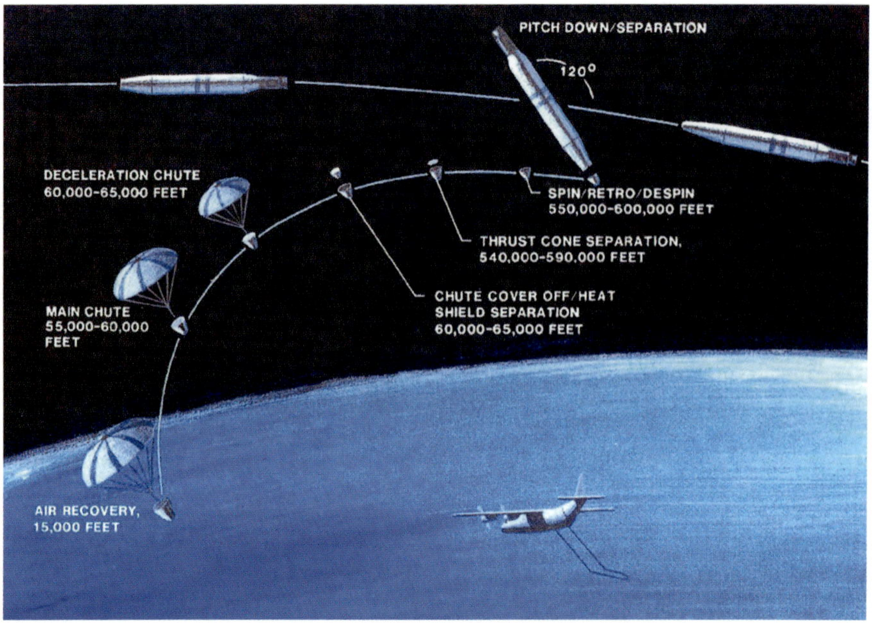

RIGHT The recovery process for CORONA film buckets involved a complex sequence of maneuvers that began with the correct attitude orientation of the satellite and continued with correct de-orbiting of the "bucket" and its heat shield. *(NRO)*

Eisenhower's predilection for quiet, unfussed, preparation and low-key intelligence gathering. And in one way the CIA knew that and played to the gallery.

To reinforce the secrecy, when the press got hold of snippets of the Discoverer story and began to piece together separate parts of the real story the Air Force and the CIA were not seen to react, reinforcing the view among many in the military – who knew nothing of this venture – that such a thing was impossible, knowing the procurement and development process as they did. In this way both the Air Force and the CIA learned a completely new way of misdirecting (misinforming), by way of "detached association," prying eyes – both inside and outside the military – for future classified projects and programs.

As the program developed and evolved, what had at the beginning been a rather informal effort closely guarded within the appropriate channels at the Air Force and the CIA became increasingly formal and institutionalized. Established on September 6, 1961, the National Reconnaissance Office, or NRO (see Appendix 1), which was set up as a top secret organization never publicly admitted to exist for three decades, would be the natural home of the photo-reconnaissance satellite. Tasked with management of spy satellites for the Air Force and the CIA, the first director of the NRO, Dr. J.V. Charyk, chose to leave CORONA within the CIA, since it was deemed to have a limited life remaining and would soon be superseded by SAMOS E-5. But the LANYARD system was moved across to the NRO.

The precursor camera to the system used in CORONA was designed by Prof. Walter Levison of Boston University, who would help found the Itek Corporation, and this design had been contracted by the CIA. It was a development of cameras built for the U-2 spy-plane and for the GENETRIX balloons. It had originally been expected that Fairchild would provide the cameras for CORONA but, along with the US Intelligence Board, the CIA's Richard Bissell preferred that Itek be the system designer with Fairchild working as a subcontractor for both design and manufacture. Fairchild would be phased out entirely during 1960.

Shortly before the planned flight operations, a joint press release was issued on December 3, 1958, to the effect that the Air Force was initiating a series of flights with a spacecraft that would explore the environmental conditions in space after a series of test launches and then go on to carry biomedical experiments contributing toward the day when humans would fly in space. There would be five biomedical flights, it said, the first two with mice on launches 3 and 5 and a primate on flight 7. The release went on to describe two radiometric payloads that would study the navigation of vehicles in space.

An operational CORONA flight would incorporate a General Electric Satellite Recovery Vehicle (SRV), commonly known as the "bucket" because it would be released from the forward section of the Agena and return to Earth with the film shot during orbital operations. Launched in a southerly direction by the 672nd Strategic Missile Squadron from Vandenberg AFB, the spacecraft would enter a polar orbit flying first over the South Pole. At the end of its nominally one-day mission the ejection sequence for the bucket would be initiated by radio command from the station in Alaska and recovery would be conducted by an airborne snatch executed by the 6593rd Test Squadron, training for which began while the satellite and the Agena stage were still being developed.

One drawback with the use of Vandenberg was that the Southern Pacific railroad ran close by and the Air Force was nervous about having carloads of passengers gawking at the launch site with cameras clicking while launching what only a few knew were highly classified CORONA payloads masquerading as scientific research flights. By scrutinizing the timetables, launches could be synchronized to windows within gaps in the Southern Pacific schedule. Not that there was anything to see, but so tight was the security that it just didn't seem right to have trainloads of inquisitive passengers rolling by!

Tied to this launch window was a requirement to launch in daylight and to synchronize the path so that on a typical 24-hour mission of 17 orbits, seven would cross Soviet and Chinese territory, also allowing for daylight recovery. By combining these requirements an afternoon launch was the optimum period in the day – with the precise time set by the Southern Pacific timetable!

The sequence of events necessary to get hold of the film once the camera had done its job was equally taxing. After the photo sequence was complete and the command was sent to de-orbit the SRV, the Agena stage would pitch down 60° so that the bucket would be in the correct orientation with respect to the flight path. After the SRV separated from the front of the assembly it would be spin-stabilized at 70.5 rpm by small spin-rockets to maintain it at that angle, the nose section pointing down. The retro-rocket would fire to decelerate the capsule by 1,270 feet/second (387 m/sec) some 3 minutes 27 seconds later and de-spin rockets would fire to slow the rate of rotation to 10.5 rpm. About 1.8 seconds later the retro-rocket thrust cone would separate from the blunt aft end and the SRV would begin re-entry.

During descent through the atmosphere the nose cone would decelerate due to friction with the atmosphere, kinetic energy released as heat being removed through ablation. About 9 minutes 37 seconds after thrust cone ejection the heat shield would fall away to reveal the spherical container – the bucket – with the exposed film. This would release the drogue parachute immediately followed by the main parachute in the reefed condition, fully deployed 5 seconds after reef deploy to lower the capsule to the recovery area.

The recovery technique called for the aircraft to fly over the descending capsule and snag the parachute or its shrouds in a trapeze-like hook suspended below the aircraft and winch the capsule aboard. During the test phase before flights began, only 49 recoveries were achieved in 75 simulated drops using personal

BELOW The sequence of air-snatch recovery activities shown here involves a JC-130, a variant of the C-130 transport aircraft. Several passes were feasible and the technique was honed to a fine degree where the majority of buckets were snatched at first pass. *(NRO)*

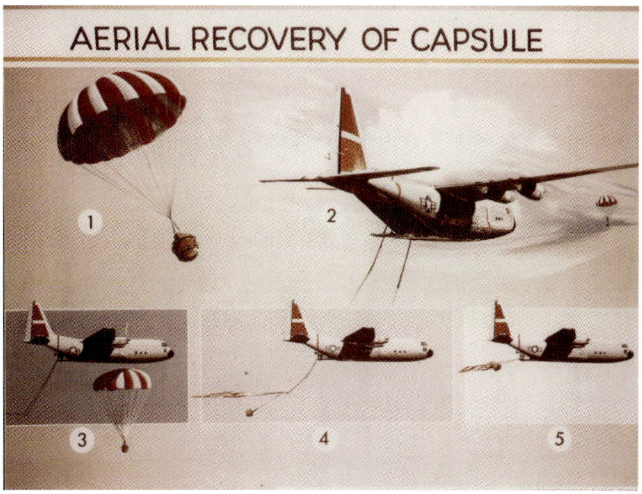

ABOVE **The Fairchild C-119 was used for the early bucket snatches, here being conducted using a flexible trapeze.** *(USAF)*

ABOVE **A test weight simulator for a recoverable capsule gives the crew of this C-119 practice runs at getting it right the first time!** *(USAF)*

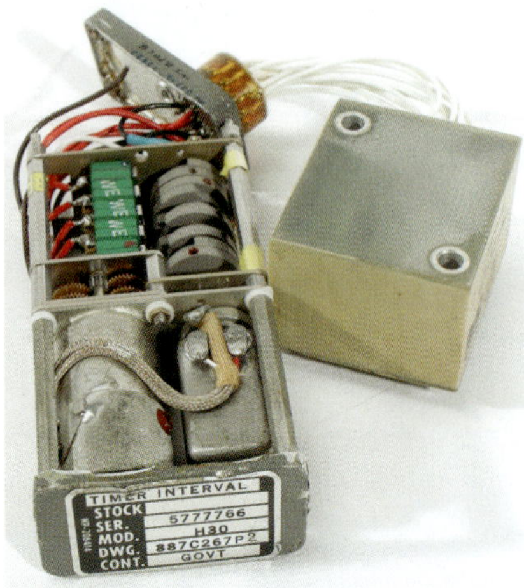

RIGHT **The electromechanical timing clock that ran several functions in the recovery capsule was built by General Electric.** *(GE)*

parachutes. And using an early type of recovery parachute only four were recovered of 15 attempts when the design of the parachute was changed with only five successes in 11 drops.

The real problem was in the sink rate of 33 feet/second (10 m/sec) with a parachute weighed down by the mass of the capsule. The ideal descent rate was 10 feet/sec (6 m/sec), during which a recovery aircraft would have time for four passes to get it right. Early flights in the operational program would use the Fairchild C-119 but later the Lockheed C-130 Hercules was inducted to conduct bucket recovery. By the time space flights started and bucket capture was required for real the parachute design had improved markedly, giving the pilots the option of two or three passes.

Flight operations

The first two scheduled Discoverer flights did not have buckets because they carried no cameras. The flights were configured to test the integration of Thor and Agena and the sequential operation of all systems during a typical mission in orbit. But it was not a good start. In an amazingly brief period the Discoverer program had reached flight status in little more than a year after departing from the mainstream development of WS-117L. The first flight was set up to go from LC-75 at Vandenberg, two years after the first flight of a Thor missile with 30 flights of which 17 had been failures. Nevertheless, the first two-stage configuration, the Thor-Able, had already demonstrated that the rocket could carry an upper stage into orbit.

The countdown was progressing as planned on January 21, 1959, when the auto-sequencer was initiated at T-60 minutes, beginning the scheduled electrical tests of the launch vehicle's hydraulic system while the Agena stage was being loaded with hypergolic propellants. The Thor was still dry at this point but a controller decided to run a check on the launch computer sequencer. A spurious electrical signal triggered an indication of stage separation that caused the Agena ullage motors to fire and the turbopumps to start spinning ready for delivering propellant to the Agena's rocket motor.

A reaction from an alert controller sent a signal to shut down the Agena start sequence and the stage settled down on to the Thor main stage, collapsing the adapter connecting Thor to the Agena but not deforming it sufficiently to cause it to fall to the ground. As corrosive and highly toxic propellants spilled from the Agena it ran down the sides of the Thor and caused some damage. It was several hours before the onboard batteries ran dry and technicians could access the pad to begin dismantling the configuration. Thor would be returned to Douglas for refurbishment but the Agena was wasted.

This attempt was designated Discoverer 0 but the first launch occurred (as Discoverer I) on February 28 after several postponements and a 24-hour delay due to problems with tank pressurization and propellant loading. At precisely 13:49 local time the Thor rocket (serial no 163) burst into life and slowly climbed away from LC-75. Due to a low injection angle there was some uncertainty as to whether the Agena A (serial no 1022) had made it into orbit, as no radar tracking was obtained and no telemetry signals were received. For several hours tracking stations in Alaska and Hawaii tried to raise it.

This was an exacting and drawn-out process. As the Earth rotated on its axis, the ground track would appear to move with each 90-minute orbit, placing the spacecraft approximately 1,500 miles (2,400 km) further west each time it crossed the same spot on the equator, returning to approximately the same location 24 hours later. Despite successive bids to acquire a signal, and some reports that a faint response had been detected, an investigation determined that Discoverer I had re-entered over Antarctica before achieving its planned polar orbit.

Next up after the engineering verification flight, not altogether a success, was to launch Discoverer II with a bucket but no camera system. The objective was to secure an effective operational orbit and then de-orbit the SRV and recover it by air-snatch. The launch took place at 13:18:39 local time on April 13 with Thor 170 burning for 159 seconds before separation and ignition of Agena 1018 for a burn of 120 seconds, Discoverer II entering an orbit of 124 miles (199 km) x 148 miles (238 km) with an orbital inclination of 89.9° and an orbital period of 88.9 minutes.

The orbit was slightly different to the planned one, the orbital period a little shorter than intended, but in orientating itself base-forward the satellite was the first from anywhere to achieve attitude stabilization about roll, pitch and yaw axes. This was crucial for stabilization and pointing angles essential for fixed camera alignment with the surface of the Earth. It was a great step forward but one which could not be publicly revealed for its true function.

The slightly lower orbit had an impact on the outcome of the flight because the separation of the SRV and the entire recovery procedure was triggered by an on-board timer which was set to a 94-minute orbital period. Tracking stations could uplink a corrective signal to alter the separation sequence and this was done as the satellite passed over the Kodiak, Alaska, station but the displays showed that the command had not been received on board the satellite. This was erroneous and the controller sent it a second time, but on receiving a repeat of the signal already accepted it reverted to the installed time.

Programmed to remain in space a day, instead of being aligned in orbit for a recovery in the region of Hawaii the shorter orbital period placed Discoverer II for a drop close to the Norwegian island of Spitsbergen, located at 78.5°N, just 760 miles (1,220 km) from the North Pole, within the Arctic Circle. It was always understood that errors in orbital positioning and timing could prove problematic, if not downright embarrassing, should a bucket come down where it could be retrieved by a foreign power. Spitsbergen hosts a Russian mining camp which was also the landfall for a Soviet undersea hydrophone line monitoring the movement of US and NATO submarines in and out of the region.

The recovery operation expecting the bucket to arrive close to Hawaii was the 6594th Test Wing led by Lieutenant Colonel Charles G. "Moose" Mathison, a man who got his well-earned nickname from an uncompromising determination which usually demolished any opposition. He called Major General Tufte Johnsen of the Norwegian Air Force Northern Command and requested permission to access the area and search for the bucket. Ironically, Mathison was not privileged to know anything

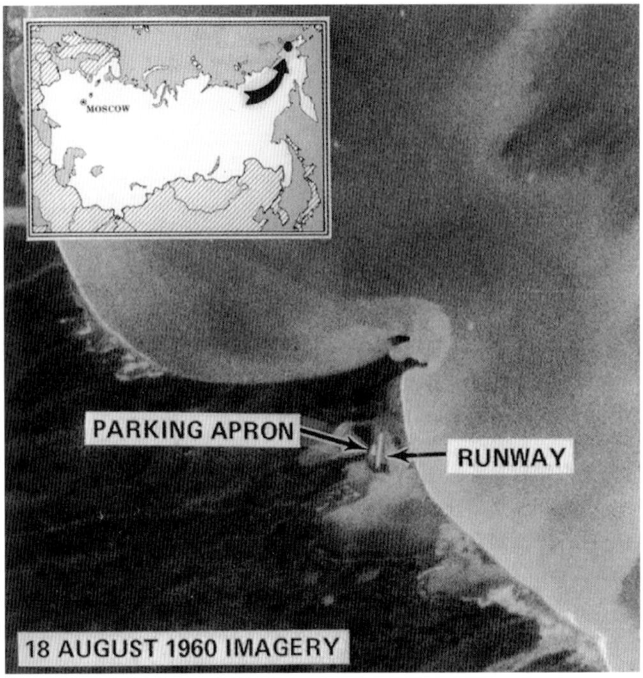

ABOVE The first successful picture returned from a CORONA satellite showed a runway that was completely unknown until observed in the processed film during August 1960. *(NRO)*

about CORONA but thought the satellite was returning to Earth with science instruments.

Telemetry from the still orbiting Agena about attitude and changes in the satellite's center of gravity indicated that separation had been

RIGHT The GRAB-1 satellite sits above the Transit 2A satellite with which it was launched as the first electronic spy over Soviet territory. *(NRO)*

achieved but there was never any evidence that it safely re-entered the atmosphere. Despite strenuous efforts to find it, nothing was discovered, although snowshoe tracks were spotted circling the area it was predicted to land. This is moderately significant because only the Russians wore snowshoes in that area; Norwegians used skis.

Some years later there were rumors that the Russians had recovered the capsule but, if they had, there was nothing inside it to compromise the Americans, only a simulated biological payload – this was, after all, an engineering verification flight. In fact, it might have helped allay suspicion if the Russians had recovered the Discoverer II capsule, seeming to confirm the professed purpose of the program and its recoverable satellite pods widely discussed in the press. But the achievement was notable in itself, for if it had successfully returned to Earth, it was the first man-made object to do so.

The CORONA/Discoverer SRV was shaped like a dome with angled sides, circular cross-section and a slightly convex base to which was attached the retro-rocket. The shape of the SRV was driven by the work of engineers crafting the warheads that would spear back into the atmosphere on ballistic trajectories carrying nuclear devices to their targets. The SRV capsule had a diameter of 33 inches (84 cm), a length of 27 inches (68 cm) and a weight of 160 pounds (72.5 kg). Located inside the kettle-shaped re-entry vehicle, the assembled SRV had a mass of 300 pounds (136 kg).

The re-entry vehicle inherited a great deal of research work on shape and materials from the General Electric work on warheads, and development of the SRV was equally as challenging as the Agena or the KH camera systems. GE's Ingard Clausen managed the SRV program before Edward A. Miller took over and Hilliard W. Page was responsible for overall facility management, making immense contributions to the CORONA program. Many people populated the CORONA story and were equally important in this effort which even today is eclipsed by the more publicized achievements of the space program.

If Discoverer II was in fact a success it was the last for almost 16 months. In the period between June 3, 1959, when Discoverer III was launched, and August 10, 1960, when Discoverer XIII lifted off, there were ten successive failures due to malfunction with the Thor, the Agena, on-orbit systems or, once, with the SRV retro-rocket. Four failed to reach orbit at all.

Despite publicity to the contrary, Discoverer III was the only one to fly a biological payload, consisting of four mice. They had replaced four other mice that were poisoned and died before launch when they gnawed toxic materials in the bucket. The flight was a failure when the vehicle did not reach orbital velocity and fell back through the atmosphere, but the repercussions were more significant than the single loss. Both this and the following flight were to have carried mice but the media pressed Air Force officials to answers that brought wide publicity and a formal complaint to the US ambassador from the British Society Against Cruel Sports.

Biological flights had been introduced to the Discoverer program to satisfy public curiosity as to the nature of these flights. Suddenly it appeared to be working against that cover story. Discoverer VII was scheduled to carry a monkey up but the attention drawn to these activities began to take on a negative feel, and although the engineering development for this flight continued it was eventually dropped and plans changed. There were to be no more biological flights carrying live animals in the Discoverer program; plans were restructured and the decision was made to start flying the spy cameras on the very next flight.

The first KH-1 camera system was carried by Agena 1023 on Discoverer IV, launched on the afternoon of June 25, 1959, the first complete CORONA package carried, but it too failed to reach orbit. Less than two months later Discoverer V could not operate its camera when the batteries failed and the attitude of the Agena was incorrect when the SRV separated, raising the orbit instead of lowering it.

Seven days later, on August 13, the camera on Discoverer VI failed and the SRV failed to separate when the retro-rocket malfunctioned, and on Discoverer VII, launched November 7, the Agena lost power preventing any of the systems from operating. A worse fate struck Discoverer VIII after launch on November 20: the Agena lost guidance during powered flight and achieved a high orbit but the camera failed; the SRV separated but came down long on the ground track and the bucket was not recovered.

But these were the obvious signs of a program in deep trouble. Added to the existing uncertainties of the time regarding the ability

LEFT Eerily similar in appearance to a Vanguard satellite, the GRAB provided proof that it was possible to map and analyze Soviet air defense radars from an orbiting detector in space. *(NRO)*

of rockets and launch vehicles to perform as expected were fundamental flaws in the design and operation of the cameras and associated equipment.

At the time a lot of rockets were failing and satellites were prone to sudden catastrophic malfunction. The learning curve was exceptionally steep and even in the experimental days of the late 1950s and early 1960s, had such a program been under open and public scrutiny it is doubtful it could have survived. On December 15, 1959, Bissell met with senior White House officials and Pentagon managers to analyze the problems and it was decided to keep flying because the problems being encountered were impossible to simulate since they were unknown until experienced in flight or in orbit. But while failure was costly the solutions were frequently even more expensive.

BELOW Launched on June 22, 1960, on a Thor-Able-Star launch vehicle from Cape Canaveral, GRAB and its accompanying Transit satellite opened new areas for exploitation in the use of space for detection and observation. *(NRO)*

Yet there were some areas where changes could raise the odds of flying a successful mission, one of which was to reduce weight and increase the margins for a successful orbital injection. Engineers set to work to pare off tiny amounts of metal and unnecessary pieces of material, insignificant on their own but which, cumulatively, began to grow a credible weight-reduction bonus. There was still a lot of engineering information needed from each flight and it would be some time before that instrumentation could be removed. One obvious solution was to increase the performance margin by moving to the planned Agena B and its dual-burn capability, but that stage would not be ready before the end of 1960.

Further improvements and weight-saving were made when Eastman Kodak replaced its acetate type 4401 film with a new product based on polyester, known as "Estar" by the manufacturer. Loaded with 3,600 feet (1,100 m) of film, there was considerable weight-saving potential by adopting Estar for each KH-1 camera assembly. Moreover, the acetate film had been a very real problem in tests, jamming and tearing being a common fault, which in turn caused the roll mechanism to jam.

Several minor issues helped shave off other problems, including the use of variable paint patterns to affect thermal reflection and emissivity, as maintaining an appropriate internal temperature had become a very real problem. In the absence of thermal convection in weightlessness and the absence of an atmosphere to ameliorate the extremes of temperature in space, thermal problems inside and outside the Agena/payload assembly was a knotty problem.

In a very real sense, the frequency with which these military satellites were being launched – the Discoverer series as well as others – was putting the Pentagon and the CIA at the cutting edge of satellite technology development. Of the 34 satellites and space probes launched into orbit by the United States to the end of 1960, 18 were operated by the military. Much of the information that would improve the reliability of the satellites and space probes was gleaned from the failures in these military flights. But improvements were also made to the SRV and the recovery processes, including adding chaff that would reflect radar signals to assist locating the bucket

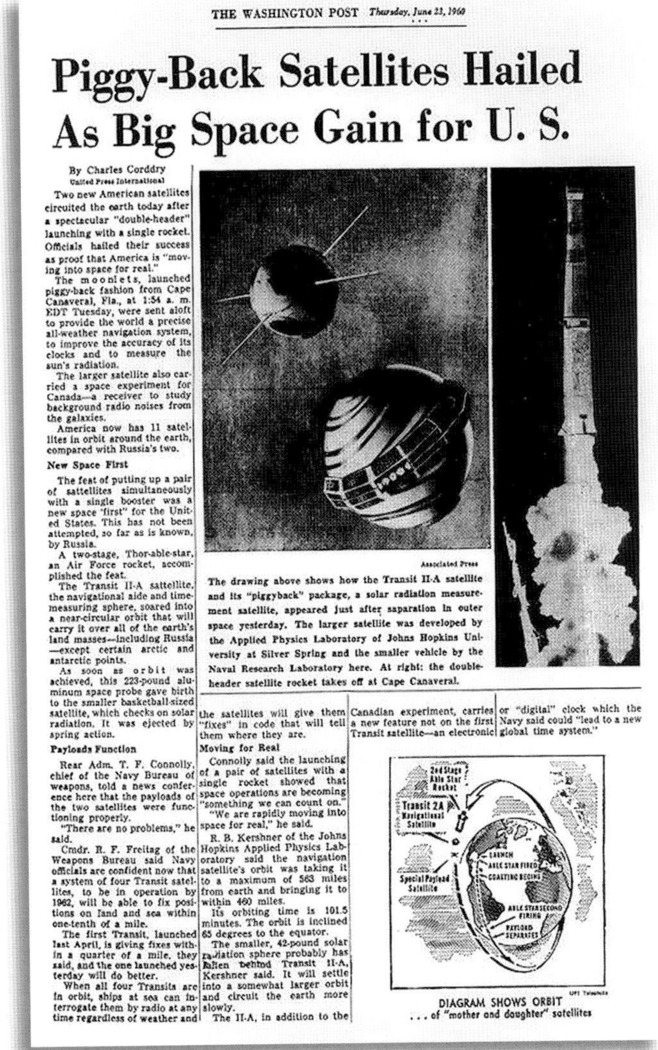

THE WASHINGTON POST Thursday, June 23, 1960

Piggy-Back Satellites Hailed As Big Space Gain for U. S.

By Charles Corddry
United Press International

Two new American satellites circuited the earth today after a spectacular "double-header" launching with a single rocket. Officials hailed their success as proof that America is "moving into space for real."

The moonlets, launched piggy-back fashion from Cape Canaveral, Fla., at 1:54 a. m. EDT Tuesday, were sent aloft to provide the world a precise all-weather navigation system, to improve the accuracy of its clocks and to measure the sun's radiation.

The larger satellite also carried a space experiment for Canada—a receiver to study background radio noises from the galaxies.

America now has 11 satellites in orbit around the earth, compared with Russia's two.

New Space First

The feat of putting up a pair of sattellites simultaneously with a single booster was a new space "first" for the United States. This has not been attempted, so far as is known, by Russia.

A two-stage, Thor-able-star, an Air Force rocket, accomplished the feat.

The Transit II-A sattellite, the navigational aide and time-measuring sphere, soared into a near-circular orbit that will carry it over all of the earth's land masses—including Russia—except certain arctic and antarctic points.

As soon as orbit was achieved, this 223-pound aluminum space probe gave birth to the smaller basketball-sized satellite, which checks on solar radiation. It was ejected by spring action.

Payloads Function

Rear Adm. T. F. Connolly, chief of the Navy Bureau of weapons, told a news conference here that the payloads of the two satellites were functioning properly.

"There are no problems," he said.

Cmdr. R. F. Freitag of the Weapons Bureau said Navy officials are confident now that a system of four Transit satellites, to be in operation by 1962, will be able to fix positions on land and sea within one-tenth of a mile.

The first Transit, launched last April, is giving fixes within a quarter of a mile, they said, and the one launched yesterday will do better.

When all four Transits are in orbit, ships at sea can interrogate them by radio at any time regardless of weather and the satellites will give them "fixes" in code that will tell them where they are.

Moving for Real

Connolly said the launching of a pair of satellites with a single rocket showed that space operations are becoming "something we can count on."

"We are rapidly moving into space for real," he said.

R. B. Kershner of the Johns Hopkins Applied Physics Laboratory said the navigation satellite's orbit was taking it to a maximum of 563 miles from earth and bringing it to within 460 miles.

Its orbiting time is 101.5 minutes. The orbit is inclined 65 degrees to the equator.

The smaller, 42-pound solar radiation sphere probably has fallen behind Transit II-A, Kershner said. It will settle into a somewhat larger orbit and circuit the earth more slowly.

The II-A, in addition to the Canadian experiment, carries a new feature not on the first Transit satellite—an electronic or "digital" clock which the Navy said could "lead to a new global time system."

Associated Press

The drawing above shows how the Transit II-A satellite and its "piggyback" package, a solar radiation measurement satellite, appeared just after separation in outer space yesterday. The larger satellite was developed by the Applied Physics Laboratory of Johns Hopkins University at Silver Spring and the smaller vehicle by the Naval Research Laboratory here. At right: the double-header satellite rocket takes off at Cape Canaveral.

UPI Telephoto

DIAGRAM SHOWS ORBIT
. . . of "mother and daughter" satellites

as it descended and adding a strobe light to assist with recovery from an ocean splashdown.

During this period of self-analysis, the Discoverer program halted flights, resuming again with the launch of Discoverer IX on February 4, 1960; but the Thor stage malfunctioned when it shut down prematurely yet again. Discoverer X launched 15 days later and suffered a similar fate when the main stage engine gimballed back and forth, causing the rocket to weave an erratic path before tumbling and exploding as it disintegrated. Neither had reached orbit. But things seemed to go well with Discoverer XI, launched on April 15. The satellite achieved its correct orbit, the camera operated as planned, all the film was exposed and the SRV separated. Seconds later the spin rockets exploded, destroying the capsule before it re-entered. It was not recovered because the pointing angle pushed the SRV into a higher orbit instead of safely bringing it down through the atmosphere.

Paradoxically, President Eisenhower looked to CORONA with increasing support as the sole means by which he could legitimately and without compromise spy on the Soviet Union to assess its military capabilities and even, perhaps, its readiness for conflict. Accordingly, it was comparatively easy to get an extension of the Discoverer program to 29 planned flights with the possibility of a further six added later. But inside the "need to know" camp there was increasing frustration, which caused letters of concern to be sent to Lockheed's senior leadership from former SAC commander, and now Air Force Chief of Staff, General Curtis LeMay, who wanted detailed information on the Soviet war machine.

But then something else happened, outside the Discoverer/CORONA program but well within the intelligence community. Following a limited resumption of spy flights over Russia, a U-2 piloted by Francis Gary Powers was shot down near Sverdlovsk on May 1, 1960. It was less than three months after Eisenhower had mused over the high risk to these flights from Soviet air defenses and pondered the nightmare of a show trial with wreckage placed on public display. But the dire need for robust intelligence would not go away and the president had been pushed to the edge by his own determination to gather information.

In the intense fervor that gripped the program following the Powers incident, it emerged that a disproportionate number of failures were occurring with the spin/de-spin rockets and that faults here were causing several failures to get a recoverable bucket home. The rockets fired unevenly, sometimes sending the capsule in the wrong direction or even exploding and destroying the SRV. A solution was to replace these solid propellant charges with cold-gas jets using nitrogen and Freon gas expelled under pressure, exerting a thrust of 867 N for 0.8 seconds.

ABOVE Public awareness of the expanding role of space applications for national security began to flood out during 1960, with the press lauding the achievement and beginning the legitimization of space budgets and the value of the technology. *(The Washington Post)*

ABOVE The bucket capsule from Discoverer XIII is recovered by the crew of Colonel "Moose" Mathison, with General Bernard Schriever looking at the camera approvingly. *(USAF)*

The new motors were retrofitted to Discoverer XII, which was a pure engineering flight and had no camera system on board but instead carried a large number of diagnostic systems for engineers to fault-tree every minor discrepancy and in effect, for the first time, to provide a full performance analysis. Air Force officials used to forensically examining every piece of a wrecked airplane were upset by their inability to get their hands on failed hardware in space, left abandoned in orbit or destroyed during re-entry. The radical new form of in-flight monitoring and real-time readout pioneered by the North American X-15 rocket research aircraft was now being applied to satellites and specifically to the Discoverer satellites and their CORONA packages.

BELOW The first intact return of an object from orbit shared headline news with the trial of U-2 pilot Gary Powers, chillingly bringing an end to one era and marking the beginning of another. *(The New York Times)*

"All the News That's Fit to Print"

The New York Times.

LATE CITY EDITION

NEW YORK, SATURDAY, AUGUST 20, 1960. FIVE CENTS

SPACE CAPSULE IS CAUGHT IN MID-AIR BY U. S. PLANE ON RE-ENTRY FROM ORBIT

FLIERS ARE CITED

Vehicle Is Recovered 8,500 Feet Up in C-119's 'Trapeze'

SECURITY COUNCIL MEETS TOMORROW ON CRISIS IN CONGO

Lumumba Lays 'Blackmail' to Hammarskjold, Who Assails Incidents

POWERS GETS A 10-YEAR SENTENCE; SOVIET ASSERTS PENALTY IS MILD, BUT EISENHOWER FINDS IT SEVERE

U-2 TRIAL ENDED

3 Years to Be in Prison —Rest May Be Spent Working in Russia

Russians Orbit a Satellite Carrying 2 Dogs and TV

U.S. BARS LOAN USE FOR CUBA'S SUGAR

Forbids Purchases With Aid From Washington—Cites 'Difficulty of Business'

Discoverer XII was launched on June 29, but horizon sensors on the Agena misread the measurements when the telemetry signal interfered with the structure and the stage pitched down instead of up, driving it back to destructive re-entry. During this period, and up to the date of the next launch, an exhaustive series of tests with a modified SRV and its new cold-gas jets was conducted with parachute tests in a simulation of an actual re-entry from space. Lessons were learned there and the technology for bucket recovery advanced on a range of fronts. Tests that should have been conducted earlier in the program – instead of satellites being rushed into operational flights long before the equipment, or the technology, was ready – were now being conducted.

Discoverer XIII was launched on August 10, 1960, when Thor 231, carrying Agena 1057, lifted off at 13:38 local time. Throughout the flight there was a series of minor problems but none were of sufficient magnitude to impede the sequence of events that helped engineers better understand the behavior of the systems on board. It carried no camera, its aim being to verify the modifications and changes made in preceding tests. Charles Mathison had very good reason to want this to be a good flight – he had been promoted and was about to leave his post as commander of the 6594th Test Wing for a new job in Washington DC.

As programmed, Discoverer XIII's on-board timer started the recovery sequence after 17 orbits of the Earth, 26 hours 37 minutes after launch, during which it had passed over the USSR on a simulated spy flight. Signals picked up at the Kodiak station confirmed that SRV separation had taken place and that it had been safely pushed away from the Agena by springs. Without any further radio contact the SRV descended, releasing the bucket as it should, a tiny camera inside the base of the capsule taking pictures of parachute deployment.

Radio signals picked up by the recovery aircraft confused the operating personnel and the bucket splashed down into the Pacific Ocean some way off from the expected location, 288 miles (460 km) west-northwest of Hawaii. Converging on the splashdown point, now accurately pinpointed, the USNS *Haiti Victory* steamed to the recovery zone, launching a helicopter to where two C-119s were circling the spot in the sea where the strobe light and a yellowish-green dye marker revealed the tiny bucket floating in the 12-foot (3.6 m) swell. Some three hours after it splashed down the first Discoverer SRV bucket successfully recovered was plucked from the sea.

So fine a line had been drawn between the Discoverer "science" missions and the CORONA KH-1 camera flights that it had always been the plan to make a grand public display of the first capsule recovered from space. However, had the first recovery been of a camera-carrying flight there was a plan to swap it for an engineering capsule devoid of any associated equipment which would identify it as a spy flight. In the dying months of his administration the president was still nervous about letting the Russians know there was a major, well-funded, program to spy on their country on a routine basis. As it turned out, Discoverer XIII was an engineering flight and the genuine capsule was put on display, alongside a US flag carried aboard the satellite and a beaming president!

With the first successful bucket recovery behind them, CORONA officials decided to make the next flight a fully operational spy flight, packing a 20-pound (9 kg) roll of Ester film into the KH-1 camera payload. With the cessation of U-2 penetration flights over the USSR, the CIA began what was, in effect (although not formally), to convert all their rationales for overhead photography targets to a defined list of objectives. Of paramount importance to the CIA was the need for strategic intelligence on the magnitude of Soviet missile production and deployment, but the Air Force wanted to pinpoint targets it would have to attack in a pre-emptive strike to prevent the Russians launching their missiles.

The CIA calculated that of the total surface area of the USSR, approximately 65% would be suitable for the deployment of ICBMs in fixed launch sites. This was reduced to 24% of total area when factoring in road

LEFT Discoverer personnel celebrate achievements believed impossible a few years earlier, their names remaining unidentified for their role in CORONA for four decades. *(NRO)*

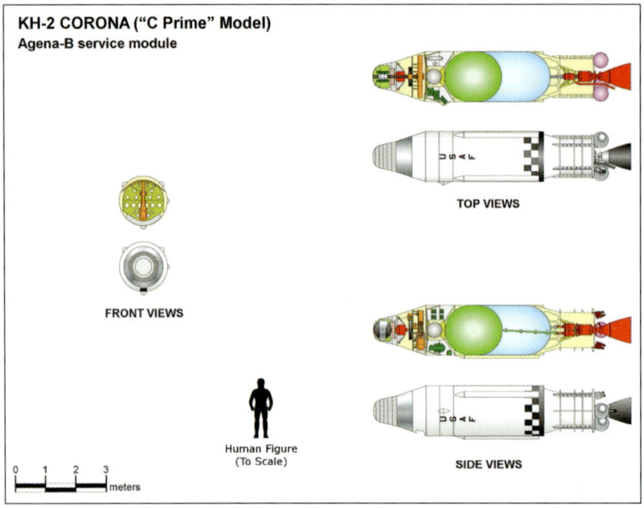

ABOVE The KH-2 CORONA camera schematic with the improved Agena B stage capable of restart. *(Giuseppe de Chiara)*

and rail transportation lines, stations, nodes and available track linking machine building installations (rocket factories). That left a total surface area of 2,081,000 square miles (5,390,000 km^2) over which to search for possible launch sites, which, when mapped, the Air Force would translate into targets for US ballistic missiles.

There had been so little photographic coverage of the USSR from the U-2 that vast areas were largely unknown. For a long time US intelligence agencies used captured German maps of Russia compiled from high-altitude photographs taken by the Luftwaffe during the Second World War. They revealed the incongruities in Soviet maps of Russian territories, deliberately falsified to confuse an invader. The job of mapping the USSR would have to be done from external sources and most of the work would be done by satellites.

By the summer of 1960 the newly established Committee on Overhead Reconnaissance (COMAR) short-listed 32 high-priority areas where there was significant evidence to suggest ICBM activity and which CORONA cameras should address. There was significant uncertainty about the magnitude of the Soviet missile force and rumors ran rife as the US closed in upon a presidential election due to take place on November 8 with platforms substantially different on reaction to what was perceived as a Soviet threat. Both Richard Nixon, Republican nominee as successor to Dwight Eisenhower, and John F. Kennedy promised expansion of America's nuclear deterrent but facts were few and

RIGHT An aerial view of launch complex 75-3-5 which would later be redesignated Space Launch Complex 11 (SLC-11), with the Thor rocket horizontal and its servicing shed at left capable of being moved back and forth on a track. The missile resides on an erector and launch table and this configuration is typical of RAF stations in the UK where the missile was deployed. *(USAF)*

LEFT A display model of the KH-4 CORONA payload elements as arranged in sequence but without the Agena stage, which would be to the left. The heat shield for the recovery capsule is at right with shroud. *(David Baker)*

hyperbole was in the ascendant.

Fully equipped as a CORONA flight with the KH-1 C system, Discoverer XIV was launched at 12:57 local time on August 18, 1960, and entered a normal orbit with a period of 94.5 minutes. However, rounding the North Pole close to completing its first orbit, telemetry indicated that the Agena was pointing in the wrong direction; but it soon corrected itself and the first photographic pass over the Soviet Union began during the second orbit. As the Earth rotated beneath the fixed orbit of Discoverer XIV successive passes shifted farther west on each pass and by the ninth orbit it was passing across Eastern Europe. It worked perfectly, taking pictures as planned, and with a full load of exposed film it began its re-entry on the 17th orbit.

Fairchild C-119s were rotating around the racetrack path ready for the air-snatch but it took three tries to snag the parachute lines, down around 8,000 feet (2,400 m). Radio silence prevented an exuberant crew announcing their success but a call from a ground station provided opportunity to claim the very first air-recovery of a retrieved CORONA bucket with a very full load of telltale images across several successive swathes of the Soviet Union. The ironic twist was that on the very day the US obtained the first spy satellite pictures of Russia, in Moscow Gary Powers was given a ten-year prison sentence for spying from the air in Soviet airspace.

The 3,000 feet (914 m) of film exposed by Discoverer XIV covered an area of 1.65 million square miles (4.3 million km^2). This equated to a greater area in seven orbits lasting a total of just over ten hours than had been photographed in the 24 overflights of the USSR by the U-2 spy-plane. Many places had been photographed for the first time, particularly areas in central Siberia, albeit at a resolution much less than had been obtained by the U-2. Nevertheless, the information was invaluable and allowed the mapping of facilities, buildings, airfields and runways completely unknown at the time. Missile test ranges, lengths of runway, weapons storage locations and fuel depots in Eastern Europe were visible.

Generally the quality of the film was good, but streaks of light and dark running across the film puzzled scientists until they recognized that these were "coronal" (sic) flashes from solar activity. At one stroke the quality of the images encouraged further flights, pointed toward more advanced cameras and opened the possibility of new capabilities using bigger and more powerful vehicles. It also called into question the need for a dedicated organization to operate the new system, and the National Reconnaissance Office was born (see Appendix 1).

In fact, CORONA was not the first spy satellite to reach orbit and deliver information about the Soviet Union. Back in 1958, when NASA got the Vanguard program from the Naval Research Laboratory, a concerted examination was made of what role the NRL could play in space activities. It had a lot of expertise and had Navy-unique requirements that could be accommodated by exploiting that research. It would benefit the Navy, and be of use to the Air Force too, if better knowledge about Russian radar sites could be obtained directly from space and it was in this area that the Navy, among others, focused its attention.

The opportunity came immediately after Gary Powers was shot down in the U-2 on May 1, 1960, quickly followed by a public display of the wreckage in Moscow and a show trial. That prompted Eisenhower to halt U-2 overflights of Soviet territory and to seek acceleration in the CORONA program. But there was a universal "hurry-up" for all military space projects, and that included an electronic intelligence gathering satellite originally developed under Project Tattletale and put under a strict security system known as Canes. Just four days after the U-2 incident, Eisenhower gave approval for the launch of the first electronic intelligence (ELINT) satellite, which took place on June 22, less than two months later.

An acronym for Galactic Radiation and Background, the cover name for what was now known as Project Dyno, GRAB was carried into space along with the Transit 2A navigation satellite by a Thor-Able-Star rocket from Cape Canaveral and placed in a 383 miles x 639 miles (616 km x 1,028 km) orbit inclined 66.77° to the equator. This was the launch in which the first SNAP nuclear power plant was orbited. Aircraft flying close to Soviet borders could not "see" the transmitted pulses from Russian radar, which went in straight lines across the horizon and into space. As GRAB orbited the Earth its path carried it through the beam of the radar projecting into space at an inclination and that would provide intelligence information on the frequency and on the width of the beam as well as its strength.

Powered by nickel-cadmium batteries and with solar cells, GRAB-1 operated for three months with a total of 22 data passes of 40 minutes each over the Soviet Union and China. The second attempt to get a GRAB satellite into orbit failed on November 30 when the rocket malfunctioned, but GRAB-2 was orbited on June 29, 1961, along with Transit 4A and another small satellite called Injun, which was for geophysical research. This time the ELINT satellite continued to operate for 14 months. Another launch vehicle failure occurred on January 24, 1962, as did a fifth satellite carried on a solid propellant Scout rocket on April 26, 1962.

As GRAB satellites passed through a Soviet radar beam they captured the signal within a specified beam-width using small antennae, which information was transmitted to small collection sites within the satellite's field of view manned by intelligence personnel. This information was recorded on magnetic tape and then sent by courier to the Naval Research Laboratory where it was examined and a duplicate set sent to the National Security Agency at Fort Meade, Maryland. Other tapes were sent to Strategic Air Command headquarters at Omaha, Nebraska. Both the NSA and SAC used the information to characterize the nature of Soviet radar signals and to pinpoint their location.

When the National Reconnaissance Office was established in secret in August 1960 its ELINT satellite system was also designed to target Soviet radar installations and to garner information about Russian naval vessels. In all, seven POPPY launches, as they were code-named, took place between December 13, 1962, and December 14, 1971, using Thor-Agena rockets, with or without strap-on boosters. The POPPY program ended in 1977 and was succeeded by the Naval Ocean Surveillance System (NOSS), which has had three generations of satellites to date.

Growth

With the recovery of the bucket from Discoverer XIV in August 1960 all doubts about the ability of the CORONA system to provide useful intelligence was erased and confidence was high that the system could become a reliable source of photographic reconnaissance. Next up, Discoverer XV was launched on September 13, but the bucket was not air-snatched, hit the water, sank and could not be recovered. It was the last of the C-series (KH-1) cameras. Discoverer XVI, launched on October 26, carried the first of the C' (KH-2) cameras, but the Agena failed to separate from the Thor and the stack fell back through the atmosphere. Discoverer XVII launched on November 12 also failed, when after achieving orbit the film tore loose.

Discoverer XVIII was launched on December 7, the first successful flight of the KH-2 payload. It had almost twice the amount of film and potential photographic targets as the KH-1, covering more than 3,800,000 square miles (9,842,000 km^2) of Soviet territory. Moreover, with 65 lines/mm compared to 55 lines/mm for KH-1 cameras, resolution was 20% better, with some objects on the surface as small as 25 feet (7.6 m) just visible. The satellite remained in space for three days, versus the previous one day for KH-1 flights, and that allowed the gradual migration of the orbital ground track farther west with each pass, successive slices of territory coming into view.

What Discoverer XVIII proved was the low level of Soviet long-range ballistic missile deployments, beginning a realization that the United States was already far ahead of the USSR in strategic nuclear weapons and their rocket-boosted delivery systems. Soviet bravado and extravagant claims bolted to a closed society had overdone the job of putting fear into the hearts of potential enemies when in reality its propaganda campaigns had been baseless and untrue. Only selected space spectaculars created a false canopy of alarm and over-reaction.

The early months of 1961 were to inaugurate the first flights with the KH-5 system alongside continued flights with the KH-2. But prior to that, on December 10, 1960, Discoverer XIX launched a test package for the MIDAS missile detection system. MIDAS had been configured for launch on Atlas-Agena and the first flight had taken place on February 26, 1960, but the Atlas stage failed and the vehicle was lost. Another flight took place on May 24, 1960, but this was relegated to a test shot for sensors carried by the fully developed satellite.

MIDAS was precursor to the later, more advanced, space-based early warning systems that would give an early indication of Soviet ballistic missile launches against Western targets, supplementing the Ballistic Missile Early Warning System (BMEWS), which was

LEFT A KH-3 ready for launch as Discoverer 37 on January 13, 1962. The erector/ launcher has been lowered and the servicing shed retracted (left). *(USAF)*

a series of ground stations stretching across North America from the Canadian border and on to the UK. Eventually these would involve "Cobra" over-the-horizon (OTH) radar facilities that could, theoretically, provide trajectory information for incoming warheads and massed bomber formations.

The first two MIDAS flights launched from

BELOW A schematic of the KH-3 camera system and Agena B. *(Giuseppe de Chiara)*

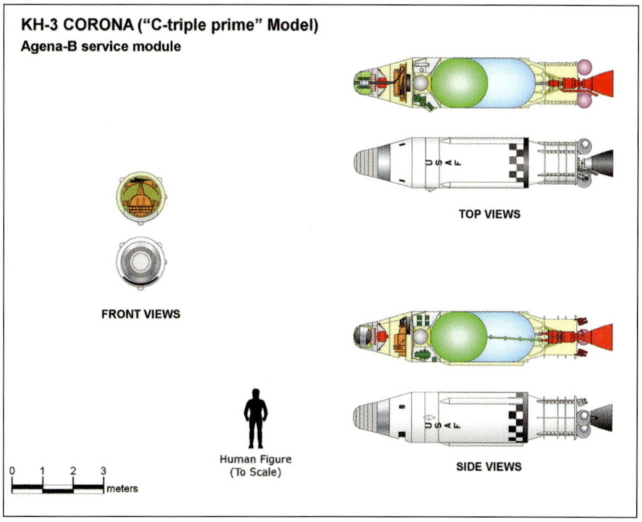

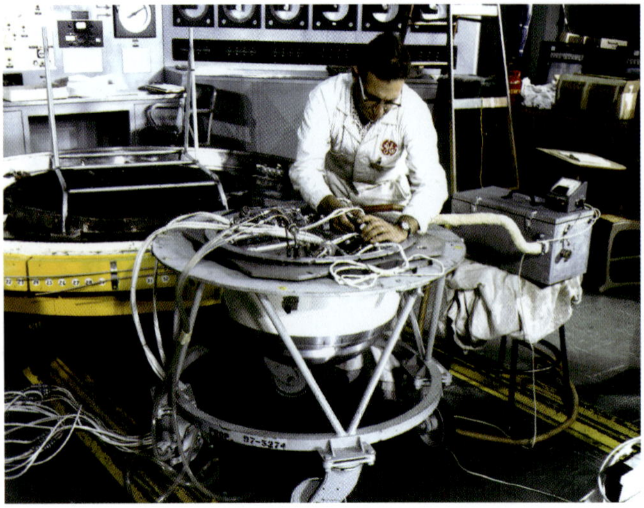

ABOVE **A rare example of a Discoverer re-entry capsule with biological payload, living up to the generalized nature of the program openly discussed with the public.** *(GE)*

Cape Canaveral, but the program shifted to the West Coast and Vandenberg Air Force Base, where the flight of Discoverer XIX carried more development sensors. Another flight, Discoverer XXI launched on February 18, 1961, carried infrared sensors, and the first flight of a MIDAS satellite from Vandenberg, using the Agena B, took place on July 24, 1961. It was a success and periodic MIDAS satellites were launched subsequently, until the project's cancellation in favor of a more technically advanced system. But the Discoverer program had satisfied one of the publicly lauded rolls of the program: to test new technologies for space systems.

RIGHT **A MIDAS sensor package as part of the missile defense system. MIDAS sensors were lifted into orbit aboard the Discoverer XIX flight launched on December 20, 1960, the system initially flying from Cape Canaveral before shifting to Vandenberg Air Force Base.** *(David Baker)*

Another way in which Discoverer became a "catch-all" for a variety of prime and piggyback payloads for the military and the CIA was with the introduction, under the cover name Discoverer XX, of the first KH-5 ARGON camera system. KH-5 was a mapping system using a frame-type camera built by Fairchild and with Fairchild lenses. It had a line resolution of 0.14 inches (3.5 mm) per scan on to 5-inch (12.7 cm) wide 3404 Estar film, shot through a 3-inch (7.6 cm) focal-length lens. KH-5 was also equipped with a 3-inch (7.6 cm) stellar camera.

Covering an area on the ground 345 miles x 345 miles (556 km x 556 km) with a resolution of 459 feet (140 m), the satellites were suitable for wide-scale mapping of very large areas and as such provided the Army with valuable and relatively detailed photographs. The spacecraft weighed an average of 2,866 pounds (1,300 kg) including the Agena B stage, the mass varying according to the specific piggyback payloads, and operating life ran to a few days in orbit.

Launched on February 17, 1961, the first ARGON (Discoverer XX) failed when the capsule was unable to separate from the Agena. The second KH-5 launched as Discoverer XXIII on April 8, 1961, but an attitude problem with the Agena dumped the re-entry capsule in the wrong orbit. After two more launch failures (Discoverers XXIV and XXVII), the first success with the system came on May 15, 1962. Over the next seven launches of the KH-5 system, five were successful, two of them carrying electronic intelligence-gathering satellites released into independent orbits. The last ARGON was launched on August 21, 1964.

In all, across 12 launches there were six successes, but the system proved its worth despite having a limited value overall. It is also worth noting that the Army benefitted from this program and achieved a "first" when a contractor under its employ used KH-5 photographs to assemble the first mosaic of an entire continent – Africa – using its 1:4 million scale to effectively provide the first in a long and evolving series of satellite imagery, increasingly from the mid-1970s emanating from civilian and, eventually, commercial programs.

Meanwhile, flights continued with the KH-2 (C') CORONA satellites with Discoverer XXV (9017) launched June 16, 1961, also carrying a range of small experiments into radiation and micrometeoroid hazards. The flight went well but the descent was off target, the bucket splashing down in the Pacific Ocean where it was spotted by the crew of a C-119. Divers jumped from a US Air Force Air Rescue Service Douglas SC-54 search and rescue aircraft and bundled it into an inflatable life raft, but they were required to spend the night there until picked up by the destroyer USS *Radford*.

Having retrieved what was only the second successful KH-2, analysts were ecstatic. The weather over the USSR had been picture-perfect, the atmosphere had been crystal clear, and the ground track carried the satellite over areas that disclosed the first ICBM site being built. Essential to establishing their own ballistic missile bases, the trans-Siberian rail line was used to deliver the men and the materiel essential to that effort, and the network of Soviet ICBM silos would straddle the famous route across the vast expanses of Russia.

But what the pictures revealed was considerably more refined than the earlier capsules. The information from 9017 was the first to carry detailed photographic evidence of the scale and magnitude of the Soviet missile fields and it directly resulted in a new National Intelligence Estimate (NIE) titled "Strength and Deployment of Soviet Long Range Ballistic Missile Forces." The first NIE was issued in 1950 and made available to senior intelligence staff and to the senior levels of the White House. They are intended to convey a consensus of analytical judgement from all available sources about the immediate present and future state of threats to the security of the United States.

The new NIE was released on September 21, 1961, and concluded that, "We now estimate that the present ICBM strength is in the range of 10–25 launchers from which missiles can be fired against the US, and that this force level will not increase markedly during the months immediately ahead. We also estimate that the USSR now has about 250–300 operational launchers equipped with (theater range) ballistic missiles. The bulk of these...are in the western USSR, within range of NATO targets in Europe."

In reality, as determined after the collapse of the USSR in 1991, there were in fact only 12 R-7 ICBMs operational at the time of the flight, using liquid oxygen as an oxidizer and therefore requiring several hours of pre-flight preparation. Not until the end of 1961 would the USSR begin to field the R-16 (SS-7) using storable propellants and available for launch at short notice. By this date the US had already fielded 78 Atlas and Titan ICBMs (all with liquid oxygen/kerosene motors) with 80 solid propellant Polaris missiles aboard five submarines, more than 1,500 long-range nuclear bombers and around 7,000 nuclear weapons.

It is worth noting here that this revised NIE

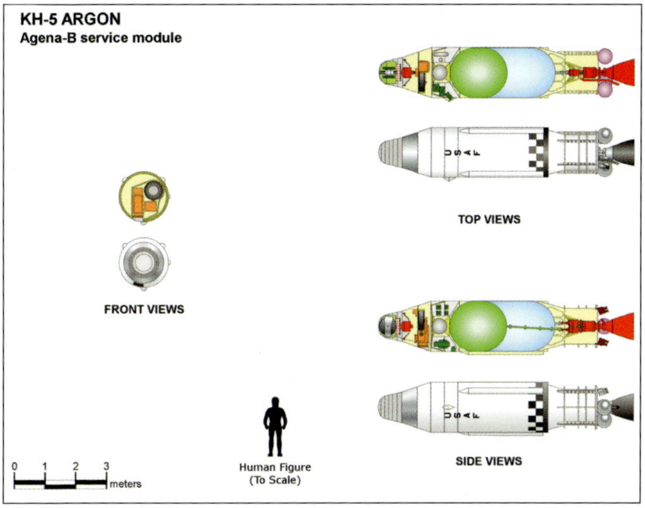

ABOVE The KH-5 ARGON followed in 1961, as shown here on an Agena B. It was a mapping camera system much sought by Army cartographers. *(Giuseppe de Chiara)*

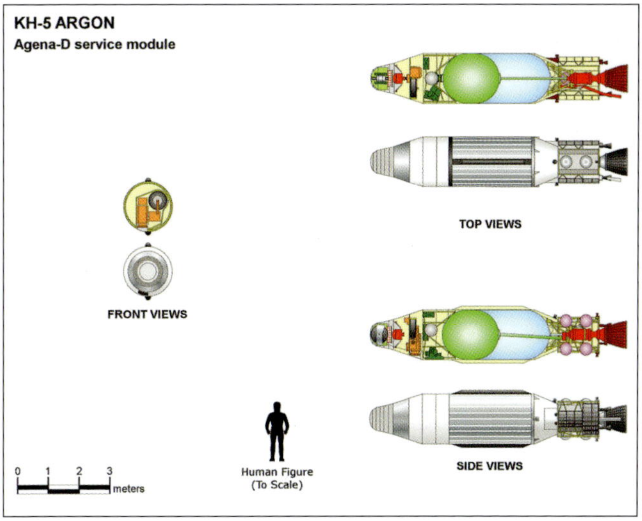

BELOW Later models of the KH-5 were launched on a Thrust-Augmented Thor-Agena D. *(Giuseppe de Chiara)*

ABOVE **The Lockheed JC-130 replaced the Fairchild C-119 in later Discoverer air-snatch operations, as seen here during a test flight with a dummy drop and a simulated mass model of a CORONA bucket.** *(USAF)*

landed on President Kennedy's desk just four months after he had reacted to the flight of Yuri Gagarin as the first human to fly in space by authorizing NASA to send astronauts to the Moon by the end of the decade. Only a few months after receiving this apparent debunking of any notion that America was behind Russia in this most visible of technological sprints, he began to recant on his Moon challenge and openly started to speak of cooperation with the USSR.

BELOW **Radio hams around the world benefitted from the OSCAR 1 relay module carried into orbit with Discoverer XXXV on November 15, 1961.** *(David Baker)*

The reality check on the balance of military power also informed his robust reaction to the Berlin crisis of October when the Russians closed the frontier and built a wall to prevent East Berliners from escaping to the western sector under Allied control. The Russians responded by dropping a 58 MT thermonuclear bomb on the Semipalatinsk test range but there was no means of delivering this device as a weapon. Through CORONA, the Kennedy administration increasingly came to see the overt threats from the Soviet Union as a bluff.

Moreover, only a year after this revised intelligence assessment, Kennedy faced down the Russians over their delivery of nuclear-tipped missiles to Cuba, certain in the knowledge that the US was a superior nuclear power and that the Soviet Union could not risk a nuclear exchange and come out as a survivable and self-governing state. The implications of photographs from Discoverer XIV in August 1960 and Discoverer XXV in June 1961 were disproportionate in their immensity and profound in the consequences. Yet, for all the effort so far, this was only the third KH-1/KH-2 capsule recovered with film, the other launches being development flights or failures. Now the C''' (KH-3) satellites were ready for flight.

The first KH-3 was launched by Discoverer XXIX (9023) on August 30, 1961, but all the images were out of focus, caused by an incorrect scan head, and the mission failed to produce any useful result. The second attempt (Discoverer XXX) 13 days later suffered the same scan head problem and the third, as Discoverer XXXI on September 17, suffered a total power failure and the loss of attitude control gas before the capsule could de-orbit. The fourth attempt proved no more fruitful when Discoverer XXXII, launched on October 13, was recovered on orbit 18 with less than 4% of the film in focus.

The next flight never got a chance. Launched on October 23, Discoverer XXXIII held on to its Thor booster and fell back to a watery grave, while Discoverer XXXIV, sent up on November 5, entered a useless orbit when a gas valve failed. The only recordable progress in this litany of seven failed KH-3 launches was the shift to the turboprop Lockheed JC-130B, replacing the hardy piston-engine C-119s, for air-snatch operations carried out by the 6593rd and their highly experienced crews, who had flown countless missions without a single loss of aircraft or life.

The first completely successful KH-3 flight, albeit with a grainy emulsion, was launched on November 15 as Discoverer XXXV. The flight went as intended and operated as planned. It was followed by the penultimate KH-3 (9029) as Discoverer XXXVI on December 12 along with the OSCAR 1 amateur radio satellite carried on the Agena as piggyback. An acronym for Orbiting Satellite Carrying Amateur Radio, OSCAR was shaped to fit within the Agena, standing in for a little ballast necessary to get the appropriate mass distribution.

Discoverer piggyback payloads were there to take the place of an inert mass that would be required to give the satellite and its Agena stage the appropriate balance. With a weight of 22 pounds (10 kg), OSCAR 1 was the first in a running series of satellites specifically aimed at radio hams and their esoteric pursuits. It comprised a sloping rectangular box 12 inches x 10 inches x 5 inches (30 cm x 25 cm x 12 cm) and incorporated a battery powering a 120 mW transmitter operating at 144.983 MHz in the 6.6-foot (2 m) band. The satellite was released from the Agena, operated for 22 days and stayed in orbit until January 31, 1962, the first of many that have merged with successor satellites and piggyback packages to this day.

Discoverer XXXVI was the perfect KH-3 flight, in fact the only one because the final launch of a camera of this type, as Discoverer XXXVII on January 13, 1962, failed to reach orbit. Of the nine KH-3s launched only two could be considered to have been a success. But the camera had been a marginal improvement on the KH-2 and was the first both manufactured and to have lenses provided by Itek.

The 24-inch (61 cm) f3.5 lens was of the Petzval type, with a 70° pan and vertical reciprocation. It shot on to a 3400 Estar film with 0.1 inch/line (2.5mm/line) scan producing a resolution of around 35 feet (11 m) compared with 40 feet (12 m) for the KH-2 and 50 feet (15 m) for the KH-1. At 7,800 feet (2,377 m) the film supply was the same as the KH-2.

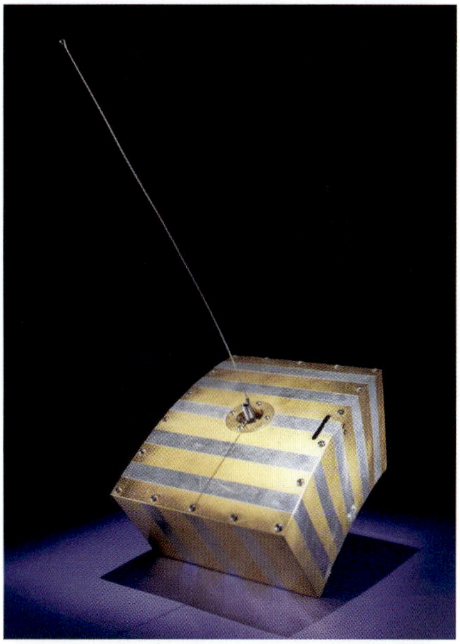

LEFT Shaped to fit within one of the weight balance segments on the Agena B stage, OSCAR was the first in a continuing series of relays for amateur radio enthusiasts. *(David Baker)*

The technical capabilities of the C''' camera were well proven through the two highly valued missions in which it was a great success and it was integral to the next development. But there were changes in the offing, ones that would propel the space-based intelligence and surveillance satellite technology into a new era.

It was around the time that the CORONA C''' (KH-3) program was winding down that the full spectrum of classified defense satellites came under review, with a decision made in early 1962 that the cover name Discoverer would be dropped and, while launches would be acknowledged with a public statement, there was to be no discussion of payloads unless specifically authorized. A memorandum from deputy defense secretary Roswell Gilpatric on March 23 approved a recommendation from NRO boss Joseph Charyk that all military programs were to be classified "Secret," with varying levels of grade above that according to the program in question. The intelligence-gathering community was about to ramp up a notch and, although very few knew the full gamut of programs under way, some would become very public knowledge by intention.

Under the new system of designations, the Discoverer CORONA flights would operate as Program 162, SAMOS E-2 camera flights became Program 101A, the E-5 system was

Program 101B and the E-6 was to be known as Program 201. The CORONA C-series cameras were redesignated under the KH-series as noted and described earlier.

A new year and a new camera: when the first KH-4 was launched as Discoverer XXXVIII in February 1962 it was a development of the C''' but carried the new title MURAL due to the change in nomenclature and because of the significant change to its operating protocols. Much like CORONA had begun development as a quick-reaction interim project until a film read-out system could be launched under the original expectations of WS-117L, so too was CORONA-M expected to be an interim program to take existing equipment (the C''') and fill a need to access denied regions through a stereo camera capability versus the two-dimensional images of the KH-1, KH-2 and KH-3.

The idea to combine two CORONA cameras into a single stereo-capable system arose in mid-1960 even before the first film had ever been recovered from space. Lockheed came up with the idea to pair existing cameras, with the C''' design being favored, particularly because it was lighter and therefore could be engineered within the lifting capacity of the Thor-Agena. The Air Force soon gave CORONA-M approval and work began.

Lockheed at first called the new stereo concept Gemini (completely disassociated with the spacecraft of that name begun by NASA at the end of 1961), because it was a "twin" camera system. The idea was to pair the two C''' cameras – the aft one looking forward, the front one looking aft – in a faired module on the front of the Agena and employ two recovery spools to a single capsule, assessed to weigh 94 pounds (43 kg) loaded with 15,600 feet (4,805 m) of film.

Approval to move ahead was granted by Charyk on February 24, 1961, and work started on six pairs of C''' cameras, subject to final approval by the newly installed President Kennedy, with further orders following. The program evolved rapidly and independently but under a very tight security veil, only 300 out of 2,700 CORONA personnel even knowing of its existence. Officials in the National Photographic Interpretation Center were informed in mid-July 1961 and by the time of the first launch six months later all CORONA personnel knew about it.

Quite late in the development phase it was decided to add a stellar indexing camera to the C''' pair which many thought to be an added complication paying lip-service to the requests of the mapping fraternity for an E-4 capability that Charyk had been developing as an alternative to ARGON. As justified, the 3.1-inch (80 mm) stellar index reference camera would be employed plotting and rectifying the longer focal length high-resolution panoramic photographs and could be of use in map-making. In reality it was equal in length to that of the ARGON system and had better resolution, albeit largely due to improved film quality.

To an extent this debate over who should provide the mapping capability and which satellite should be assigned responsibility for that, appeared as a result of the widening circle of invested intelligence agencies. The Defense Intelligence Agency (DIA) had just been formed and it was keen to develop its own system independent of the NRO, which it felt it could not trust to give it the priority it wanted. The Army was being squeezed out of space projects.

At the time there were too many competing concepts to accommodate all the potential users and the Army would have to look elsewhere for its mapping system. But CORONA-M was also considered a stopgap because of the existence of the E-5 system and this itself would merge with future requirements in the form of LANYARD.

Because it was rated as an interim system, MURAL had to be made to fit in with the existing mainstream CORONA program and the plan was for MURAL to launch every two weeks until the 16 initially contracted satellites had been exhausted, so that they would not impede flights with the C''' series cameras (KH-3) cameras. But all that would change.

The MURAL camera would achieve its stereo imaging by aligning the two cameras at a 15° converging angle and two 40 pound (18 kg) reels of film identical to the film used with the C''' cameras on the KH-3 flights. The cameras afforded a lateral angular coverage of ±35° with a forward angular coverage of 5.25° at the center of the format. The coverage had a 10% overlap on a format size of 2.15 inches x 29.32

inches (5.46 cm x 74.47 cm) with a cycle rate of 2.15–6.0 seconds.

Cross-track coverage was 133–334 miles (214–537 km) depending on the altitude of the satellite, 92–230 miles (148–370 km), along-track coverage varying between 8.9 miles (14.3 km) and 22.24 miles (35.8 km) depending on similar altitude variables. The total linear track coverage per satellite was 43,745 miles (76,226 km) at lowest altitude, with a total operating time of 2 hours 49 minutes.

The dual spools would feed in through separate apertures and emerge on to a double-reel rake-up spool in the recovery capsule. Each area would be photographed twice, the forward-pointing aft camera taking the first exposure and about six frames (or so) later the forward, aft-pointing camera would take an exposure of the same area, thus providing two perspectives of the same location that could be viewed through a stereoscope after processing to obtain a three-dimensional picture.

One interesting aspect for photo-interpreters was the improvement in visual acuity through a stereo image compared with a two-dimensional one. While there was only a marginal improvement in the theoretical ground resolution of each image, the stereo effect allowed a significant increase in the ability of the analyst to "see" objects that would normally disappear into the grain of a two-dimensional picture. In fact, photo-interpreters take it for granted that stereo images provide more than twice the visual acuity of a non-stereo image.

Equipped with the first KH-4 dual C''' camera system (9031), Discoverer XXXVIII was launched on February 27, 1962. The nominal life of a KH-4 was expected to be around five days, but the re-entry capsule was separated and de-orbited on revolution 65, four days into the flight. It was recovered safely, albeit with its jettisonable heat shield still attached. The photo-interpreters were ecstatic over the quality of the pictures, despite some being apparently out of focus.

RIGHT A Thor-Agena D lifts off with a KH-4 camera payload as CORONA flight 74 on November 27, 1963, long after the name "Discoverer" had been buried. *(USAF)*

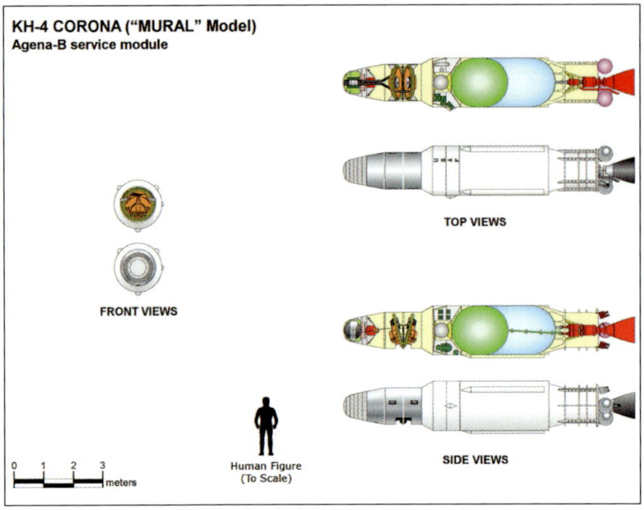

ABOVE The KH-4 MURAL system launched on an Agena B, which remained an integral part of the system on orbit. *(Giuseppe de Chiara)*

In addition to the twin C''' cameras, an Itek index camera was carried on this first KH-4 flight. It had a downward-looking terrain lens of 1.5 inches (38 mm) but the stellar index camera on later flights had both a 1.5-inch (38 mm) lens and a 3.1-inch (80 mm) focal length stellar lens, the former using 2.8-inch (70 mm) film, the latter using 1.4-inch (35 mm) film. The main function was to provide supplementary information to the images from the main camera system allowing greater and more accurate geographic orientation. A calibration of the 90° included angle between the index and the stellar index camera was accomplished using a precision goniometer, also providing a calibration of relative distortion between the two.

This information would allow a bulk calibration between the three camera systems so as to establish the exact pointing angles and position in a space-frame reference and for each frame from the primary stereo cameras. This did allow cartographers to produce some relatively small-scale maps of selected areas. Missions carrying only the index camera ran through to the flight of satellite 9044 launched on August 29, 1962, the 12th KH-4 flight.

The use of terrain imagery helped diagnose an apparent anomaly where film would appear blurred or smeared or out of focus, when in reality it was haze, thin fog or transparent cloud. A separate CORONA Performance Evaluation Team monitored such anomalies and with the terrain camera on the KH-4 they were able to determine which atmospheric obscuration was responsible. The two-dimensional pictures did not allow analysts to determine that and the stereo imagery added a new dimension. This was of particular interest to engineers puzzled over lack of clarity in images and excellent technical performance from the cameras. Photo-interpreters were likewise on a learning curve, as most had been trained on aerial photography where the dynamics of atmospheric obscuration were very different.

The CORONA pictures were the first taken of the Earth from orbit on a routine basis and interpretation was a completely new science. The first American to orbit the Earth – John Glenn in the Mercury MA-6 spacecraft – made his flight one week before the flight of the first KH-4, and over the next three Mercury missions, up to mid-1963, both astronauts and ground personnel were stunned by the visual perception of the human eye over the sometimes muddy appearance of photographic products. It took time to convince some managers and senior personnel that look-angle, Sun-angle, and varying combinations of the two would compromise fixed filter settings, exposure times and film quality.

The second KH-4 flight, Discoverer XXXIX (9032), launched on April 17, 1962, was the last to carry that cover name and henceforth all spy satellites would be publicly identified by launch number alone but internally by space vehicle number. The Discoverer program had supported 39 launches of which 25 had successfully reached orbit, a success rate of 64% which was, for the time, fairly good. Of the total in orbit all but two were attempted recoveries, of which 13 were successful, a failure rate of only 52% for a sophisticated and somewhat precarious procedure.

Discoverer XXXIX added to the education of analysts by taking pictures of the Sacramento, California, airport where visual calibration of known features displayed runway markings, cars, buses and small buildings and even allowed differentiation between two- and four-engine aircraft, endorsing the claims of camera engineers that the system could discriminate objects 7 feet (2.1 m) long on a side.

By the end of June 1962 a total of six KH-4 satellites had been orbited with the loss of only one capsule, when an extended boom on a recovery aircraft struck the collapsed parachute, sending the bucket spinning 12,000 feet (3,650 m) into the ocean, where it sank. However, the terrain framing camera operated correctly on only one flight, although these failings were attributed to design as well as to manufacturing and installation difficulties.

During the year a total of 17 KH-4 satellites were launched of which 13 had provided varying levels of photography, the first stellar camera flying on 9045 launched September 29, 1962. The first flight of a Thor-Agena D with a KH-4 occurred on June 28, 1962, for a mission that was notable for bad static affecting the quality of the photographs. Static electricity caused by the complex dual-camera system would plague the KH-4 program and never be fully and totally resolved.

What had begun as an interim program had become highly successful and would extend for several more years to come. The last KH-4 MURAL system would launch satellite 9062 on December 21, 1963, completing 26 successful launches and 20 recoveries. But MURAL would spawn a new series of spy satellites that followed the increasingly more reliable KH-4.

New eyes

MURAL had been providing a highly detailed picture of the USSR despite an increasing demand for more target areas and better resolution. The expansion of Soviet military activities, while slow during 1961, had accelerated in 1962 and the year itself brought new tensions via the Cuban missile crisis and a general chill across the Cold War world. During 1963 a new generation of camera technology would introduce two new satellite systems while launch vehicle evolution increased the lifting capacity and therefore the options for satellite designers.

The story of the first new system is enmeshed within the GAMBIT history and is picked up in Chapter 6 but the reason for what was known as LANYARD (KH-6) was a direct result of a perceived threat to US security in early 1962 when Secretary of Defense Robert McNamara grew concerned over intelligence reports that the USSR was developing an anti-ballistic missile (ABM) system. Such a system could render the Soviet Union impervious to attack by US ballistic missiles, unseating the balance of terror that underpinned the concept of mutual assured destruction (MAD).

Under MAD, each super-power had to believe that they would be destroyed in a nuclear attack and that a second strike (following a pre-emptive surprise attack) would be similarly destructive – so no one would start a nuclear war for fear of self-annihilation. If the Soviets deployed an ABM system it would allow them to strike without fear of total destruction as only a handful of warheads would get through. McNamara wanted to examine physical evidence for any such screen around Moscow by launching satellites with high-resolution cameras.

At the time, the only such system in development was the KH-7 GAMBIT system, but when asked about its launch availability McNamara was told that it could not be expected to fly for at least another year.

BELOW A TAT-Agena D launches a KH-4 satellite as CORONA flight 75 on December 21, 1963. The method employed in erecting and launching Thor-based launcher derivatives had changed greatly in preceding years. The Castor solids provided a significant increase in lift capability. *(USAF)*

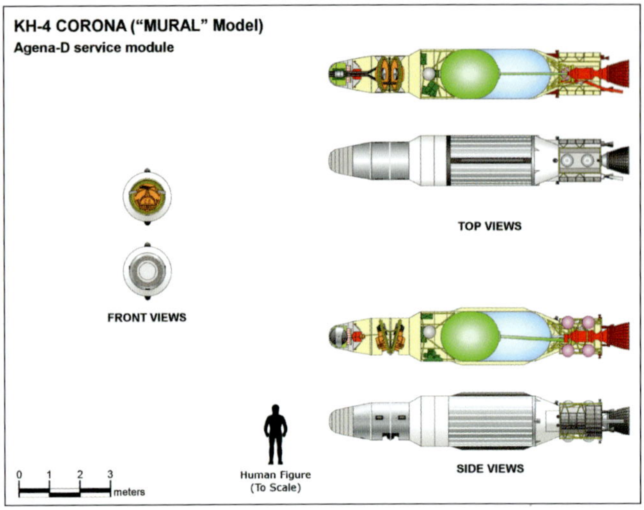

ABOVE CORONA KH-4 configuration with an Agena D. *(Giuseppe de Chiara)*

Accordingly an agreement was quickly signed for development, and launch, of the KH-6 LANYARD system. It was not a fortuitous decision and was one that would fail to deliver.

The first launch of an improved system preparatory to LANYARD occurred on February 28, 1963, when a Thrust-Augmented Thor (TAT-Agena B) lifted off from Vandenberg AFB carrying a KH-4 on a flight that failed and had to be destroyed by the range safety officer. The new Thor carried three solid propellant Castor 33 strap-on booster rockets, which increased the lift capability to 2,200 pounds (1,000 kg) to polar orbit. It was available in time for the first system to use it successfully, the KH-6 LANYARD satellite, which sought to resurrect the E-5 camera and which aimed to provide an interim capability pending availability of the KH-7 GAMBIT system.

LANYARD weighed about 3,307 pounds (1,500 kg) and was a follow-on to the SAMOS program, providing a panoramic capability using an oscillating lens cell and a large viewing mirror aimed at a 45° angle to the ground. The mirror could be moved to provide stereo or two-dimensional photographs on 5-inch (12.7 cm) film fed from a spool with a capacity of 8,000 feet (2,465 m). The camera had an effective focal length of 66 inches (167 cm). To increase the scan angle of the lens a roll joint in the Z axis was incorporated within the structure. The camera had a ground swathe coverage of 9 miles x 46 miles (14 km x 74 km) and a resolution of 6 feet (1.8 m).

Three KH-6 LANYARD satellites were launched on TAT-Agena D vehicles, with the first (8001) getting off the pad on March 18, 1963, before a failure in the hydraulics in the upper stage doomed it never to reach orbit. The second vehicle (8002) was successful in achieving orbit but the camera never received the command to begin operating and was recovered on the 33rd orbit. The last KH-6 (8003) launched on July 31, 1963, and managed to return with exposed film, but it was brought down early on orbit 32 when telemetry indicated that the camera had failed.

A significant problem with the LANYARD system was the lack of an active thermal control for the focusing system, and for the film returned from 8003 there was inadequate focus control. Nevertheless, the pictures were of some use. Each flight also carried a stellar index camera and some additional value accrued from that last recovery.

The TAT-Agena D had been developed in part to lift the KH-6 LANYARD satellites and although beset by early development problems, the uprated launcher began a progressively more robust series of enhancements through extended lengthening of the core stage and additional strap-on boosters. But the availability of a more capable system prompted a wider review of what was required next from reconnaissance satellites.

Just as the C''' camera had doubled up for the KH-4 MURAL series, so too could there be an increase in the number of re-entry elements carried by each vehicle. With additional lift capacity, two spools of film could be carried, each feeding a single SRV, with a substantial increase in capacity. Moreover, with the restart provision of the extended-capability Agena D the system could be used in a radically different way. Instead of returning to Earth after a few days, the dual-SRV system could enter a quiescent mode for up to 21 days before resuming operations.

This quiescent, or "zombie," mode would allow the orbit of the satellite to migrate, or to be adjusted with the Agena restart capability, so as to revisit the same area several times. Or it could go quiet in space and operate silently, progressing its orbit until required. There was almost no possibility of the Russians skin-tracking the Agena by getting a reflection off its surface and a quiescent satellite could therefore appear to have either returned its recovery capsule or to have malfunctioned, only turning itself back on by command when required.

There was increasing awareness that the Russians, knowing when a launch had taken place, could calculate the path of the orbit and discreetly hide or camouflage objects or small buildings, denying plausible interpretation of the site. The zombie-mode could therefore work to the advantage of the intelligence analysts by getting the jump on the Russians, lighting up an apparently dormant and useless piece of space hardware and taking photographs.

The design of what was now known as CORONA-J (for Janus, the Roman god of transitions and of two faces), designated KH-4A, was an outgrowth of the KH-4. Approval was not granted before October 1962, when Lockheed were given authority to begin development. But as the concept was examined the zombie role was modified so that SRV-I would be recovered after four days, just as it would be for the single-bucket KH-4, whereupon the satellite would go into a controlled tumble for more than two weeks. All electrical power and stabilization systems would be turned off to conserve consumables and a second four-day period of activity would follow, after which the SRV-II capsule would return.

The practical side to this operating mode was that it effectively did the work of two separately launched satellites on a single mission, saving the money of another satellite and another launch. The two separate film spools would each have dedicated loops to their respective recovery vehicles and each would be completely independent of the other, feeding through the two stereo cameras as they would in a single-bucket KH-4. This made it highly attractive, as the cost of increasingly frequent flights was taking its toll on the budget for military satellites.

Although many of the clandestine projects had, and still have, classified budget levels – so only a generalized idea of the importance placed on space by the affected agencies can be had from publicly disclosed figures – in 1959 the space departments of the Department of Defense and the intelligence services were spending a total of what would be $3.45 billion in 2016 money. By 1963 that had risen to almost $12 billion in current terms. By 1988 (the peak year) that total would be $34.5 billion in today's money. Within such soaring allocations, putting two satellites into one was a very good idea.

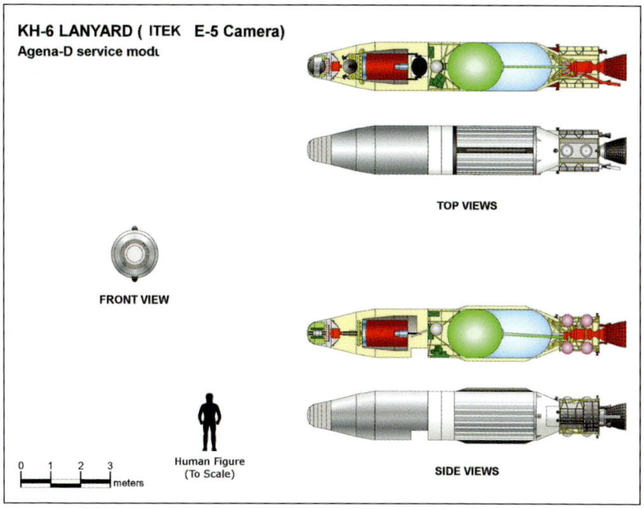

ABOVE A KH-6 LANYARD configuration with Agena D. There were three launches to orbit but only two successful recoveries. *(Giuseppe de Chiara)*

Behind the seemingly simple idea of doubling up the buckets lay a complex revision of the operating procedure. The CORONA-J system would carry a total of 32,000 feet (9,750 m) of film required to wend a circuitous path while maintaining proper tension and first passing through the rearmost SRV and out to the second capsule. When the forward capsule was full a cutter would sever the film thread, sealing the SRV for return to Earth. The second SRV would then receive its film load when appropriate and go through the same process.

So secret was the design that no one individual in the manufacturing and assembly process was allowed to "see" the entire mechanism. Each component and specific unit of elements within a discrete system would be manufactured separately and only brought together when the assembly process had itself been hidden within the overall design, thus avoiding the possibility of any one individual being able to visually reverse-engineer the design.

To make the system work effectively there had to be modifications to the Agena D, which was now required to support two individual missions within a single flight as well as provide unique power, stabilization and orbit make-up tasks. This latter accommodated the tendency of the Agena to encounter trace molecules at the fringe of the atmosphere that would act as a drag-brake and gradually lower the orbit. Small solid propellant rockets were provided to give the stage a nudge back-up to counter this effect and restore the planned orbit.

Launched on August 24, 1963, the first KH-4A (1001) got into orbit and operated effectively, returning the first capsule after four days, but the second capsule failed to return due to a collapse in the on-board electrical inverter. The second JANUS, launched on September 23, resulted in a similar story, the second bucket failing to separate, indications of extreme heat conditions in the cameras plaguing the system. Launched on February 15, 1964, the third KH-4A was a resounding success, returning both buckets to Earth, but only after a decision to abandon the zombie mode and run the two film sessions in sequence, SRV-I coming back on February 19 followed by SRV-II three days later.

By now the MURAL system had been retired and, despite the third KH-4A flight launched on March 24 being a failure, operations switched to the JANUS satellites. But the fifth flight, on April 27, 1964, had a harrowing journey. When the Agena separated from the Thor core stage several electrical surges were seen on telemetry received at ground stations, although all other aspects of the mission proceeded as planned. Then film in one of the two stereo cameras broke and it was decided to bring the first bucket back home. A command was sent but nothing happened.

For the next 26 orbits of the Earth the same command was sent repeatedly, but although the satellite acknowledged receipt still nothing happened and the SRV remained firmly attached. Engineers even resorted to repeating the separation command through a newly installed system that would send instructions direct to the pod rather than through the Agena, but without any luck. There were no further signals after it fell silent on May 19, some 22 days after launch.

Over the next several days the Agena degraded back down through the atmosphere and provided a fiery spectacle in the sky over the mountains of south-western Venezuela, KH-4A 1005 plunging to the ground outside the town of La Fria close to the border with Colombia. While the stage and the main structure of the KH-4A had disintegrated and strewn its debris across the re-entry path, the heat shield for one of the buckets remained intact. It was retrieved by two farm laborers.

On seeing a mass of strange components the farmer began to disassemble the capsule for toys to occupy his children, hoping to sell the other elements as curios, not knowing exactly what it was he had hold of! As word got out, despite the patent lack of interest in buying what he had hoped to sell as a souvenir, a growing trickle of visitors tramped the countryside to visit him and his find. Until a commercial photographer saw it and called the US Embassy in Caracas.

Government officials from the embassy bought it from the farmer for a nominal sum, explaining that his find was part of a NASA satellite and had scientific interest without real monetary value. News broke and US newspapers reported the story with apparent disinterest and lack of attention to its true purpose, which they did not in fact know. The reason for the lack of interest? Earlier that same day the press was anxiously reporting an attack on two US warships by North Vietnamese patrol boats in the Gulf of Tonkin; the Vietnam War had begun.

As a result of this event the Air Force switched the internal identity of the KH-4A to Program 241 and proceeded to the next launch on June 4, which was a complete success for each of two four-day photographic surveys. The program had turned a corner, and while it had been felt prudent to abandon the zombie operations, the regular use of two back-to-back imaging sessions and sequential bucket recoveries worked very well. Two photo-loads out of a single mission advanced by several months the completion of full photographic surveys of the USSR.

Over the course of 1964 a total of 13 KH-4A flights took place, of which 11 were a success, albeit two only partially, and by March that year a full inventory of Soviet ICBM sites had been compiled showing 23 locations, with a further two added during June. For the first time the CIA could claim, with certainty, that no other sites existed and that these could be monitored on a routine basis.

By this time the Air Force GAMBIT program was getting into its stride and, together with CORONA, the intelligence community was acquiring assets unprecedented in capacity and scale. The KH-4A continued to serve until the final one, 1052, launched on September 22, 1969, but long before then the final CORONA configuration had been introduced. Throughout their service these satellites had supported several clandestine projects for a variety of purposes, one of which was electronic intelligence gathering.

Hitch-hiker I was carried piggyback on the CORONA flight of June 27, 1963. It was a science satellite that carried a small solid-propellant rocket, placing it in a highly elliptical orbit from where it reported significant data on radiation, a threat to satellite electronics and to optical equipment. Three SIGINT rides were given by CORONA missions during that year, first operationally on Atlas-Agena missions in subsequent years, and some on GAMBIT flights.

Throughout this period the number of launches and the range of tasks accorded to satellites went up dramatically, with most of the flights being military missions increasingly identified merely by a number and a letter designation. While the public was awed with space spectaculars from the government's civilian space agency, NASA, an equal amount of development was taking place far from the public gaze, much of it directly tuned to providing detailed information on the Soviet Union and on the increasing pressure for support to military operations in South-East Asia, Vietnam in particular.

During the mid-1960s, with direct overflights by manned aircraft of communist countries now relegated only to client states of the USSR, an interchange of intelligence utilization and asset allocation began to spread out of the space program and into the refined and highly sophisticated intelligence gathering aircraft now being deployed. Moreover, with the increasing sophistication of networked intelligence, overlays of visual, signals and radar intelligence, a comprehensive three-dimensional box of intelligence data was becoming normal.

With the service introduction of the Mach 3+ Lockheed SR-71 Blackbird at Beale Air Force Base, California, in January 1966 the intelligence community had a fast-reaction asset which was mission-integrated with area intelligence from the KH-4A, technical intelligence from GAMBIT (Chapter 6) and highly detailed diagnostic intelligence from Blackbird intruder flights. It was rare, but on occasion SR-71 missions were triggered by satellite intelligence from photographs of Third World countries of client state status.

The need to expand flexibility in the JANUS system resulted in a raised confidence about returning to a zombie-mode operation. After a year of successful activity, on December 19, 1964, the KH-4A 1015 vehicle was operated as normal before it was placed on standby for four days, reactivated and operated for the second four-day period, each SRV being returned as planned.

There was increasing demand to make the system more flexible if, for instance, weather moved in over a high-priority target and the satellite paused operations to allow the conditions to change. Moreover, there was an increased sophistication about the way the

BELOW The considerable growth in length and capability provided by the long-tank Agena D, the extended length of the Thor core stage and the three strap-on solid propellant Castor boosters facilitated a growth in satellite weight. *(Douglas)*

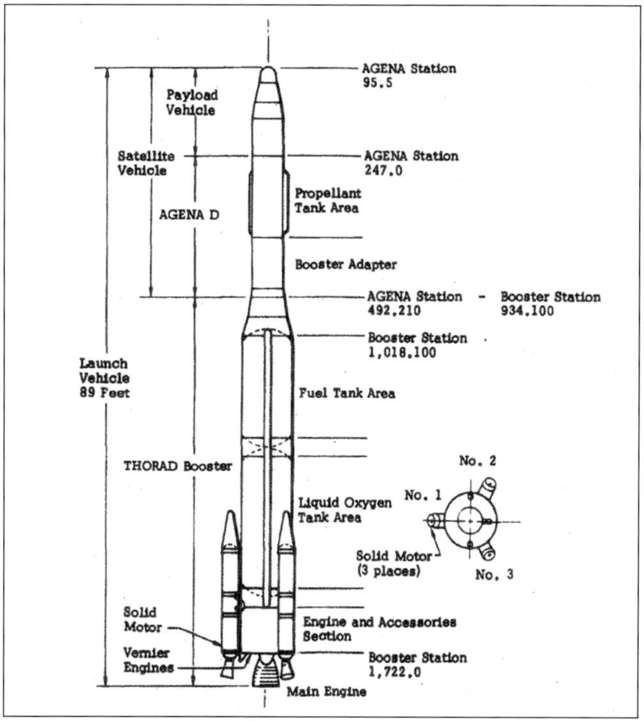

various government agencies were working with each other. Requests would emerge from other forms of intelligence about an upcoming event for which satellite coverage was required, necessitating that it suspend operations to await the unravelling of predicted activities so that it could photograph them.

Better eyes

As indicated earlier, expanded requirements and demands for better and bigger satellites resulted in moving ahead with improved and uprated launch vehicles, and the KH-4B system would make use of another stretch of the basic Thor. Requested by the Air Force Space Systems Division in January 1966, the basic Thor stage, which had remained largely unchanged throughout, was extended in length, allowing it to carry additional propellant, with the forward RP-1 fuel tank now having a constant diameter rather than tapering as before. Substantial refinements in the engineering and manufacture of the stage added to improved and more powerful strap-on solid propellant booster rockets.

Known as Long Tank Thrust-Augmented Thor (LTTAT) rockets they were more frequently designated as simply Thorad-Agena D, and the first of these carried KH-4A 1036 into orbit on August 9, 1966. The new launcher could lift 2,900 pounds (1,315 kg) into polar orbit, more than 660 pounds (300 kg) greater than the TAT-Agena D, significantly expanding the operational flexibility of the system and making ready a weight increase for the final CORONA development, the KH-4B or JANUS-3.

For some months during 1964 there had been plans to further improve the KH-4A but these stalled on proposals sponsored by the CIA, known as Fulcrum, and S-2 proposed by the NRO. Eventually the S-2 design would metamorphose into a new system approved on April 22, 1966, with the name HELIX, changed to HEXAGON eight days later. But the debate over what to do about a replacement for CORONA ran on into 1965.

For the period from March 1963 to February 1964 the performance record of the CORONA system showed significant improvement: its success rate, which had previously been little more than 50%, increased to 69%, with

RIGHT Further extension of the Thor tank with the LTTAT-Agena D facilitated launches with the improved KH-4A J-1 camera system, as carried with CORONA 119 launched on August 7, 1967. *(USAF)*

nine successes in 13 launches. Over the next 12 months that increased to 82%, with 23 successes out of 28 attempts. In 1966, with the new KH-4B system known as JANUS J-3, the previous series was retroactively designated J-1.

While modest in improvement KH-4B got its own numerical production lot series number starting with 1101 through to 1117, with the last flight in May 1972, versus the J-1 series which ran from 1001 through to 1052 by the time of the last KH-4A flight in September 1969. J-3 had its own management staff, its own personnel and ran a separate, parallel development cycle.

Meanwhile, the KH-4A went from strength to strength, expanding the eight days of operation it demonstrated in 1964 to 15 days by 1967. Slowly, but effectively, technical improvements were being incorporated, lessons learned and the performance expanded until, from 1966 to 1970, it demonstrated a straight run of 28 successful flights and recoveries – 100% success. But the system could do more, and give better service, so justifying J-3.

One of the new requirements was to improve resolution by lowering the perigee of the orbit to get closer to the target. Other, technical, requirements were addressed too, among which were: a reduction in vibration within the camera system ("sputter"); better velocity/height matching to cut the amount of smear on photographs; better film carriage along the guide rails to prevent it jumping; enhanced exposure control using a variable slit selector; and a flexibility to install and operate a range of different filters and to separate the film loads as well as the use of ultra-thin base films to reduce weight.

Careful calculation using a wide range of data sets from numerous satellites in different orbits, plus a very much more refined model of the Earth's outer atmosphere, gave operators the confidence to plan flights as low as 98 miles (158 km). But it was improvements to the operation of the cameras that gave the KH-4B its distinctive edge and produced the truly definitive CORONA.

All previous camera systems had operated where the lens assembly constantly rotated as the shutter unit and the slit oscillated. This rocking motion had caused some vibration when the combination came to a halt, reversed direction and started again. This had an effect on the stability of the Agena and on the quality of the photographs. The revised configuration was called a "constant rotator." A rotating drum incorporated the lens assembly, shutter and slit and the film was only exposed during

LEFT In April 1964 Venezuelan agricultural workers got hold of a CORONA camera film bucket when it came down in a remote part of the country and brought visitors from miles around to see the strange object before US government officials were alerted and retrieved it. *(NRO)*

BELOW By 1964 activity at Cape Canaveral had expanded and the general momentum of the space program was accelerating. Military payloads, too, were launched from the Florida launch site, while Discoverer flights originated at Vandenberg AFB. *(USAF)*

RIGHT During the early 1960s, development of the solid-propellant Minuteman ICBM eclipsed the Atlas launch vehicle and the Titan 1 – both of which had non-storable propellants – with a series of test flights from Cape Canaveral and Vandenberg AFB. *(USAF)*

70° of arc rotation.

To start the filming, the two separate drums of film and the drum assembly itself would rotate in opposing directions, and to compensate for the orbital motion of the satellite the two separate camera assemblies would rock back and forth, also in opposite directions. This opposing rotation was necessary so as to neutralize gyroscopic motion from the mass of the drums, which were each over 5 feet (1.5 m) in diameter and 7 inches (18 cm) deep.

Improvements were also made to the lens units which, while retaining the same system as the KH-4A, increased resolution to 160 lines/mm. All these refinements and qualitative improvements stacked up to move the ground resolution to 6 feet (1.8 m) compared to an actual capability of 9 feet (2.7 m) for the KH-4A – a staggering performance upgrade which would shift several small targets into focus, moving the resolution into the range of the KH-6 LANYARD system.

All other aspects of the satellite were the same as the J-1 although each camera had two changeable filters and four separate exposure slits, which would allow appropriate exposures for varied lighting conditions. This compared with only one slit on the KH-4A, which had frustrated photo-interpreters when viewing images shot at dusk, early morning or during winter, with poor-quality pictures.

Changes were also introduced to the stellar index camera, which had never really performed as expected on the KH-4A. The 1.5-inch (3.8 cm) lens from early satellites was replaced with a 3-inch (7.6 cm) lens similar to the one installed on KH-5 satellites; this was given the new name Dual Improved Stellar Index Camera (DISIC). As with earlier cameras of this type it was employed locating targets amid major geographic features to get a precise position fix useful for mapmakers and battle-plan plotters. It was located behind the second SRV. Finally, an additional pair of horizon cameras was attached

LEFT A test launch of the Minuteman missile from Vandenberg Air Force Base. The Minuteman was made plausible in its deterrent role by technologies that made it deadly accurate, including precise targeting achieved through CORONA imagery. *(USAF)*

RIGHT The twin recovery buckets from the KH-4A afforded new opportunities, seen here as a payload attachment to a production-line Agena D. *(Giuseppe de Chiara)*

to the Agena for greatly improved, and more precise, attitude control.

The introduction of the KH-4B provided stereo coverage for traditional reconnaissance duties with the added capabilities originally flown on the unsuccessful KH-5, where only six recoveries were accomplished. In that ARGON program, mappers had been able to get accurate elevation scales to within 164 feet (50 m) and to locate a specific point to within 30 feet (9 m). Geodetic measuring with this data allowed mappers to place two locations on opposite sides of the Earth to within 1,000 feet (305 m) of each other. This activity was essential for the next development in nuclear deterrence and war-fighting strategies.

Nuclear weapons evolved dramatically during the first half of the 1960s. The miniaturization of warheads developed during the end of the preceding decade had placed nuclear weapons on single-engine strike aircraft, ground attack aircraft, up the muzzles of artillery pieces and down the barrels of tanks. These weapon delivery systems were appropriate for visual targeting and theater warfare where armies were within sight of each other. But the relative inaccuracy of early ballistic missiles such as the Atlas and Titan I improved with the deployment of Minuteman and with the later Titan II.

Improvements with guidance systems were also increasing the accuracy of the ballistic intercontinental delivery systems, cutting down the average miss distance from around 5 miles (8 km) at the dawn of the missile era to around 3,000 feet (900 m) by the end of the 1960s. But accuracy must translate into known geodetic locations at positions of launch and of arrival at the target. It was therefore axiomatic that all these technical improvements had to be matched by an equally refined knowledge of exactly where, on the three-dimensional

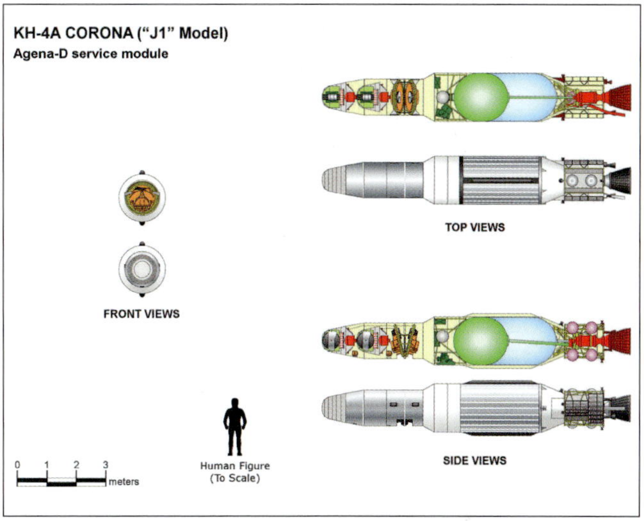

RIGHT An early KH-4A launch on a TAT-Agena D on March 24, 1964, CORONA flight 77. *(USAF)*

TOP A KH-4A photograph of Poznan, Poland, showing urban and rural areas, roads, waterways and man-made structures. *(NRO)*

ABOVE This part of Poland observed by a CORONA KH-4A shows wispy clouds scudding, or sweeping, across a pastoral scene below, from which intelligence data on ground facilities can be obtained. *(NRO)*

geodesic reference, the target was located with respect to the launch site.

This detail was significantly enhanced with the KH-4B system and the DISIC. In fact, by the mid-1960s the J-3 system was providing incredibly accurate maps of the USSR, much better in fact than those that existed for North America, which had been prepared using Army mapping techniques of the Second World War. Before the age of the spy satellite, maps of the USSR were highly inaccurate and what were available had been plundered from the mapping units of the Luftwaffe during the German invasion of Russia between 1941 and 1945.

Russian maps were inherently inaccurate by intent, to confuse invading enemies. Now even battle management planners had highly accurate knowledge of the country's cities, towns and villages, streets and roads, and could place those locations on an elevation map vital for invading armies and occupying forces. Now, were it to come to that, US forces would move across the USSR with more accurate maps than they had available to get between any two military facilities in the United States!

One of the primary advantages of the DISIC was that its star calibration capability was largely unaffected by the attitude of the Agena stage, unlike earlier stellar index cameras which were compromised by the orientation of the vehicle to achieve its primary photographic role. With the DISIC, one camera would always be pointed 90° away from the direct Sun-line. Combined, the stellar and index cameras could place the attitude of the Agena to within 3–5 arc-seconds, calibrated before flight at an observatory in Cloudcroft, New Mexico, where they photographed stars and then compared those with the known, and highly accurate, positions from the observatory index.

One aspect that taxed the camera designers and engineers working on the J-3 system was the tolerances of film running through the rollers and to the distortions that were tolerable. Aerial cameras worked to an acceptable tolerance of 20 microns; the KH-4B had a tolerance of 1–2 microns. Because of the very thin base film employed, for weight-saving reasons, it tended to stretch and was held in place by reference marks that would allow a compensation for the distortion when the film was processed. In turn, this brought fresh demands for more advanced computers and better and more efficient use of solid-state electronics, another push on the state of the art.

The existing computer technology was too slow and far too cumbersome. The intelligence-gathering requirements of the Air Force and the CIA became the single most influential factor, along with ballistic missile development, in the rapid advancement of computers. In the 1960s they were large room-size machines with slow mainframes and used punch cards and ribbon tape for delivering the product of their calculations. Engineers and technicians relied on slide rules, trigonometry and standard calculators, even using pocket devices to do basic mathematical calculations.

Launched on September 15, 1967, by Thorad-Agena D, the first KH-4B (1101) was the

120th CORONA satellite and the mission went as smoothly as could be hoped for. The flight duration was 19 days and both SRVs were recovered as planned. The second followed on December 9 when 1102 followed a KH-4A that had gone up just over a month earlier. The year closed having seen seven KH-4As and two KH-4Bs launched; the following year there were five KH-4A missions and three with KH-4B, all successful. How different now was the reliability and performance of a system that had begun almost 15 years earlier.

During 1969 six CORONA satellites were launched, an even split between the two systems, and some of the KH-4Bs were carrying sub-satellites as piggyback payloads for classified missions. The only significant difference to anyone tracking the satellites was the lower perigee of the J-3 flights. Over this period scientists worked with a variety of film emulsions to improve operability of the system in space and some infrared film was flown on 1104, launched on August 7, 1968. Two other missions (1105 and 1108) launched on November 3, 1958, and December 4, 1969, incorporated color film, while special thin film was flown on several J-3 missions with success.

While the technical standard of the processed image from color film was problematic, the optics did not allow for appropriate color correction and the reduced resolution from the multiple layers of emulsion was less than optimum. But something else was gained that would add a completely new dimension to satellite reconnaissance: the ability to evaluate the balance between dry land and water, farmland and general waste areas, between natural vegetation and managed land, in a way that was totally impossible with monochrome film.

Thus began a new use of information, which would be exploited by the CIA and other government agencies to broaden the application for intelligence information toward multi-spectral imaging that could deliver

ABOVE Launched on June 4, 1964, this vehicle carried a KH-4A with the J-1 system, its two buckets retrieved from orbits 66 and 128 respectively. This launch marked a change in code designation from Program 162 to Program 241. *(NRO)*

RIGHT In parallel with the expansion of satellite photography, the Air Force began operations with the SR-71 Blackbird, assembly of which is seen here in the company's "Skunk Works." *(Lockheed)*

ABOVE Capable of speeds in excess of Mach 3 and extreme altitude, the SR-71 supplemented information from satellites and was frequently targeted to specific sites in denied areas, based on CORONA photography. *(USAF)*

information on the scale and magnitude of a country's crop yield, on the health of those crops and on the capacity of a nation to feed itself. Color photography of wide areas of the world, including North America (which was used for calibration of photo data), farms, forests, woodland and waterways revealed a detailed index of the natural world.

It was also possible to determine mineral deposits and to photograph geological formations and assess their hydrocarbon potential. And so began an entirely new way of looking at the world, its environment and its resources, one which was developed to incredible lengths over the next several decades and which continues today to provide scientists with valuable information about the planet.

It became readily apparent that surveys of large areas carried out by satellite would be much cheaper than comparable coverage by aerial survey. Dedicated civilian Earth resources satellites, the first of which was launched by NASA in 1972, would provide an inventory of the planet emanating from the pioneering work of the military reconnaissance satellite.

The last KH-4A satellite (1052) was launched on September 22, 1969. It was the 135th CORONA flight in less than ten years, it lasted 20 days and it was a complete success. Some 52 systems had launched and 93 bucket-loads of film had been recovered. The KH-4A had taken reconnaissance photographs covering 273,047 square miles (707,189 km^2), compared to 149,258 square miles (386,577 km^2) by KH-1, KH-2, KH-3 and KH-4. In addition it had covered 37,509 square miles (97,149 km^2) of territory with mapping function.

The CORONA program was sustained by

BELOW This CORONA image of a Russian air base for strategic long-range aircraft deployment provided information on the operability of one part of the Soviet airborne nuclear deterrent. *(NRO)*

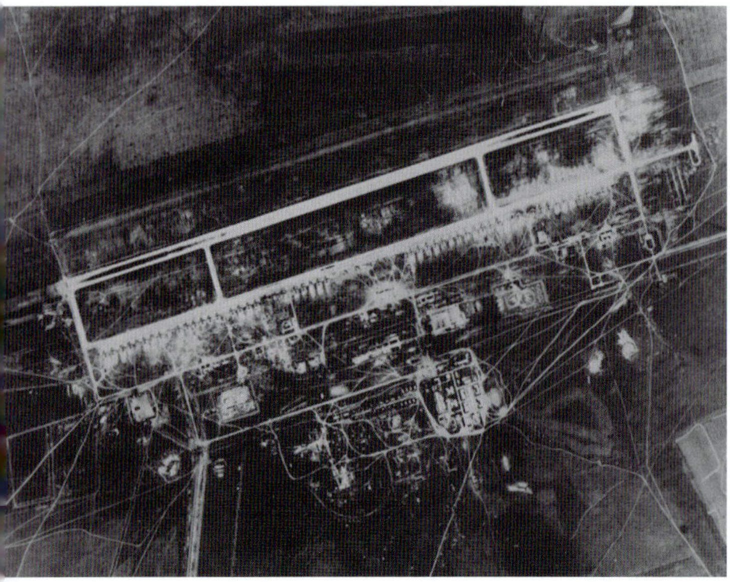

BELOW Very occasionally CORONA photographs would show areas of archaeological interest, such as the remains of a Roman fort in Jordan. *(NRO)*

the KH-4B alone for almost three years, four flown in 1970, three in 1971 and two in 1972. The last KH-4B (1117) was launched on May 25, 1972, another successful mission with its two buckets recovered despite one of the two Agena solar panels failing and some minor technical problems with the satellite payload. There had been 17 launches and 32 bucket recoveries. Added to the KH-4A total was coverage of 253,653 square miles (656,959 km^2) for reconnaissance and 38,034 square miles (98,509 km^2) for mapping purposes.

The total area coverage of all CORONA satellite photographs amounted to 676,555 square miles (1,752,270 km^2) for reconnaissance (including KH-6 LANYARD) and 132,307 square miles (342,676 km^2) for mapping purposes, the latter including the KH-5 ARGON series.

As the CORONA program worked toward its natural conclusion, the existing system design having reached the end of its evolutionary potential, a flurry of plausible upgrades and adaptations were posed to senior management as a means of keeping the system alive. The KH-7 GAMBIT program commenced launch operations in 1963 and would endure four years, and the KH-8 GAMBIT-3 model would continue that line through the early 1980s while KH-9 HEXAGON would evolve in parallel. But a CORONA J-4 was proposed during the very early flight phase of the KH-4B. It owed its origins back several years and to the development of the KH-4 MURAL.

Because it was considered an interim system, in March 1962 Lockheed proposed an improved M-2 system (MURAL-2) which would have been a completely re-engineered system merging the functions of the two cameras into a single 40-inch (102 cm), f/3.5 optical telescope serving two platens. Itek was convinced it could produce a camera with a resolution as low as 4 feet (1.2 m). It would not be adopted, the technology was considered too risky, but it was kept on the shelf until 1963 when it would be taken down and employed as the genesis for CORONA J-4.

Not until 1967 did the J-4 appear as a strong candidate for further development. The new system, as proposed, would have one or other of two Itek designs, the old MURAL-2 camera and one with a focal length of 32 inches (81 cm), both providing a resolution of at least 4.5 feet (1.4 m) and a stellar indexing camera with a 12-inch (30.5 cm) focal length and a more powerful launch vehicle. The collective capability would provide an 18-day on-orbit life.

At the time it was believed the J-3 system would retire in June 1971 and it was proposed that it be succeeded by 20 J-4 satellites to sustain CORONA operations through mid-1973. But initial optimism began to dissipate when new estimates said it would not be ready until mid-1970, and even then could not be relied upon as the camera technology was proving difficult to develop and might require additional work before the system could completely replace CORONA. As time wore on the J-4 concept became a very real competitor to HEXAGON and, as budget demands for the latter began to rise appreciably, it was even proposed that HEXAGON be scaled back to a two-bucket system with further extension of CORONA.

To a large extent enthusiasm for J-4 polarized around Itek's desire to continue to remain at the core of US reconnaissance satellite optics but even in 1966 it was faced with an end to work in this sector. At this time it only had the S-2 program and the possibility of J-4 to look forward to. The Fulcrum concept incorporated an Itek camera but that had gone when Eastman Kodak backed DORIAN and the

BELOW A KH-4A photograph of the Polish military test area of Gryzcye, an image taken by CORONA 98 launched on August 17, 1965. *(NRO)*

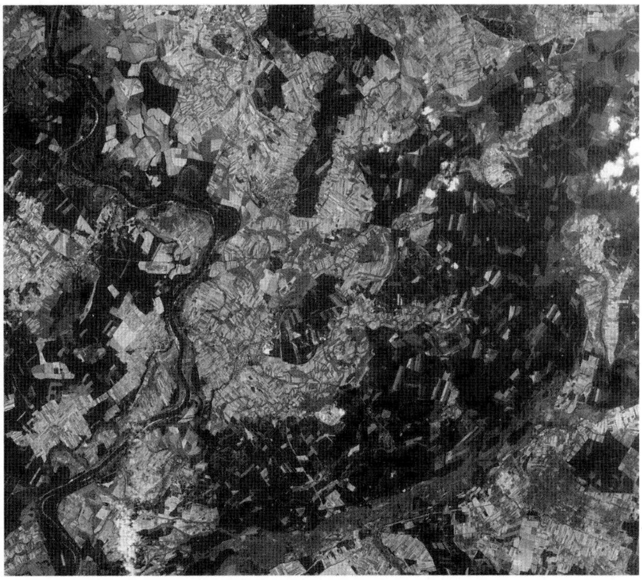

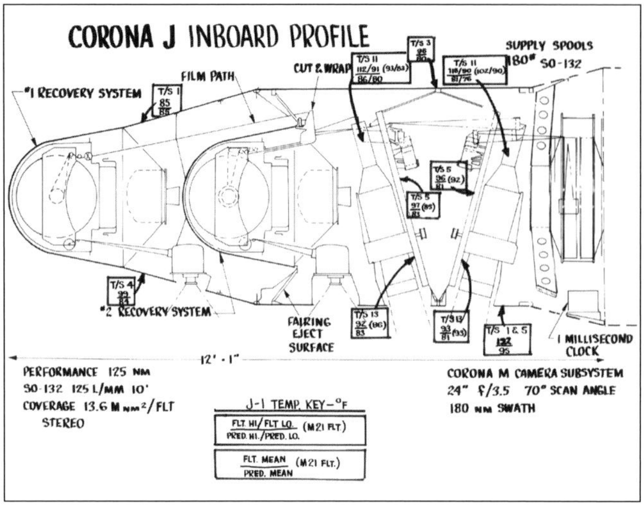

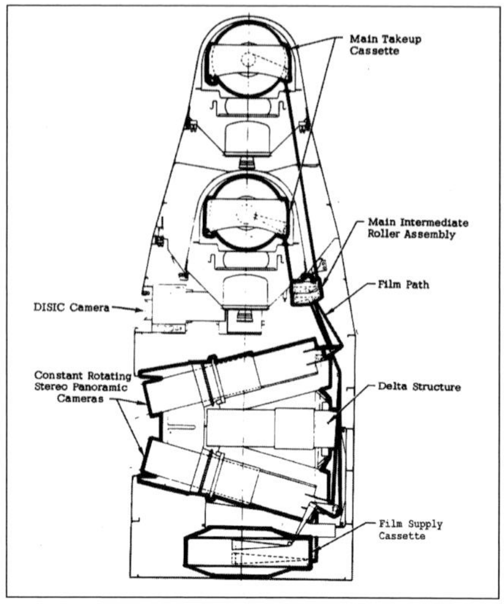

ABOVE Side-elevation drawing of the CORONA KH-4A system, showing the direction of travel of film to the two recovery vehicles. *(NRO)*

ABOVE RIGHT A view of the KH-4B with the Dual Improved Stellar Index Camera (DISIC) as indicated. *(Lockheed)*

Fulcrum was passed to Eastman Kodak. Itek would find work with HEXAGON, but only as a subsystem contractor, an ironic twist since the S-2, on which HEXAGON was based, was originally an Itek design proposal.

In November 1968 the NRO concluded that CORONA had reached the end of its life, and despite the fact that in theory J-4 could have produced photographs with a resolution of at best 4 feet (1.2 m), the HEXAGON system promised 2 feet (61 cm). On balance it was thought better to have a slowly evolving successor than push hard for the last stretch on an already aging system. But for a while it looked as though that position might be reversed.

When Richard Nixon entered the White House in January 1969 he sought major cuts to defense and space spending – playing a significant role in winding down NASA's Apollo program and in delaying a successor, which eventually was approved in 1972 as the Space Shuttle. But in January 1969 he reopened the possibility of cancelling HEXAGON and reverting to a combination of GAMBIT-3 and CORONA. The CIA rebounded with a rebuttal of that logic

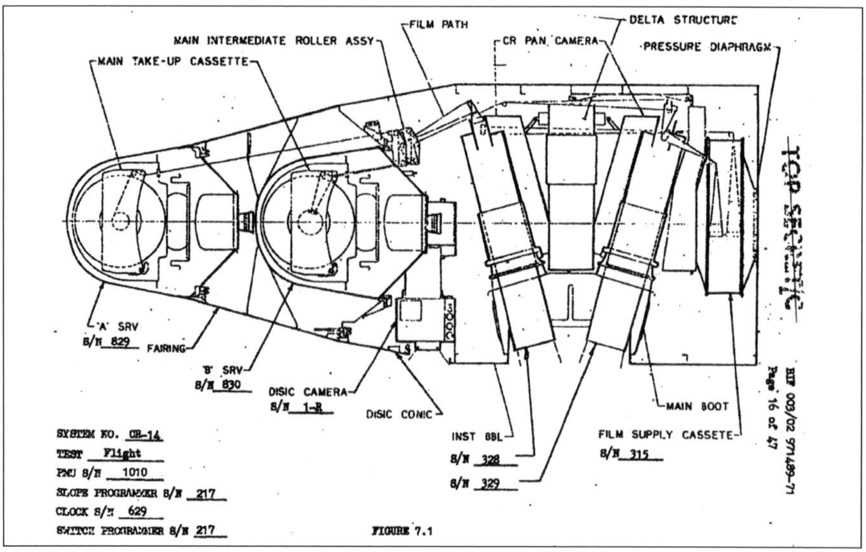

RIGHT A schematic of the KH-4A J-1 camera system with two recovery vehicles that doubled the amount of film available – an increase made possible by the advent of more powerful Thor-derivative launchers. *(Lockheed)*

but over the next several months the position hardened as the new administration criticized the apparent proliferation of programs.

There was not only KH-9 in development but also the much more ambitious Manned Orbiting Laboratory (MOL) and its KH-10 DORIAN system, which anticipated launch in 1972. Universal agreement was reached by the new government that the sheer scale of the programs had to wind back, and – to the chagrin of the NRO, the CIA and the Air Force – the very cost-effectiveness of the proven CORONA series worked against its demise.

On April 9, 1969, President Nixon authorized cancellation of HEXAGON and a reduction in the MOL program by emphasising DORIAN flying early missions without astronauts. The net effect was to sustain CORONA and invest in the J-4 system. But, in one of those unfathomable reversals that afflict many political decisions and edicts, on June 6 Nixon did a *volte face*, cancelled MOL and reinstated HEXAGON (work on which had, in fact, never been halted). A public announcement to that effect was made on June 10, a day after the principal contractors had been informed.

While the main story of DORIAN resides in Chapter 8, the linked CORONA, HEXAGON, MOL/DORIAN story is a seamless tale and decisions made in that fateful year of 1969 would never have occurred had President Nixon not forced a reduction in defense spending and occasioned a complete re-examination of the several reconnaissance satellite platforms in operation and under development. Paradoxically, the success of CORONA worked to bring about the demise of MOL but a key player in that decision was Dr. Edwin Land, a powerful figure in the development of reconnaissance satellites.

On May 6, 1969, Dr. Land wrote to Richard Nixon and urged cancellation of MOL while supporting the DORIAN concept of digital image transmission. Land wanted an unmanned vehicle and a robotic telescope providing continuous imagery over an extended lifetime unachievable with bucket-carrying satellites restricted in potential by the number of SRVs carried, which was the limiting design feature of the KH-9.

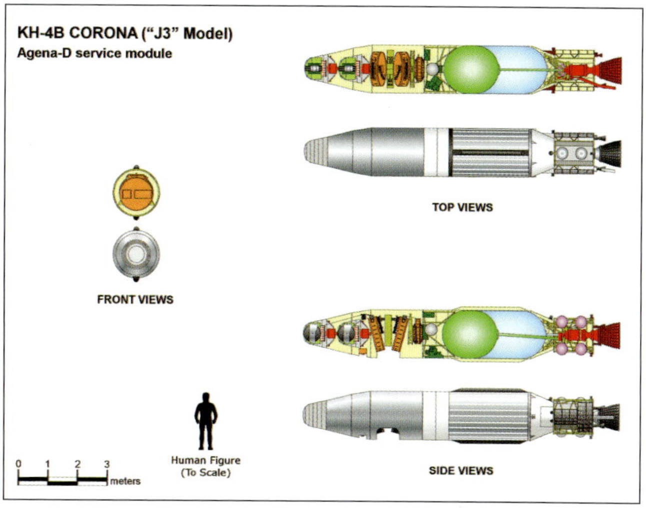

ABOVE The KH-4B and Agena D configuration, the definitive CORONA satellite evolution. *(Giuseppe de Chiara)*

A diagram of the geometric relationship of the forward- and aft-looking cameras, the horizon camera, the stellar camera and the index camera on the KH-4B configuration. *(NRO)*

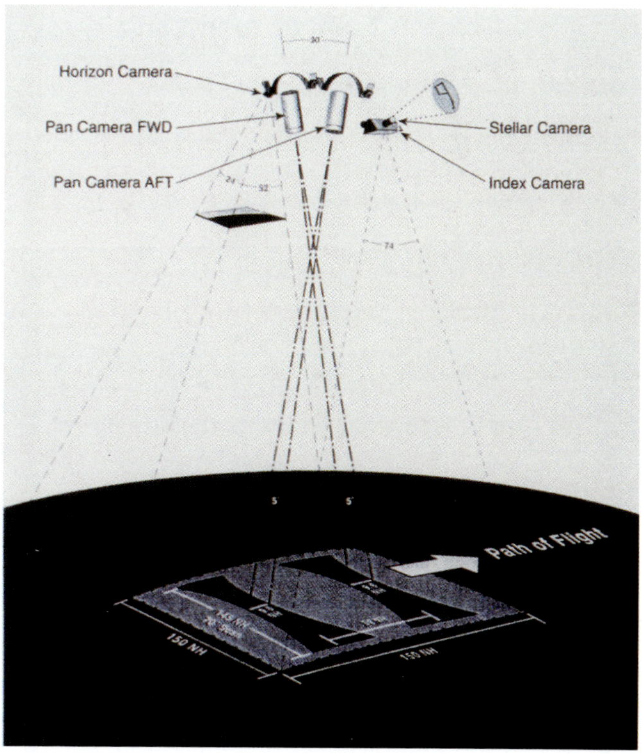

Chapter Five

SAMOS

The SAMOS system emerged from the dismantled WS-117L program and its separate tentacles. There were many competing concepts, and because satellite design and launch vehicle technology was still in its infancy the ground rules had to be written on the back of exploding rockets and flawed designs that had all seemed like a good idea at the time and for which there was no alternative. There was a perceived need for images retrieved quickly, and for satellites to remain in space longer, for a more extended duration of service in orbit and for a greater flexibility in targeting sites of interest.

OPPOSITE **The launch of a SAMOS payload integrated with an Atlas-Agena B.** *(USAF)*

RIGHT A briefing chart for the SAMOS program – named after a Greek island (contrary to numerous other claims) – that resurrected the TV record and read-out system which had been a part of WS-117L program but which proved too challenging for the early return of photographic images. *(NRO)*

Several studies very early in the evolution of the spy satellite concept, back before WS-117L, had prioritized the transmission of pictures from space direct to the ground, but as we have seen that was far from practical when transmission rates and bandwidth were so low and the frequencies were limited. Nevertheless, a legacy of the earlier concepts lived on and, as discussed earlier, WS-117L left a legacy of varied applications, some practical and some which – while thought difficult to accomplish – spawned a series of failed projects and similarly afflicted programs. One such type was the SAMOS surveillance system which would incorporate both readout and film recovery.

BELOW The general configuration of the SAMOS E-5 system, with internal layout of equipment in the nose of the Agena stage. *(NRO)*

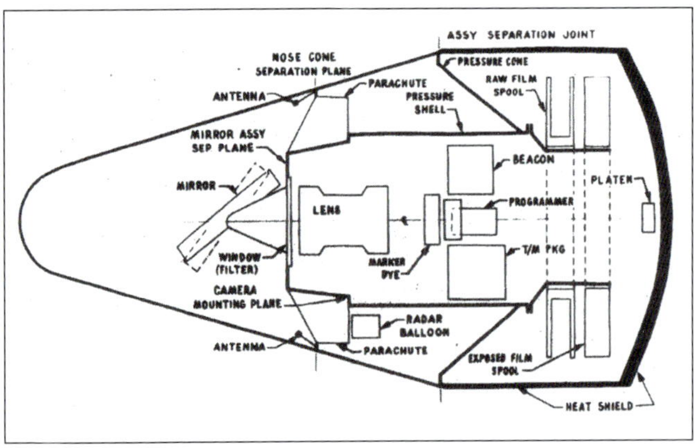

The original readout system was designated E-1, for no other reason than it was the first in a sequence of separate satellite systems, each designated by a letter from the alphabet: A for airframe; B for propulsion; C for auxiliary power; D for guidance and control; E for visual reconnaissance; and so on. As the inaugural readout technology for satellite applications, the E-1 was expected to provide 100 lines per millimeter of fine-grain film using an f/2.8 lens. The system assumed that the satellite would have five minutes of operation over the target area, store the images and transmit them over ground stations. These were located at Fort Stevens, Oregon; Ottumwa, Iowa; and New Boston, New Hampshire. Operations were to be conducted from SAC headquarters at Offutt Air Force Base, Nebraska. In this way, it was believed that up to 10% of the data thus obtained could be in the hands of analysts within one hour of observing the target, the remainder within eight hours.

RIGHT Fine-pointing accuracy was critical for SAMOS and this schematic shows the location and distribution of its attitude-control systems. *(NRO)*

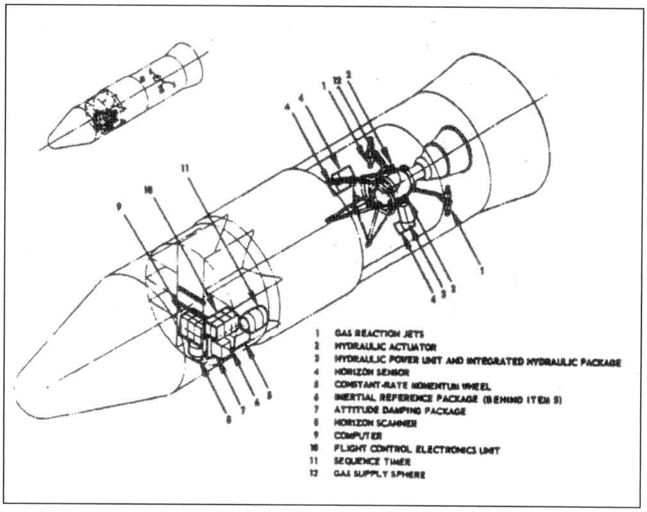

Limited by available battery power, the lifetime of each satellite was intended to be 10–30 days and with a small number in orbit at the same time this was also expected to give SAC a useful "early warning" of impending attack, as well as detailed characterization of large equipment. To satisfy this requirement, the initial E-1 camera system was designed to observe objects 100 feet (30 m) across, with a focal length of 72 inches (1.83 m) across a swathe of 100 miles x 100 miles (161 km x 161 km). An improved E-2 system would enhance surface resolution to 20 feet (7 m) with a camera focal length of 36 inches (0.91 m) covering a swathe of 17 miles x 17 miles (27 km x 27 km). The desired power provision for the E-2 was assumed to be nuclear or solar.

BELOW LEFT The location of the pitch, roll and yaw gyroscopes for the SAMOS satellite, with axial orientation and torquing layout. *(NRO)*

BELOW RIGHT Batteries, regulators and power distribution circuits for the SAMOS system took advantage of the tailored Agena B layout. *(NRO)*

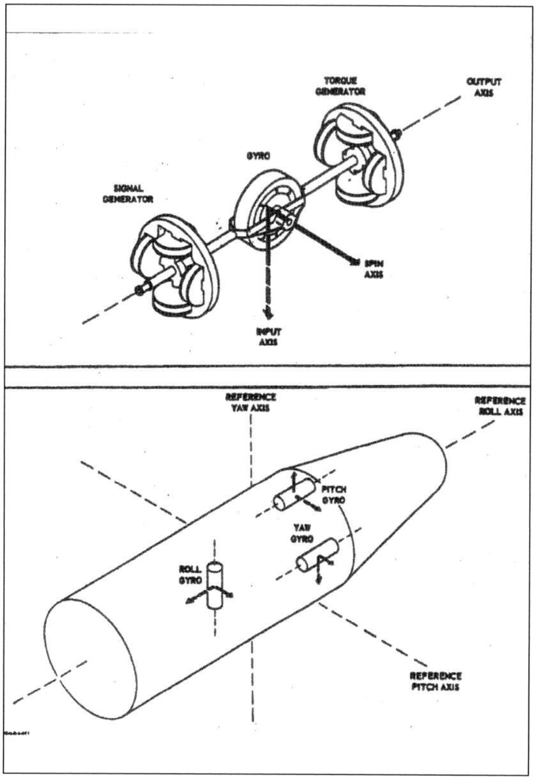

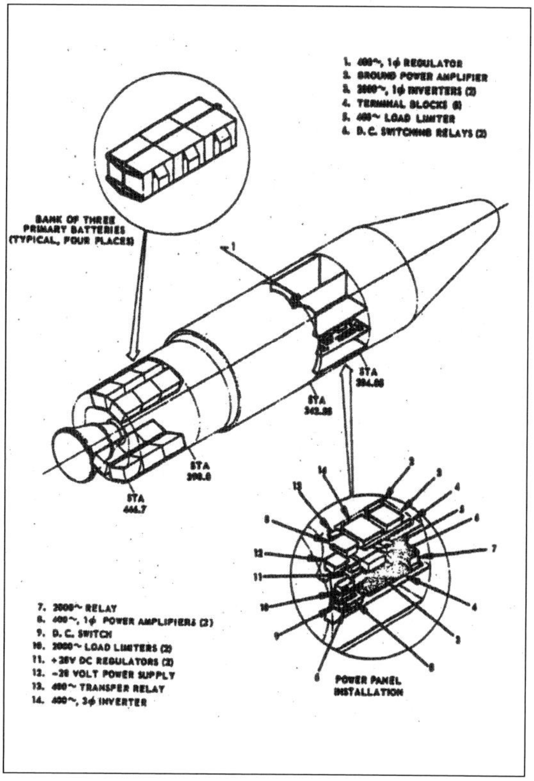

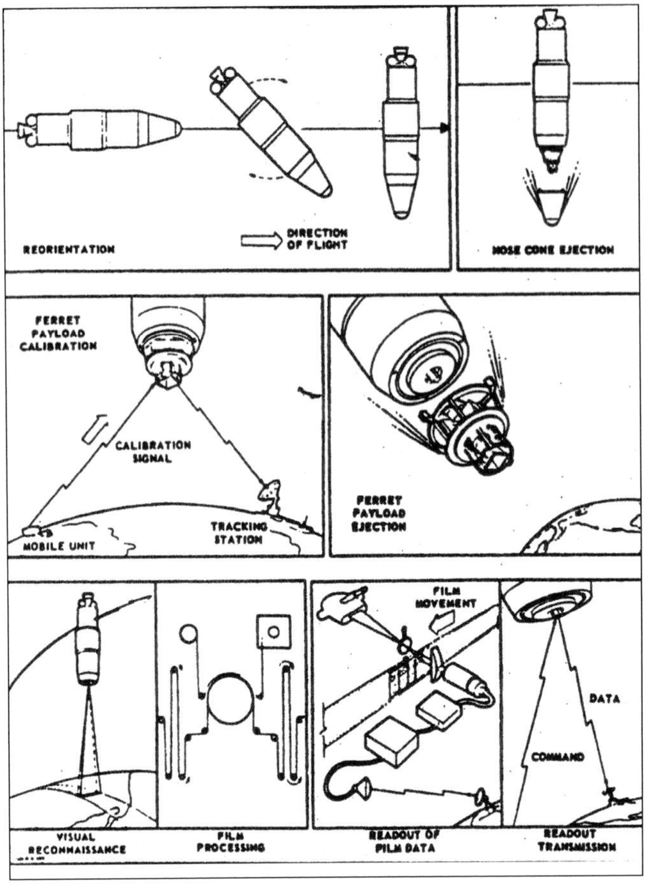

ABOVE The operation of SAMOS was different to CORONA in that the satellite pointed directly down at the Earth and could also carry a ferret sub-satellite on its nose. This sequence shows the release and calibration of the ferret prior to the SAMOS conducting its planned objective – taking photographs, processing them, scanning the images and transmitting them when over a ground station. *(NRO)*

When the original SAMOS design was drawn up in March 1958 it was designed for integration with the Agena stage (like CORONA) launched by an Atlas rocket. It was expected to have a length of 19 feet (5.8 m), a diameter of 5 feet (15 m) and a payload of 2,680 pounds (1,215 kg). The Agena stage would carry 5,080 pounds (2,304 kg) of propellant for a total stage mass of 9,300 pounds (4,218 kg). These technical requirements would change over time but, eventually, they were consumed by the inability of the technology to match the expectations of the user community.

In the late 1950s the physical ability to match the requirement was evident and the dynamics of orbits meant that very little coverage would be available each day. Moreover, the film would have to be exposed on orbit, transported to a scanning device, each negative frame digitized into analogue signals, those signals transmitted to the ground, reformed into images at the receiving end and distributed to the user. By 1958 much thought had been given to the readout system and the preferred method began with a strip camera spool loaded with 4,500 feet (1,370 m) of 2.75-inch (70 mm) film. This compared with CORONA carrying 15,000 feet (4,570 m) of 3-inch (76 mm) film.

SAMOS film would move across a slit, consisting of a line scribed through the aluminium coating on to a glass plate, essentially a shutter, at a rate proportional to the required motion for image compensation. The emerging film would be pressed against a chemically impregnated web containing the appropriate chemicals for developing and fixing it at separate intervals for a period of 16 minutes. The developed film would then move to a storage section consisting of a series of loops where it would await scanning and transmission.

The readout system incorporated a revolving drum line scan tube, the scanning lens system, a light collimator lens, photomultiplier tube and a video amplifier. An electron beam was focused on the inner surface of the drum, coated with phosphor, and would pass through an optically flat window, the beam itself passing through a scanning lens moved vertically by a motor-driven cam. The lens would move a bead of light across the width of the processed film as it moved laterally through a readout gate. The motion of the beam took the form of a square wave so that it could move from top to bottom and bottom to top without returning to a null point for repetitive scanning. The beam bead that passed through the film was captured by another lens that relayed 75% of the transmitted light to the photomultiplier tube, which converted the energy into electronic signals. After passing through a video amplifier the signals would be sent to the SAMOS communication equipment for transmission to the ground station.

All the variable factors such as image motion compensation, control over the level of exposure, the focus required and other settings were selectable on command from the ground. Most of this technology was at hand but problem areas were the speed and width of the scanning beam, which was limited by the available bandwidth. Without the invention of the travelling-wave-tube (TWT), which was still

RIGHT **This image of the curvature of the Earth was taken by an Aerobee sounding rocket launched on a ballistic trajectory in 1955. Images of this kind supported the belief that orbiting satellites could be of great value in planning and executing military operations by measuring the weather patterns over relevant zones.** *(NOAA)*

several years away, bandwidth was limited to 6 MHz. The first satellite to use a TWT was Telstar 1 launched on July 10, 1962.

Other limiting factors included the travel speed of the scanning beam which, restricted to only one width of film per second, scanned only 1 inch/sec (2.5 cm/sec), a complete scanning beam pass requiring two seconds. This time limitation was driven by the requirement of the scanning beam to travel slowly enough to translate the analog trace on to film. The resulting recomposing on the ground of the image taken in space transferred the signals to a 18-inch- (46 cm) wide strip of 1.4-inch (35 mm) film, with seven strips producing a single print 9 inches x 9 inches (23 cm x 23 cm) in size.

In examining the readout system, difficulties were anticipated from the outset. At a height of 230 miles (370 km) the resolution of 14-foot (4.3 m) objects would call for a scale factor of 1:400 K, providing an image covering 310 square miles (803 km^2) on each frame. Using an averaged number of sample points and a nominal grey scale factor, at one exposure every second for five minutes the readout time alone would be more than three hours! The maximum receive time per station was, at most, eight minutes for each of five passes per day. Each receive station could not download more than 62 frames per day which would represent an area of 16,740 square miles (43,357 km^2).

It was the limitations of the technology and the restrictions placed on the system by the few tracking stations available for downloading signals that caused a dramatic shift in emphasis between March and September 1958. While the requirement for surveillance rather than reconnaissance imagery remained, the means to acquire it shifted emphasis from the direct readout concept to film recovery of the type employed for CORONA. At this date ARPA retained control of the program and the Air Force began to shift toward a film recovery capability while retaining the direct readout method for more advanced derivatives. However, an electrostatic tape readout system (E-3) was introduced here and began to gather support.

The electrostatic concept was more advanced and could not be made available before the end of 1961 at the earliest but ARPA pushed for its development. A quick review of the technical requirement revealed, however, that the electrostatic system would provide only 20 lines per millimeter, one-fifth that of the film-based system. Moreover, it would require a significant redesign in the hardware as well as the Agena and it might well be a decade before the entire program could be implemented. By the end of 1958 ARPA's Roy Johnson had split SAMOS into three elements: film recovery; direct readout; and a ferret satellite concept for

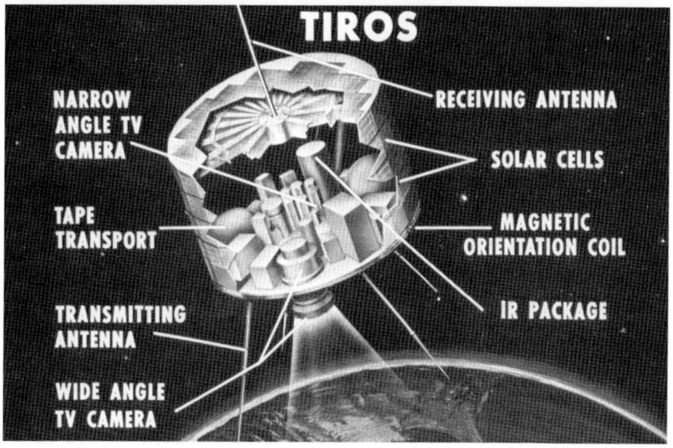

ABOVE **While the military was unable to mount an effective high-resolution TV system for satellite imagery, NASA was supporting the development of a weather satellite that would do just that, albeit with very low resolution. A briefing chart dated April 1961 shows functional characteristics of the NASA Tiros system. The name is an acronym for Television and Infra-Red Observation System.** *(NOAA)*

RIGHT Tiros weighed 280 pounds (127 kg) and supported 9,260 solar cells. It was the first satellite to have infrared lenses and TV cameras as well as being the first to transmit TV pictures of the Earth from space. *(NOAA)*

BELOW Although developed as a civilian satellite for meteorological purposes, its images being available for agencies and appropriate users, Tiros provided the military with evidence of the value of such pictures. This led to a military weather satellite program that evolved in parallel with the CORONA program. *(NASA)*

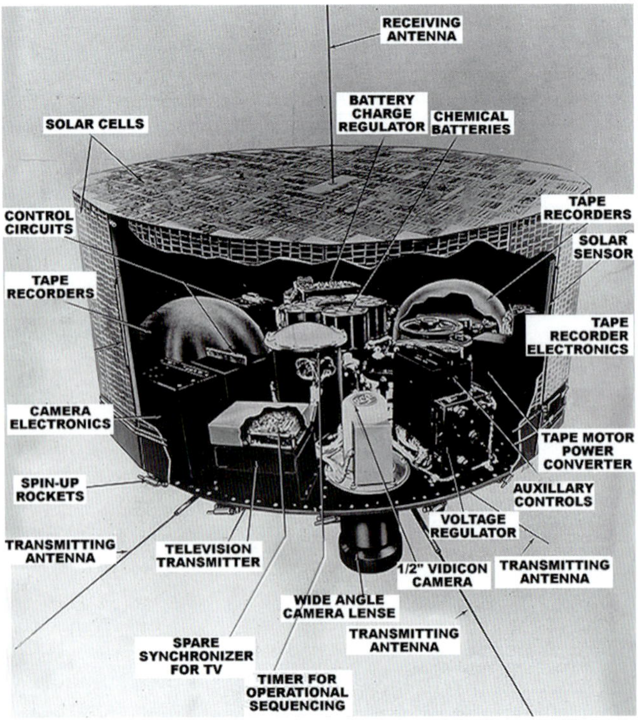

acquiring radio traffic. Acrimony set in when the Air Force exposed ARPA's manipulation of funds to push for this approach despite strong objections from the Ballistic Missile Division.

At the end of the year Johnson responded to these concerns and readjusted the program so that the E-1 system with its 6-inch (15 cm) focal length camera was replaced by the E-2, with a 36-inch (91 cm) focal-length lens. The readout system would proceed as a priority for SAMOS but the engineering flight tests of that configuration would blend with development of a recoverable capsule method. In effect, this moved toward a CORONA-style operating concept but with the surveillance camera rather than the reconnaissance type taking pictures of large areas.

Now the satellite would have a recovery capsule with a diameter of 60 inches (152 cm) and a payload weighing 1,200 pounds (544 kg), but with a heat shield that could be either the standard ablative type or a sublimation design. ARPA approved the new-style program on January 30, 1961, and by April it had been agreed to develop the E-1, E-2 and E-3 readout cameras, the E-5 film recovery type, and F-1, F-2 and F-3 ferrets. There was also to be an E-4 development for mapping and cartographic work, which ran in opposition to an Army requirement for a mapping satellite first known as SALAAM, then VEDAS and finally ARGON. In addition there was a small ARPA team working secretly on an Army-Navy satellite for geodesic survey, and E-4/ARGON programs threatened to run right into that.

The synthesis of all this resulted in a decision on May 25, 1959, to cancel E-4 to prevent an overlap with ARGON and, on June 23, to cancel E-5 but to press along with the E-3. Since intelligence analysis of requirements set a baseline resolution of 5 feet (1.5 m), there was a scramble to see which system could best be tuned to provide that. In principle the E-2 could be developed into providing that capability but it came down to a straight contest between the readout and the recovery concepts as to which could satisfy the requirement the quickest. In cancelling E-5 there was tacit approval for E-3 but the E-2 was still heavily restricted by limited readout technology. Even an advanced E-2 was considered to be capable of not more than 50 pictures a day for each ground station.

Hedging its bet that the ARPA desire for a readout system would trump the Air Force's preference for a recoverable capsule, Lockheed made a big play for the E-3 system, using results from feasibility research conducted by the Wright Air Development Center. In a proposal dated July 29, 1959, Lockheed pointed out that the electrostatic tape concept would work, that it was technically robust and was quite capable of satisfying the "new" requirement for 5-foot (1.5 m) resolution. Lockheed reminded its audience that a definition of 100 lines per millimeter was equivalent to a film sensitivity of ASA-145, whereas standard reconnaissance film had a rating of ASA-2 to -5. The photo image would be recorded on a photoelectric-sensitive electrostatic tape and read out by deflecting the modulation of the electron beam to scan a portion of the tape. The video signal would be amplified and then modulated on to a carrier wave for ground stations. Lockheed claimed this system was a great improvement over the E-2 system, although a bandwidth of 12 MHz would be needed with a readout time of 8.7 seconds per frame.

Despite cogent arguments for the E-3 electrostatic tape system, the Air Force was highly sceptical and Joseph Charyk, Air Force Assistant Secretary, pushed for the E-5 with the newly formed Directorate of Defense Research and Engineering (DDR&E), one layer above ARPA in the Pentagon. With ARPA's influence on a wide range of issues waning close to collapse, it was finally pushed from above to authorize full development of the E-5 film recovery system. On September 18, 1959, Neil McElroy, the Secretary of Defense, moved the SAMOS program from ARPA to the Air Force. The next fight was over readout versus recovery, and the technical possibilities theoretically available from readout was too great for the Air Force to pass up.

For much of 1959 the Strategic Air Command had made a big play to be the organization responsible for SAMOS, much to the chagrin of the intelligence community and the CIA in particular. With a deftly crafted countervail of secrecy and subterfuge, the CORONA program had demonstrated how a covert endeavor could be fielded under an overt wrapper of scientific and engineering investigations. Suddenly, the Air Force

LEFT Just some of the myriad array of components and equipment packaged into a small Tiros satellite. *(NOAA)*

was openly discussing its potential photo-reconnaissance program while many on the SAMOS program had no idea at all about the work already under way with CORONA. SAC had been highly sceptical of the spy satellite program. Now the Air Force was a firm advocate, and with ICBMs rolling off the production lines and rising on launch pads across the US there was a surge in demand for more information about Soviet developments and in war preparations.

By January 1960 a revised development plan anticipated seven E-5 capsule recovery flights added to an existing schedule of 18 readout and ferret missions, of which 11 would carry E-1 and E-2 systems. But changes were made yet again after the Powers incident and Charyk directed emphasis on the E-5 recovery system, sidelining the ferret systems and pushing back the E-1 and E-2 readout systems. Over the next several months dissatisfaction with the readout concept was worsened by the failures with the Discoverer program, and, by association, with the contractor, Lockheed. At SAC, plans for an elaborate readout system were quietly dropped.

It was the Air Force Ballistic Missile Committee that framed a new program structure and drew in resources from existing players and new people to consider a different satellite design with a new camera and a new recovery system – a camera to provide "the

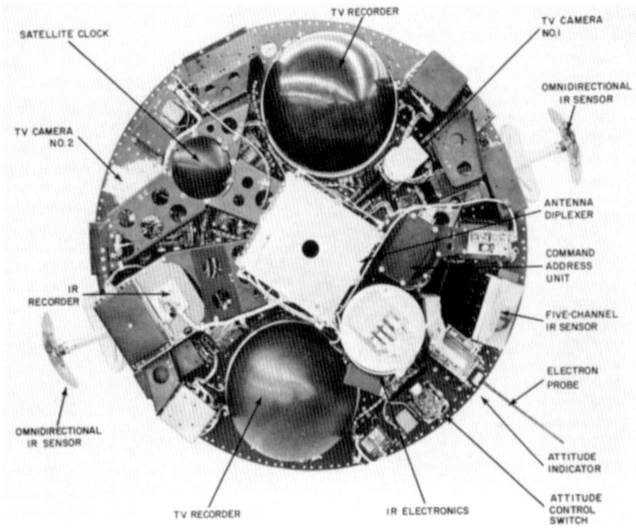

ABOVE An overhead view of Tiros showing the various instruments, command systems and sensors for taking and recording images of meteorological activities. *(NOAA)*

best ground resolution that state-of-the-art will support." As defined, the new requirement would provide a ground resolution of 20 feet (6 m) or less, secure capsule land recovery within 5 miles (8 km) of a predicted point, demonstrate high reliability and operate for eight days in orbit for large area coverage.

By the end of July 1960 the new system was designated E-6 and on the 30th of that month a new source selection board for a contractor was named for a recovery system with broad research responsibility and the highest possible resolution. But Lockheed was to be excluded, with the Aerospace Corporation appointed to manage the program. A degree of reality began to appear as the president was briefed on the technical possibilities with spy satellites in general, on the hyped expectations of advocates and on the inability of satellites in general to provide the kind of picture resolution the U-2 could produce for several years to come.

RIGHT Tiros being installed on top of the terminal stage of the launch vehicle, each satellite being an 18-sided polygon 22.5 inches (57 cm) tall and 42 inches (107 cm) in diameter. *(NOAA)*

The second half of 1960 saw major shifts in the center of gravity for SAMOS. The president approved the initial launch with the E-1 system and development of a new design moved ahead as a future development under the program umbrella. As early as March 1960, Eastman Kodak submitted a proposal to the Wright Air Development Division for a high-quality camera with a 77-inch (195 cm) focal length for satellite reconnaissance application, following up three months later with an alternative built around a 36-inch (91 cm) camera for convergent stereo coverage of Soviet territory.

Eastman Kodak were confident the system could provide a ground resolution as low as 6 feet (1.8 m) and that over a five-day operating life it could cover 97% of specified target area as defined by the Air Force. Eager to press home their technological prowess, further presentations displayed a camera that could provide spot coverage of certain targets with a resolution as low as 2 feet (61 cm). To their 77-inch (195 cm) camera they applied the name "Sunset Strip," alluding to a television show of the time. The company was certainly keen to get some work with their new designs, briefing the CIA as well. It worked, for on August 2 they were contracted to build a prototype and demonstrate the technology. The company put together a 90-day Phase I stage to provide a mock-up and a Phase II effort for design, construction, testing and flight evaluation. But there were other players.

In August 1960 Space Technology Laboratories (STL) presented the Ballistic Missile Division with a proposal for a covert spy satellite designed to compromise between resolution, design simplicity, reliable operation and quick delivery. It was based around a standard Atlas

D AVCO 52 nosecone that would be placed in a polar orbit for 16 orbits of the Earth before recovery. The satellite would be spin-stabilized, carry a 24-inch (61 cm) focal length panoramic camera and shoot pictures to a 5-inch (13 cm) film exposed to 40-inch (102 cm) strips during alternate rotations of the spinning vehicle. The nosecone was a proven design, well used, and employed reliable components that gave it similarity to the original Fairchild proposal for WS-117L.

In September, Dr Charyk chaired a meeting at which it was agreed to study the STL proposal (dubbed "Study 7"), Sunset Strip and E-6, also endorsing the 77-inch (195 cm) system as one definitely to keep in hand for later deployment as a covert system. The desire for it to be covert referred to the gradual relaxation of secrecy over the use of spy cameras in orbiting satellites, and while CORONA remained "Top Secret" under Byeman distribution rules, the general discussion of the Air Force SAMOS program was an open issue and one which was increasingly debated in the public domain.

As far as the public was concerned, however, SAMOS was the only game in town and had yet to get off the ground. In fact, the Russians were now demanding UN sanctions restricting what satellites could be used for; the Americans were already leaping far ahead of what the Russians had launched or planned to fly, and only just getting started on a manned program which would employ the same cosmonaut-carrying spacecraft, named Vostok, as their own spy satellite named Zenit. The reference to a covert system allowed the high-resolution camera to be kept Top Secret so that it would not unduly provoke Soviet responses which just might bring about international agreement prohibiting the launch of spy satellites.

The interplay between overt and generally discussed programs on one hand and covert programs on the other now received a new twist, almost a play of tactics borrowed from the Discoverer/CORONA story. Dr. Charyk agreed in November 1960 that the E-6 camera program would be used as a cover for the "Sunset Strip" system and that Eastman Kodak would develop the 77-inch (195 cm) system under the cover of a new name: GAMBIT. General Electric would develop the re-entry capsule. Both E-6 and GAMBIT would be compatible so that they

BELOW LEFT Tiros in its launch shroud with the advisory notice on the side reading "CAUTION EXPLOSIVE DEVICES ARE SET IN THIS VEHICLE. CONSULT DIRECTIONS BEFORE HANDLING." *(NOAA)*

BELOW A Delta rocket stands ready to launch an ESSA (Environmental Science Services Administration) weather satellite from Cape Canaveral in February 1966. *(NOAA)*

ABOVE **A Thor-Able launcher lifts off from Cape Canaveral with a Tiros weather satellite. While NASA was demonstrating the possibility of an effective and operational weather satellite system, the Air Force was preparing to launch precursor meteorological satellites of its own, the first successfully flown being that on a Scout rocket in August 1962.** *(NASA)*

would be interchangeable and therefore any attempt to prevent application of the more powerful camera by international treaty could be circumvented under the Top Secret GAMBIT program. Nobody would ever know it even existed. In this way "Sunset Strip" would encapsulate a secret program much as Discoverer shrouded CORONA.

But it was necessary to bury "Sunset Strip" because E-6 was going deep black, so a story was put out that it was being cancelled as the requirement had evaporated. But the covert nature of GAMBIT (see Chapter 6) meant that during the second half of 1960 the CORONA team were well aware of the other system, which was seen by some in respective camps as a competitor. This never permeated the management of respective systems who, while working hard to operate within the national interests of the country, fiercely defended their own programs and the unique capabilities of an alternate concept.

By early 1961 CORONA was heading toward a series of improvements that would significantly enhance its capabilities and the quality of its products, while GAMBIT still embraced both readout and ferret systems – as the E-1 and E-2 and the F-1 and F-2 – and E-5 was still in development, with the E-6 just starting. In these early months of 1961 Charyk moved the E-4 mapping satellite to Thor and it became a separate and quite different program. By this time the SAMOS program had entered

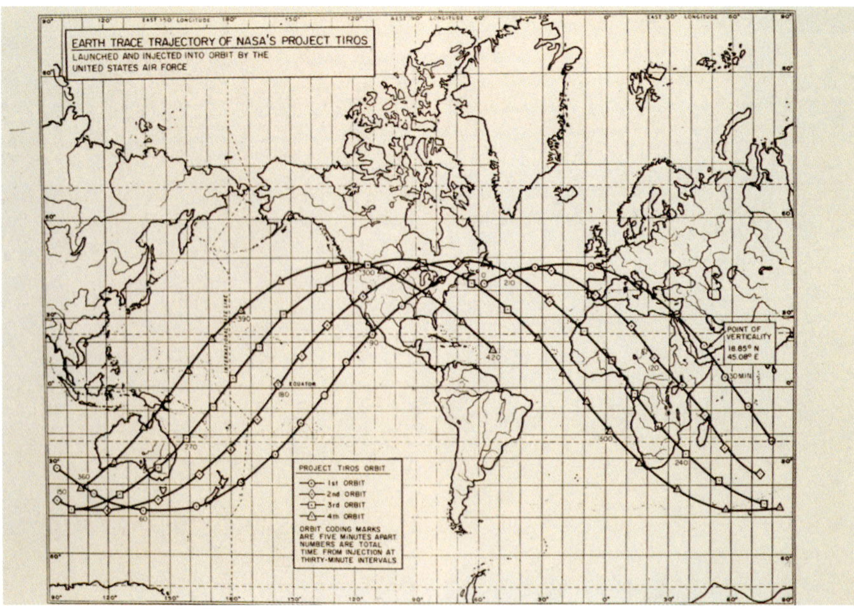

RIGHT **An orbit ground track map for the Tiros 1 satellite that shows the orbital migration.** *(NOAA)*

the flight phase, not as had been envisaged when it emerged from WS-117L but rather as an experimental program that would expose its own flaws in a manner no one had anticipated.

Meanwhile, with much public and media fanfare, the first attempt to launch SAMOS got under way on October 11, 1960, carrying both E-1 imaging and F-1 ferret signal intelligence systems. The E-1 read-out had a focal length of 72 inches (1.83 m) with a maximum theoretical resolution of 100 feet (30 m) covering a swathe of territory 100 miles x 100 miles (161 km x 161 km). Unfortunately, while the launch of SAMOS-1 provided dramatic visual coverage the mission was a failure when an umbilical disconnect failure at lift-off rapidly drained nitrogen attitude control gas from the Agena stage and when called upon to fire it tumbled out of control, never reaching orbit.

The next launch (SAMOS-2) was delayed until two captured American airmen from a downed RB-47 reconnaissance bomber spying across the Russian border were released by the Soviets; the newly installed Kennedy administration wanted a diplomatic success under their belt before taunting the Soviets with a spy flight launch, the true purpose of which was assumed to be within their knowledge.

On January 31, 1961, the third anniversary of America's first successful satellite, the 4,189-pound (1,900 kg) satellite, equipped with an E-1 system (2102), was successfully placed in a 346 miles x 295 miles (557 km x 474 km) orbit at an orbital inclination of 97.4° and with a period of 95.2 minutes. It was the first satellite placed in a Sun-synchronous orbit. This type of orbit is defined as one in which the altitude, period and inclination of the near-polar orbit are set up so that the satellite passes over any given point of the surface each day at the same local time – hence the same insolation.

Clearly, this has great advantage in that it enables flight controllers to have the satellite pass over the same spot on the ground when the lighting angles are approximately the same each day. Carefully timed, a launch can place a spy satellite in a position where it can provide daily observations of areas of interest, allowing interpreters to view the same place daily over extended periods, for instance to monitor development of new military construction sites, activity at launch locations, and the maritime traffic in and out of ports.

Dr. Charyk got his eyes on the first SAMOS direct readout pictures on February 3 and verified that the resolution was better than projected. But there seemed little functional purpose for continuing with SAMOS and the emerging consensus was that the contracted E-1/E-2 direct-readout flights would run their course but that they would, in reality, be treated as a precursor evaluation program for GAMBIT, and that one-third of the planned flights would be cancelled, with the remaining hardware returned to Lockheed and stored.

One idea was a response to the flight of Russia's Luna 2 spacecraft that, in 1959, rounded the Moon and returned to the vicinity of the Earth where it transmitted previously captured images of the far side. The Luna 2 mission roused ideas of using the E-1/E-2 system for conducting a similar Moon mission using a NASA spacecraft. While this never took hold at the time, it did result in the Air Force allowing NASA to incorporate the Kodak system in its Lunar Orbiter program of five highly successful flights in 1965–66. The Lunar Orbiter

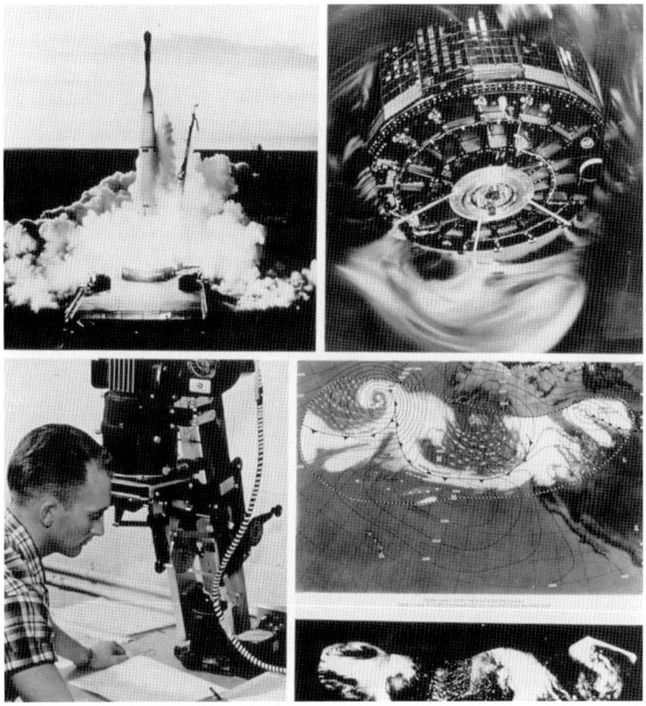

ABOVE A montage of Tiros 1 spacecraft and images as it tracked the North Atlantic storm of May 19–20, 1960. *(NOAA)*

RIGHT The Tiros satellites were covered with solar cells on every possible surface, necessitated by the comparatively low power levels available from photo-voltaic equipment of the early 1960s. *(NOAA)*

missions provided the definitive photographic Atlas from which landing sites were selected for Apollo astronauts.

Fraught with technical problems in ground tests, the number of E-2 flights was cut to two. The E-2 was essentially the same as the E-1 but with a different lens providing a focal length of 36 inches (0.91 m) for a ground resolution of 20 feet (6 m) in a ground swathe of 17 miles x 17 miles (27 km x 27 km). The first attempt to get an E-2 payload into orbit with SAMOS-3 was the first with the new Agena B, which could be restarted in space, but this failed on September 9, 1961, in a massive fireball when the Atlas rocket exploded after it lost all electrical power and fell back on to the pad, caused by a 0.2-second delay in transferring power from ground to internal systems.

The second E-2 payload (2121) was removed from its Agena and stored, replaced with an E-5 system (2202) for the next launch on November 22; but the Agena suffered an attitude problem and when it fired to achieve orbit it propelled itself back into the atmosphere and was destroyed. SAMOS-5 carried another E-5 system (2203) and return capsule, the earlier E-series having been ingloriously retired, but a problem with the Atlas after launch on December 22 put the spacecraft into a much higher orbit than planned with an apogee of 436 miles (702 km) and the retrofire system was unable to return the capsule from that great height.

Launched on March 7, 1962, SAMOS-6 carried the third and final E-5 (2204), which was successfully placed in orbit, but an attitude problem rendered it unusable. This E-5 had been significantly modified as a result of experience with the previous two and the Agena received another tranche of modifications including improved command and control systems. A plethora of failures, some the responsibility of ground stations, doomed the final E-5 system to a higher orbit than planned instead of returning as commanded.

But the technology of the E-5 was not buried, even if it had been declared dead. On December 19, 1961, the E-5 was formally submitted as a potential development for the CORONA series and this resulted in a series of developments which would eventually emerge as LANYARD. Neither was the other camera system, the E-6, totally without subterfuge; as development of this advanced recovery camera got under way it was slaved in technical direction to the very highly classified GAMBIT, but that changed during 1961 until it took on a distinctly separate technical appearance and could no longer be associated with that more sophisticated system.

The E-6 mission would begin with launch by Atlas-Agena B into a 155-mile (249 km) orbit, with orbit refinement calculated by telemetry data, angle-track data and radar tracking. Orbital corrections to precisely set up the desired orbital path would be effected from track and rate radar and applied as a burn from the Agena B. The camera section contained a small hydrogen peroxide thruster that would fine-tune the orbit.

Photographing was scheduled to start on the eighth orbit, a system incorporating two 36-inch (91 cm) focal length lenses enabling stereo coverage and horizon recording to maintain the correct attitude. The E-6 had a theoretical resolution of 8 feet (2.4 m) across a swathe 174 miles (280 km) across, preserving pictures on 3,400 feet (1,350 m) of film to be recovered like the CORONA buckets. At one time some low-funded studies had been conducted on land recovery but this was eventually abandoned.

Re-entry data would be uplinked to the

satellite based on ephemerides calculated from data received at tracking stations with Agena B orientating itself with nitrogen jets for retro-fire, also providing spin-up that would avoid the unpredictability of the solid thrusters used on CORONA. The recovery vehicle was based on the General Electric RVX-2 re-entry body developed for warheads, unlike the CORONA series that used the Mk 5 and Mk 5A designs.

All tracking and telemetry subsystems were contained within the re-entry vehicle, compatible with the Mod III systems employed at the Atlantic Missile and Pacific Missile Ranges, with the S-band tracking radar at Hawaii, Kodiak and Vandenberg facilities. Time-code binary signals were transmitted to the SAMOS vehicle by Verlot tracking link and a memory within the satellite stored commands for satellite and payload subsystems. In this area at least it carried the more sophisticated technology being built into the GAMBIT satellites.

Inevitably delays set in, and not until April 26, 1962, was SAMOS-7 launched with the first E-6 camera. All appeared tolerably well for a first attempt, despite one camera not working and the Agena suffering excessive attitude excursions, but when the Agena reconfigured itself for re-entry the attitude was incorrect and the re-entry vehicle could not be recovered. Failure also dogged SAMOS-8, launched on June 17, and again there was a multiple set of failures resulting in the Agena failing to separate from the satellite and re-entering as a single unit to impact the ocean and sink.

SAMOS-9 got off the launch pad on July 18, carrying the third E-6 payload but a different set of technical problems prevented recovery,

Spacecraft	Total TV Pictures Transmitted	Meteorologically Useful Pictures	Number of Nephanalyses	Storm Advisories and Bulletins
TIROS I	22,952	19,389	333	---
TIROS II	36,156	26,650	455	---
TIROS III	35,033	22,247	755	70
TIROS IV	32,593	22,354	836	102
TIROS V	58,226	49,236	1,843	395
TIROS VI	68,557	58,667	2,080	275
TIROS VII*	50,000	43,900	1,730	120
TIROS VIII*	8,400 1,200 (APT)	7,000	255	18
TOTAL	311,917 1,200 (APT)	249,443	8,287	980

ABOVE A log of Tiros images by satellite, current as of February 1964, demonstrates the consistency of performance. *(NOAA)*

BELOW Assembled from 450 individual photographs from the Tiros IX satellite taken in 1965, this was the first view of the world's weather systems. *(NOAA)*

up shortly after the scheduled time of impact.

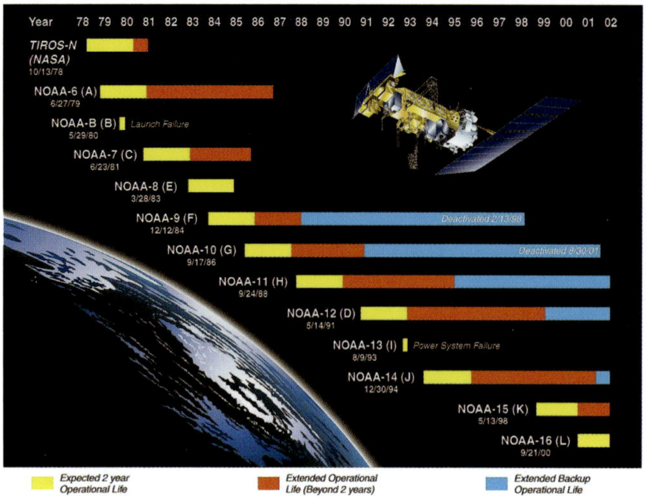

ABOVE Reliability and consistent improvements during the 1970s gave Tiros and its successor programs for the National Oceanic and Atmospheric Administration (NOAA) credible space-based performance with increasing lifetimes and enhanced durability. *(NOAA)*

prompting some engineering changes to SAMOS-10, which launched on August 5. It too suffered problems and the capsule was lost. Numerous and detailed analyses followed this succession of failures and there was talk of switching the payload to a Thrust-Augmented Thor launcher, providing increased lifting capacity through the use of strap-on solid-propellant boosters, a development of the basic Thor which was already under way.

But any changes were too far away, too costly and there was decreasing satisfaction with the system anyway. But a lot was riding on the much-publicised SAMOS program, the only one in which there was tacit acknowledgement that America was launching spy cameras in space. The E-6 cover was in fact an "open" and expendable asset which could be ceremoniously cancelled should the USSR press the United Nations to ban spy satellites in their entirety. The SAMOS could be sacrificed and Discoverer/CORONA continued in clandestine veil.

Nevertheless, it was impossible to continue with E-6, even if it was a cover for GAMBIT, and much was riding on the final launch attempt when SAMOS-11 carried the fifth E-6 into space on November 11, 1962. Everything went as planned and the satellite did its intended job. De-orbiting went well and all seemed set for the first recovery of an E-6 system. However, the capsule came down heavily and was not recovered, despite some beacons being picked up shortly after the scheduled time of impact.

Some people wanted to continue with the program and it is important to appreciate here that almost nobody associated with SAMOS – certainly not the operations people – had any idea that there were several other spy satellites flying and in varying stages of development. Secrecy was so profound that for many years afterwards some personnel believed the United States had totally given up on space-based reconnaissance, an assumption which is hard to believe today but true nevertheless.

On January 31, 1963, despite protestations to the contrary, Charyk ordered a halt to all further work on SAMOS and the E-6 program in particular. With this came an end to the E-series camera systems that since 1960 had carried the pioneering work of spy satellite evolution through to the emerging age of digital transmission. While CORONA flights would continue for almost another ten years, development of new systems was already under way. But the reality was that E-6 and SAMOS was not the only program proceeding in some level of (relatively open) secrecy.

As indicated earlier, there had been considerable enthusiasm in the Army for a mapping and charting satellite and this evolved as the E-4 direct readout system, in competition with the E-5 surveillance system and ARGON. ARPA ordered the Army to cancel the E-4 in May 1959 but the Air Force introduced into the concept their 412 camera, which appeared to be a successor to ARGON. But the Thor for ARGON provided less weight flexibility than would the Atlas for the E-4, and the latter began to gain renewed support when technical analysis showed that it would be an improvement.

The initial requirement for E-4 was a ground resolution of at least 500 feet (152 m) and was to be based on an Agena B carrying a recoverable capsule with a length of 7 feet (2.13 m) and a diameter of 6 feet (1.82 m). The camera would be equipped with a 6-inch (15.24 cm) focal-length lens and a star-mapping guidance camera with a focal length of 3 inches (7.62 cm). The satellite would operate for a planned five days from an altitude of 205 miles (330 km) with a perigee of 103 miles (166 km) over the target producing a ground resolution of about 150 feet (46 m).

The E-4s f/5.6 lens represented what photogrammetric specialists regarded as the best then available, producing a resolution of 60 lines/mm with a distortion of 10 microns reduced to 2 microns after calibration. The satellite would carry 4,000 feet (1,219 m) of 9-inch x 9-inch (23 cm x 23 cm) film. The images were to carry fiducial and reseau marks with a timer accuracy of 0.001 seconds. The f/2.5 star camera would be equipped with 4.5-inch x 4.5-inch (11.4 cm x 11.4 cm) film, exposed for four seconds at a time, to record elongated star images on 2,000 feet (610 m) of film. It was believed each mission would capture 14.16 billion hectares of Soviet territory.

To veil the application of a program, and a technology, which in theory at least had been cancelled, the program acquired the designation 1A, in part also because the Kennedy administration wanted all military space programs to go secret and to be hidden from public scrutiny. Lockheed received a contract on April 6, 1961, with Fairchild responsible for the camera and payload system for an initial approval to fly four such payloads. But technical and cost difficulties plagued the program and in January 1962 Charyk decided to mothball the hardware and cancel the E-4. It is described here only in so far as it locks into the overall story and stands as a benchmark of technical standards at the turn of the decade.

Shortly thereafter the SAMOS readout series ended and the last five flights, between April 26, 1962, and November 11, 1962, employed the E-5 film recovery system with a 28-inch (0.7 m) focal-length camera providing a resolution of 5 feet (1.5 m) over a swathe 61 miles (98 km) in length. There had been a strong synergy between the E-4 and the E-5 but the performance in 1961 was simply not good enough to warrant further application and the E-5 was cancelled in December 1961 but, as noted above, the technology had a legacy. It was not totally successful on the SAMOS flights in which it was tried and this type of camera would only be fully evaluated through the LANYARD program. By this date the CORONA satellites had provided excellent mapping and charting services and satellites dedicated to that role were unnecessary.

ABOVE The Defense Meteorology Satellite Program (DMSP) matured slowly over the decade of the 1960s, expanding rapidly in performance and capabilities alongside photographic systems such as CORONA and SAMOS. *(USAF)*

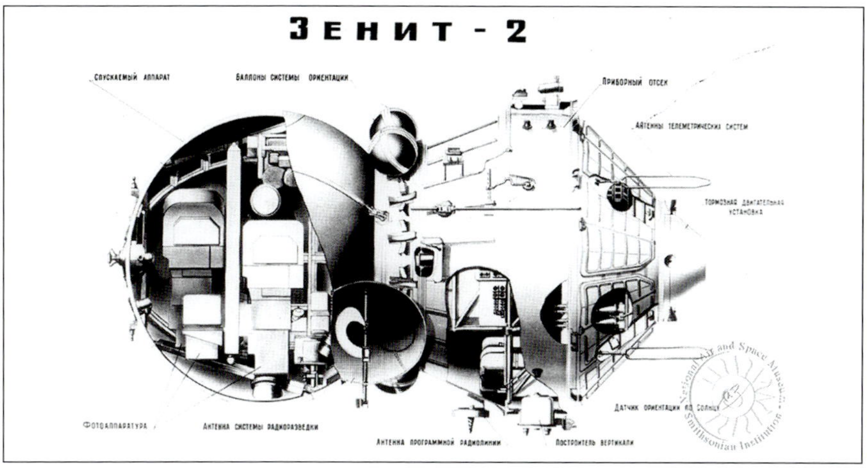

LEFT While the US was developing a range of Earth-observing systems, Russia was adapting the recoverable spacecraft it used to place cosmonauts into orbit aboard the Vostok spacecraft. Zenit was the first-generation Soviet spy satellite. Designed to carry a camera system capable of providing a ground resolution of 1.5–2.1 feet (5–7 m), the first successful return of Zenit photographs occurred on July 28, 1962. *(David Baker)*

Chapter Six

GAMBIT (KH-7/KH-8)

The need for a very high-resolution photographic system emerged early in the development of US spy satellite programs. In March 1960 Eastman Kodak sent the CIA a proposal for permission to develop a camera with a 77-inch (195-cm) focal length and three months later a 36-inch (91-cm) system for stereo imaging on to film. This system was known as Blanket and in July 1960 Eastman proposed a further development integrating the 77-inch (195-cm) camera with stereo features and importing a film recovery technique from CORONA.

OPPOSITE A "calibration" image of the US Capitol, Washington DC, taken by a KH-7 on February 19, 1966. Careful scrutiny of a well-known area allowed interpreters to get a better evaluation of the "real-world" capabilities of the optical system aboard the satellite. *(NRO)*

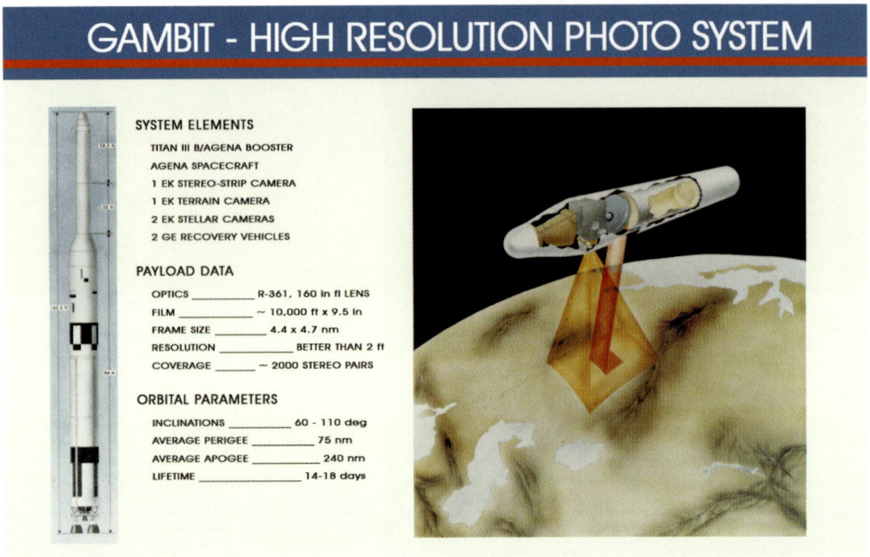

RIGHT **Exploiting all the technology developed through CORONA, a significant shift in capability was made possible by building on the Agena D stage and placing the assembly on a new launch vehicle with greater lifting ability: the Titan IIIB.** *(NRO)*

This proposal was endorsed by Edwin Land, who proceeded to support it when presented to the Air Force's then under-secretary Joseph Charyk. This went alongside similar pressure from the RAND Corporation to develop a spin-stabilized satellite. A meeting was held on July 7, 1960, to discuss a radical idea: that a satellite could be "hidden" in the re-entry body of a ballistic missile. This was a time when uncertainty surrounded the entire issue of launching spy satellites into orbit but it presaged the day when "sleeper" satellites would in reality be hidden among apparent debris from innocuous launches.

RAND recommended a 1,500-pound (680 kg) spin-stabilized satellite with a 36-inch (91 cm) lens for panoramic views at a resolution of 17 feet (5.2 m). RAND calculated that if pointing directly down from a latitude of 55°N it would view all areas between 40°N and 70°N. As the concept advanced the lens was requoted with a 24-inch (61 cm) focal length and several variations in the design were submitted for approval when on August 25, 1960, President Eisenhower decided there was merit to a clandestine satellite program.

Involved in this sequence of optional paths were the existing CORONA, E-6 and Blanket systems and their story need not be repeated here. Suffice to say that the desire for a covert program outside the CORONA/Discoverer program allowed the E-6 to appear as a covert program with the name GAMBIT. The name itself was apparently chosen by Air Force Colonel Paul J. Heran, who associated the satellite's function to that involved in the tactics of a chess game. But the initial designation was Program 307, and as such it could procure hardware without reference to satellites or reconnaissance.

Prior to significant improvements with the CORONA satellites there was little confidence that this series could deliver the high-resolution imagery essential to the needs of the intelligence community and the appalling initial launch and operational record of the Discoverer launches and space vehicles gave

BELOW **The KH-7/KH-8 series incorporated two expanded sections between the Agena stage and the satellite recovery vehicle (SRV), which allowed greater flexibility with the optics selected for each mission.** *(NRO)*

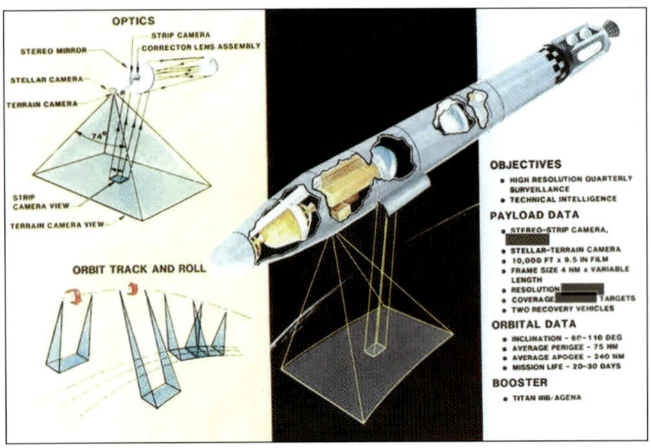

ample ground for that belief. Many experts in the field believed that abandoning the carefully crafted options under WS-117L had betrayed the intentions of the initial tranche of advocates.

Development of the GAMBIT system mirrored the E-6 in such a way that the latter veiled the existence of the former, even from CORONA people who knew nothing of their potential competitor and eventual successor. The formal cancellation of the E-6 and Sunset Strip programs appeared to signal the end of the 77-inch (195 cm) lens. At the same time the SAMOS people drew up contracts for Eastman Kodak to continue development of that system. The emphasis on the highest possible resolution came at a time when there was a profound commitment from Eisenhower to obtain the maximum amount of intelligence about the Soviet Union, and this program introduced a completely new security blanket around the promising technology.

It was agreed that the Air Force would find it virtually impossible to procure major items without going through very open and visible channels, or to be seen openly as indulging in black projects. So the system developed the concept of the "null program" whereby the orders for everything from rocket stages to satellite hardware came from the Space Systems Division and not from the office of Robert E. Greer, the boss of the SAMOS project, a man widely known to be associated with satellite reconnaissance. By not emanating from his office the open procurement of separate items, with no originating function and no declared assigned purpose, was assumed to be a general Air Force black project disassociated from spy satellites.

It is just feasible that some of the concerns expressed by Soviet officials in their dealings with American diplomats may have originated in the suspicion that the Air Force was planning to place nuclear weapons in space on standby in case of war. To those with only a smattering of knowledge about the way orbits work, such a concept is preposterous: orbits circle the globe in fixed positions while the Earth slowly spins below. Even in polar orbit, objects in space only pass over the same spot on the planet once a day – far less efficient than firing a ballistic missile that can reach its target on the other side of the world in 30 minutes. But it served the purpose of "disinformation."

The "classified" category was applied to what was originally known as Project 206 (under the new streamlined designation system of the Kennedy administration) through a code word, EXEMPLAR, given to General Bernard Schriever, Commander, Air Force Systems Command (AFSC), on September 25, 1961. Thus some wider exposure provided an identifying name for hardware procurement under the null program concept and this veiled the true intent of AFSC by ordering four NASA-style

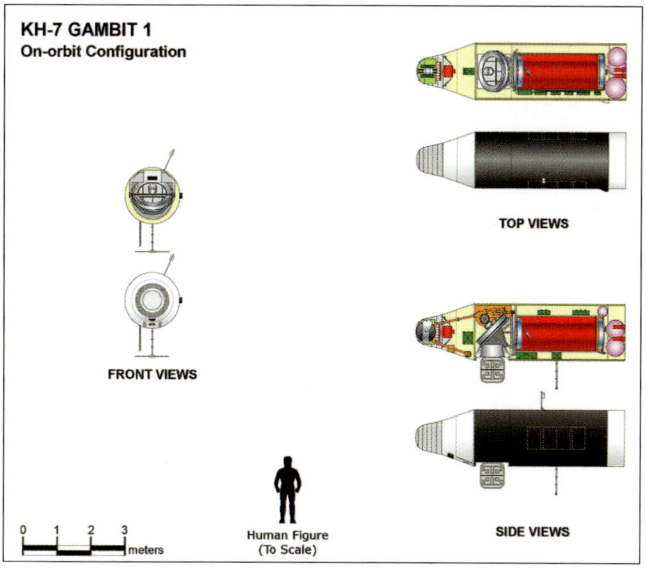

ABOVE The KH-7 system added to the front of the Agena D was a major new asset for the National Reconnaissance Office and its expanding list of customers. *(Giuseppe de Chiara)*

BELOW The fully assembled KH-7 with Agena D. *(Giuseppe de Chiara)*

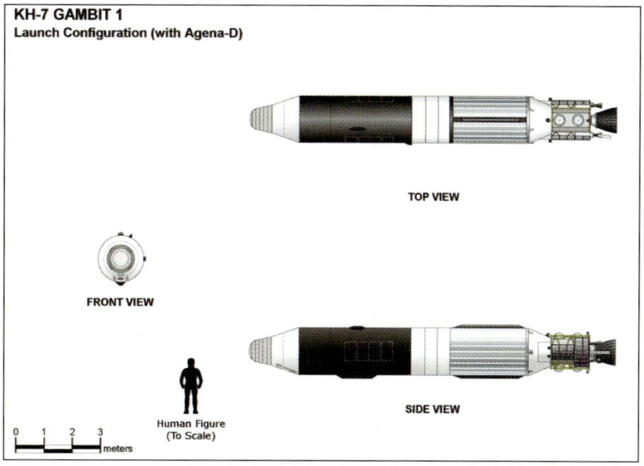

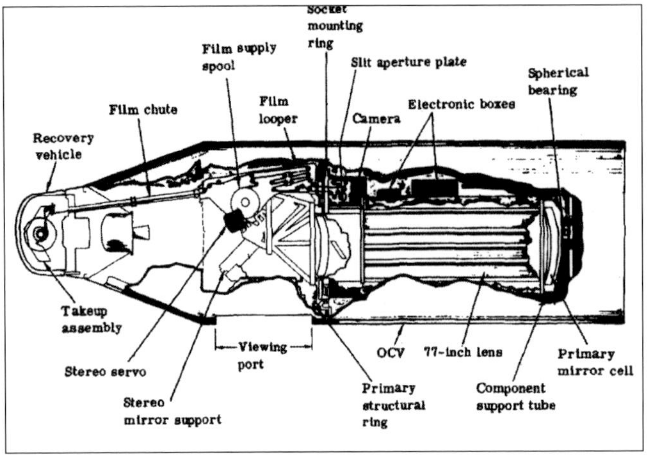

ABOVE This cutaway of the KH-7/KH-8 series shows the relative location of the new Orbital Control Vehicle (OCV) and the recovery capsule together with the film transport route and the location of the two optical systems. *(Lockheed)*

Agena B stages. At that date flight operations were to commence in February 1963.

The "white" program attached to EXEMPLAR mustered a mighty pile of documentation including costs, procurement plans and general scientific tasks, while the administrative side of the real program for what would become GAMBIT was code-named Cue Ball, directed by Colonel Q.A. Riepe. The code name appeared to indicate a program where orbiting bombs would be returned at will to prize "pockets," or targets, on the surface of the Earth, adding to the disinformation through inference. In fact, Riepe and Greer had a highly efficient (but Top Secret) channel of communication as the program developed.

Further disruption to awareness of the program's true intent came when it was split into two components: A, which included the first four Agenas procured, and B, which would include the remaining six stages supporting a ten-launch plan. Over time, the program would involve a serpentine route to funding, as not even Congressional committee members were allowed access to it. But this was not unusual and still exists today with highly classified projects.

The original idea was to have the SRV come down on land, and a considerable amount of effort went into trying to design this into the system, all to no avail. When funding was being attracted to these marginally valuable aspects of the program, it was decided to end the attempt and return to the original idea of following the CORONA method by recovery through air-snatch or surface retrieval.

When the program began there was distrust in the air-recovery method and it was felt that the high-value nature of the film, plus the fact that it would not be taking as broad an area of photography, required each SRV to have a more reliable method of retrieval. But at this time CORONA was not performing well and nobody wanted to attach GAMBIT to a flawed procedure.

As time wore on CORONA got much better and the air-snatch concept gathered respect. Moreover, the land recovery design was 500 pounds (225 kg) heavier! On August 24, 1962, Charyk authorized Greer to adopt the air-snatch concept. Central to it all, however, was the way the design of the vehicle was required to support the driving imperative for the highest possible resolution.

The way GAMBIT achieved such high-resolution imagery was to attack the problem in a different manner to that approached through

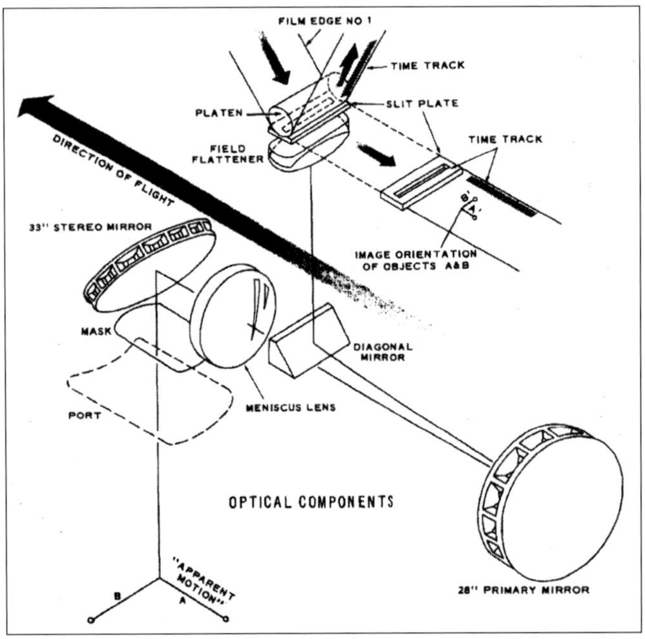

LEFT Light falling on the angled stereo mirror is reflected through a meniscus lens on the primary mirror from where it is moved through a diagonal mirror to the field flattener and film platen. *(Lockheed)*

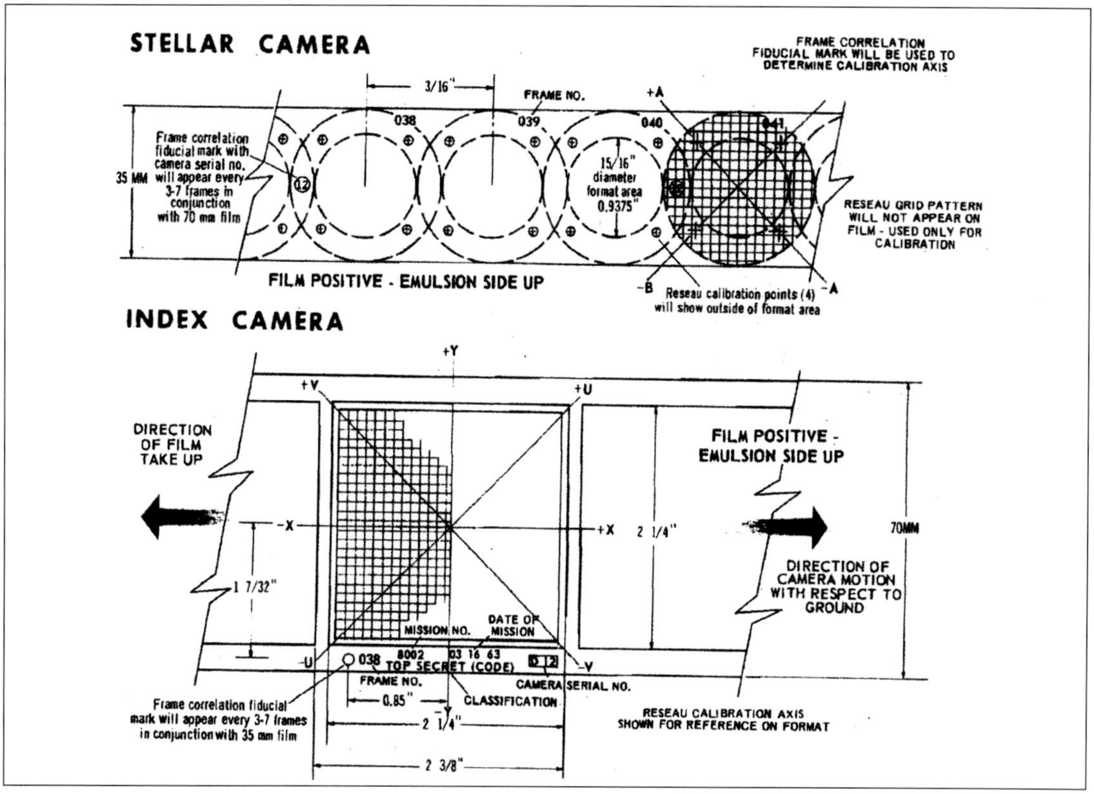

ABOVE The stellar and index camera format and titling. The index camera consisted of a Zeiss Biogon f/4.5 lens with a focal length of 1.5 inches (3.8 cm). *(NRO)*

the CORONA satellites. The GAMBIT design produced a larger image at the focal plane and featured a Matsukov-type strip camera with an aperture of 19.5 inches (49.5 cm) with an effective aperture of f/4.0 and an effective focal length of 77 inches (195 cm) as originally envisaged by Eastman Kodak. The payload incorporated both reflecting and refracting elements. With a photo resolution of 115 lines/mm this translated into a ground resolution at the nadir (closest point on the Earth directly beneath the satellite) of 2 feet (60 cm).

GAMBIT would carry 3,000 feet (915 m) of film 9.5 inches (24 cm) wide, a thin-base film that moved through the strip camera at the same speed as the projected image moved over the Earth. The camera would image a strip 10.6 nanometers wide and the total payload system had a weight of 1,154 pounds (523 kg). The format size was 8.7 inches (22 cm) wide and of variable length up to 387 inches (983 cm) but usually within the range 13–46 inches (33–117 cm). Film speeds varied from 2.022 inches (5.13 cm) per second to 3.784 inches (9.61 cm) per second in 64 discrete segments. Stereo pairs would produce 100% overlap while pairs of lateral photographs would produce parallel strips with minimal overlap.

Stereo operation would be achieved with a 30° included angle between pointing forward and then aft for an overlap. Continuous strip photography would adopt the same angular sweep between lateral pairs. Precision was vital, as the optics would be looking at a slant angle with a total ground swathe only 6.3° wide, where slight shudder or jitter would cause image distortion.

The Matsukov concept originated from the Russian-born telescope designer Dmitri Dmitrievich Matsukov (1896–1964) who, in the 1940s and 1950s, developed many different types of observing instruments and large optical systems. The Matsukov telescope corrects for spherical aberration by means of a corrector lens placed in front of the primary mirror. While similar to the familiar Schmidt telescope, the

RIGHT **The film format for the KH-7.** *(NRO)*

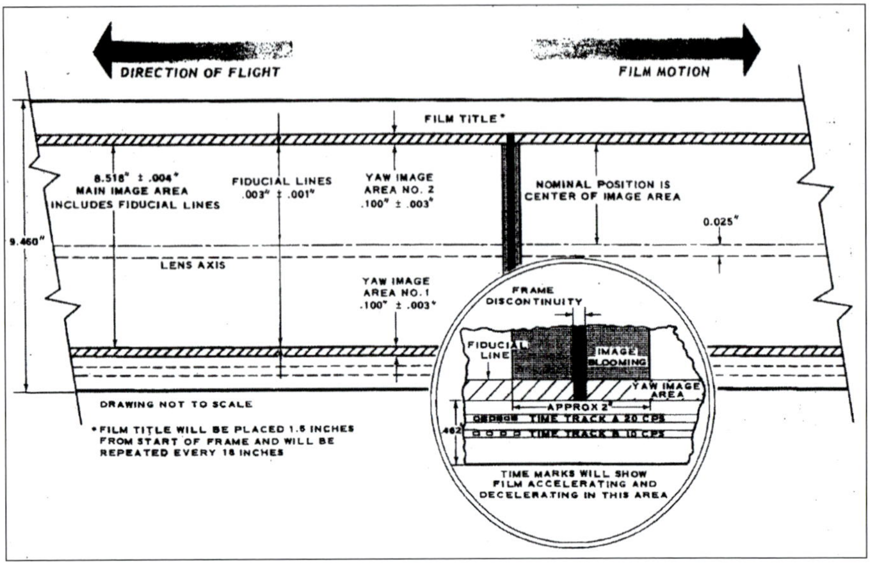

Matsukov adds a deeply curved full-diameter negative meniscus lens as a corrector shell. The design was published by Matsukov in 1944 and was quickly taken up by many famous astronomical observatories in the Soviet Union.

The strip camera continuously exposed a narrow strip on the film as the camera passed over the area being photographed. On the KH-7 it photographed a small target area on the ground through this narrow slit which was located close to the focal plane of the camera and this could produce stereo pairs, lateral pairs and strip photographs up to a maximum of 600 stereo pairs or an equivalent amount of continuous strip photography on the mission.

A further means of improving the resolution on the ground was to make improvements to the thermal efficiency of the system, which meant as much about maintaining a constant temperature as it did about cooling the system. Irregularities in internal temperatures could compromise the resolution, create tension in the film spool and

RIGHT **A KH-7 image of the Russian Plesetsk launch site obtained on June 9, 1967. Photographs showed the expanse of the facility, the number of launch pads and the capabilities of the installed infrastructure.** *(NRO)*

FAR RIGHT **A photograph of the ground radar at Sary Shagan, a major Soviet research and development center for air-defense and anti-ballistic missile radars, taken on May 28, 1967.** *(NRO)*

cause differential expansion and contraction. GAMBIT took on board a range of solutions worked out through the KH-4 program and integrated from the outset by design changes that were learned the hard way on CORONA.

But for all the technical efficiency and more advanced development going in to the camera system, the key to getting the required imagery was to have a much more stable platform from which to observe the ground. Here the design of the KH-7 departed significantly from CORONA. Not only did it have the flexibility of a more capable launch vehicle in the Atlas-Agena, it also had the flexibility of a new way of maintaining control of the vehicle in space.

The total GAMBIT system had a length of 15 feet (4.5 m), a diameter of 5 feet (1.5 m) and a payload weight of around 1,154 pounds (523 kg). It consisted of the Optics Module (OM), the Orbital Control Vehicle (OCV) built by General Electric and the Satellite Recovery Vehicle (SRV), also built by GE. The weight of the total vehicle above the Atlas-Agena D was in the order of 4,410 pounds (2,000 kg), the maximum potential lift capacity of this launch vehicle.

The OM included the 48-inch (1.21 m) diameter steerable flat mirror, the concave stationary primary mirror, an index camera of the type used on the KH-4 satellites and a stellar camera with reseau marks superimposed on the image plane. The stellar index camera was not introduced until the seventh flight. Ground tests with the optics demonstrated good performance of the entire optical system, despite inevitable delays caused by minor technical problems.

On October 30, 1962, Colonel William G. King took over management of GAMBIT and, together with Greer, incorporated an innovation to the OCV borrowed from the LANYARD program using a system which would augment the design configuration whereby the optical elements were married directly to the Agena stage, a coupling known as Hitchup. This augmentation introduced the "roll joint" concept specifically designed for LANYARD.

The roll joint was a separate interface placed between the Agena D and the optical section that could take over attitude control and fine-pointing orientation, achieving higher angular precision than was believed possible with the

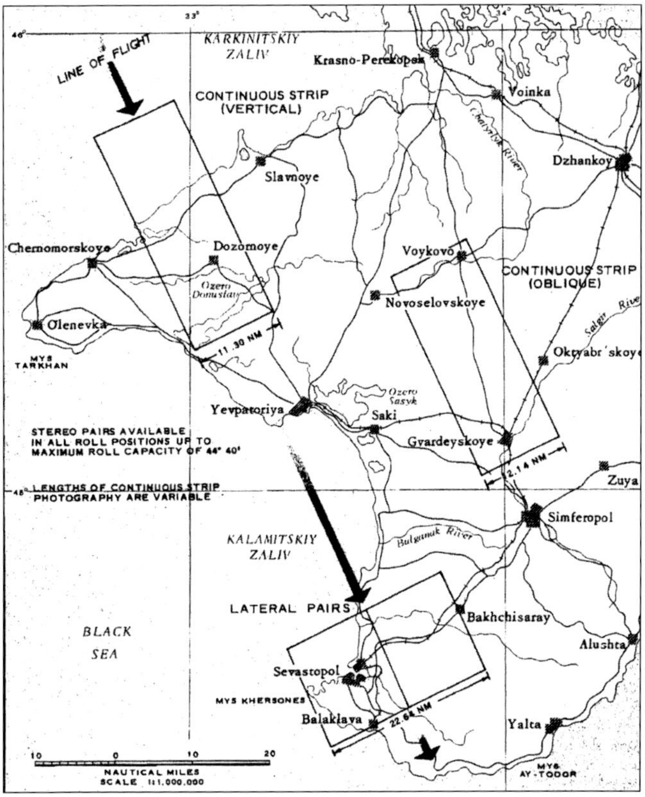

ABOVE Examples of continuous strip and lateral-pair frame coverage at a nominal altitude of 109 miles (175 km). *(NRO)*

standard Agena D. It allowed the Agena to remain stable, leaving the forward section to roll from side to side for direct imaging, obviating the need for the entire system to change attitude. This would be vital for any photography beyond pure nadir imaging. But the roll joint technology and the LANYARD program was not known to the GAMBIT people and to introduce it to the KH-7 required further subterfuge, citing it as originating from a vacant technology development program.

An additional technology transfer was introduced from CORONA, a "lifeboat" design configuration that provided independent circuitry and a stabilization gas supply if the primary re-entry system should fail, as it had done with some CORONA satellites. These separate elements would be introduced at various stages during the KH-7 program as the GAMBIT system evolved through trial and error.

The first launch of a GAMBIT satellite was in preparation on May 11, 1963, when a technical issue with the Atlas launch vehicle caused

RIGHT A KH-8 GAMBIT satellite took this picture of the research and development facility at Kaspiysk on the Caspian Sea on August 11, 1984. *(NRO)*

a loss of pressure in the propellant tanks. Because the Atlas tanks had to be pressurized to remain structurally stable the entire vehicle collapsed, spilling its RP-1 fuel and liquid oxygen over the pad from its ruptured tanks. The entire system was a write-off, but the payload was not the one scheduled for flight, although the Agena stage was.

BELOW This explosives and ammunition loading facility (Plant Raketa 392) at Kemerovo was viewed by a KH-8 on August 3, 1966. The radius of turn on road corners indicates the maximum size of lorries and freight vehicles using the facility. *(NRO)*

Operating under the strictest levels of security – even the Eastman Kodak technicians had to make a discreet approach to the pad for final adjustments, as it was not declared to be an "optical" launch – KH-7 4001 lifted off from Vandenberg Air Force Base at 13:44 hours local time on July 12, 1963, almost two years after its requirement had been urged upon the NRO by a nervous Robert McNamara. On the fifth orbit 4001 switched on and took 120 one-second light-strip exposures, followed on the eighth and ninth orbits by two stereo pairs and five two-second strips. Truncated only by premature exhaustion of attitude control gas, the lifeboat mechanism rescued the SRV from obscurity and the film was returned to Earth.

Analysis of the film showed only 198 feet (60 m) had been exposed, with an average resolution of 10 feet (3 m), although one frame had achieved 3.5 feet (1.1 m) – the very best resolution from any spy satellite thus far. The second flight also went well after launch on September 6, completed 34 orbits of the Earth and returned 1,930 feet (588 m) of film. With the resolution of the KH-7, it was possible to determine whether aircraft had a reciprocating or a turboprop engine and to identify the make and type of small vehicles. Even large maintenance rigs could be identified, giving a clue to the function of the equipment it was designed for. For the first time in three years, satellite intelligence was returning pictures previously achievable only with the U-2 spy-plane, which was now prohibited from entering Soviet airspace.

The third flight on October 25 was better still, and "calibrated" by photographs of the football field in Great Falls, Montana. The resolution was so good it showed individual players, from a place kicker to others moved into position before the teams lined up. These demonstrated an extraordinary technology and showed that it worked very well but they were not the intelligence photographs needed, and not until the sixth launch with 4006 on March 11, 1964, did the system demonstrate a level of maturity. But from then on it was downhill.

During 1964, ten GAMBIT satellites were launched, but on only half of those flights were any meaningful photographs obtained and the resolution appeared to be slowly degrading back to 7 feet (2.1 m). During this period the KH-4A J-1 was the sole CORONA type flying and there was a long way to go yet before the HEXAGON would be ready to launch – in reality seven years.

As the first few of the nine KH-7 launches sent up in 1965 began to show some improvements, significant management changes were made to GAMBIT. Out went Greer and in came Brigadier General John L. Martin, moved from chief of the NRO staff to lead the program. Uncertain about continuing, Martin decided to let 4020 launch on July 12, but the Atlas failed and the stack plunged into the Atlantic Ocean. When 4021 failed after launch on August 3 due to a power converter malfunction in the OCV, it was the third consecutive GAMBIT to suffer a catastrophe.

While the Soviets were building their forces in a way that demanded high-resolution monitoring, only the less capable KH-4A series was holding the line, albeit with good results. Martin sought a solution by attacking apparently systemic problems with the OCV and went to GE in Philadelphia to sort it out. Commandeering a secure room, a large table and ten assembled electronic boxes he proceeded to open them in turn with a screwdriver and counted the substantial bits of debris and foreign objects that fell out.

Martin also discovered that it was routine for only partly assembled and tested equipment to be delivered to Vandenberg for launch, the finished work being done close to the launch site. He also found a disincentive for quality work by contractual reward (and a bonus) given for work delivered on time and under budget; there were no rewards for successful operation in space. Martin rewrote the contract to place incentive on performance, on pain of GE losing its highly valued status. Once a contractor gets a reputation for shoddy work their teaming potential for really, seriously big contracts has evaporated.

GAMBIT 4023 launched on November 8 with all the bells and whistles of stricter test regimes and higher quality control, but while it remained in orbit for 18 revolutions, it returned hardly any photographs. But the attention paid off and the next ten launches – beginning with 4024 launched on January 19, 1966 – were successful, with the best resolution at 24 inches (61 cm). The last of the standard GAMBIT flights got off the pad on June 4, 1967, when 4038 returned excellent results. By then it had been replaced by an improved variant, built not by Lockheed but by General Electric using a Lockheed Agena D as the platform.

Known as GAMBIT-3 (when the original design was renamed GAMBIT-1), this greatly enhanced derivative started life in late 1962 when it was referred to as Advanced GAMBIT or simply G³. With the retirement of GAMBIT-1, the G³ became simply GAMBIT, although it was a very different vehicle. Because of that it was to receive the designation KH-8 and would evolve through three generations. The new version was based around a camera system using a

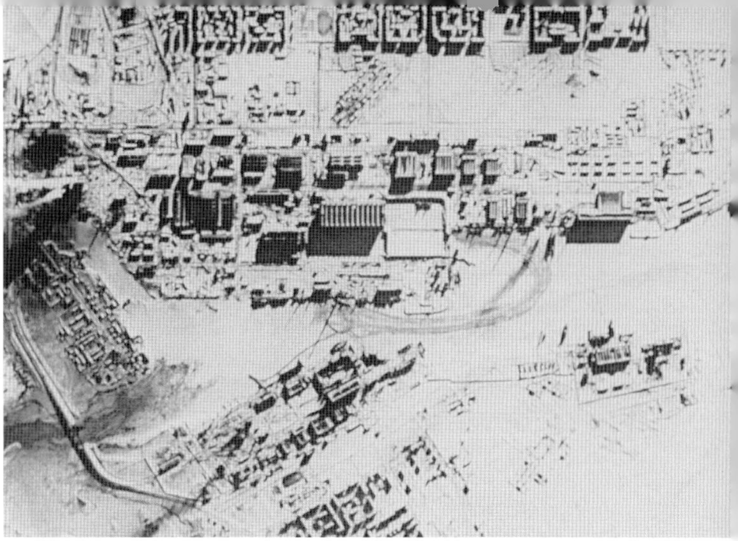

ABOVE A GAMBIT image of Sverdlovsk, a major military complex where biological and chemical weapons were developed during the Soviet era. *(NRO)*

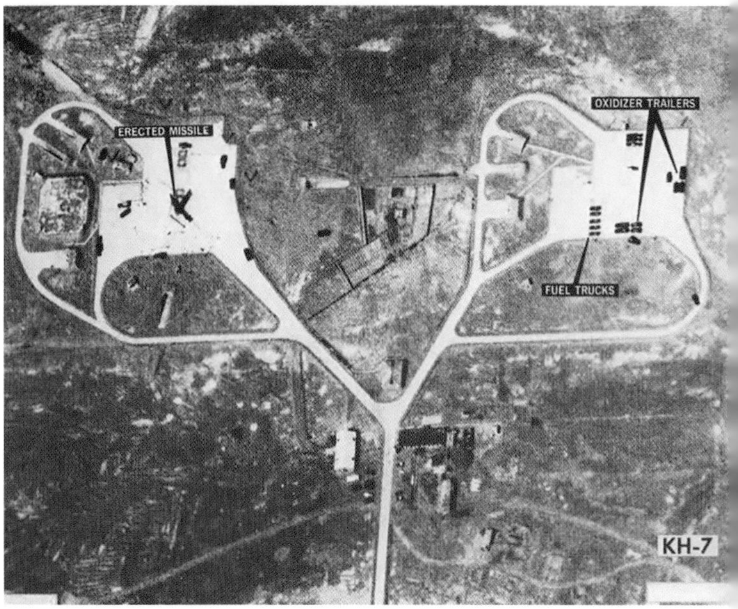

BELOW This missile launch and control center at Shuancheng was photographed by a KH-7 on May 29, 1967. *(NRO)*

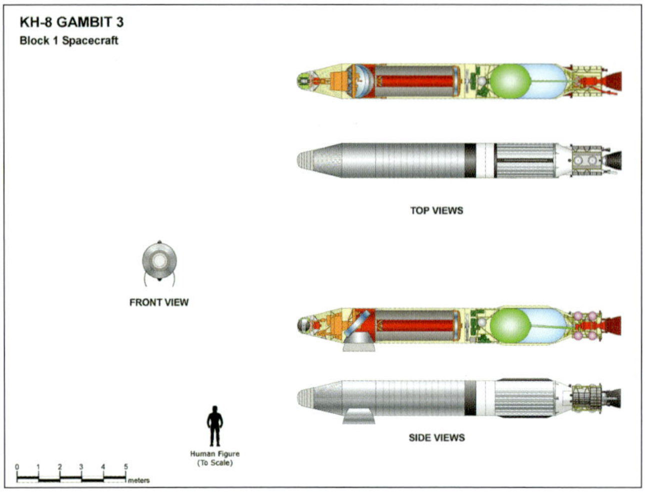

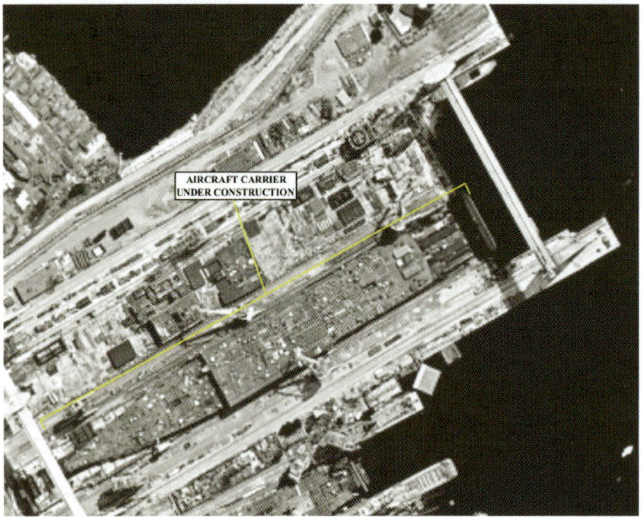

LEFT The Block 1 KH-8 GAMBIT-3 satellite was a developed version of the KH-7 incorporating a roll joint like its predecessor, and with a long focal-length lens. *(Giuseppe de Chiara)*

CENTRE The photographic payload section of the KH-8 was considerably modified from the KH-7, as seen here during assembly at Lockheed. *(NRO)*

long focal length lens, and Eastman Kodak was working on a system known as VALLEY. It was the combination of this research and the initial tranche of flights with the GAMBIT-1 system that got the interest of the NRO.

In December 1963 Eastman Kodak technicians Charles P. Spoelhof and James H. Mahar briefed NRO officials on an advanced system, and this was quickly approved. The basic technology was to replace the OCV with two modules, one carrying the camera system and the SRV and the other containing propulsion, propellant tanks and subsystems to control on-orbit operations. The roll joint device from GAMBIT-1 was incorporated as standard, located between the two modules.

Kodak also came up with an idea for a special Invar, a nickel alloy, for manufacturing the optical barrel and some associated assemblies, as well as a new thin-base high-resolution film with an exposure index of 6.0 providing approximately three times the sensitivity of the film used in GAMBIT-1. Hedging against delays due to unforeseen technical issues, the NRO approved a parallel development of alternative technologies and there was much discussion about the type of launch vehicle to use.

Having migrated from Thor and TAT launches for CORONA, to Atlas-Agena D for GAMBIT-1, was it now time to move up a notch and go for a more powerful Titan? The argument was persuasive – the enhanced lifting capacity of the Titan IIIB, while only marginal over the Atlas-Agena D, would allow

LEFT This photograph shows the aircraft carrier *Kiev* under construction at the Mykolayiv facility on July 4, 1984. *(NRO)*

some modest growth potential as the program developed. In July 1964 Greer requested compatibility studies on that marriage, effectively increasing the lift potential to 7,500 pounds (3,400 kg). Approval was granted in October 1964.

Eastman Kodak ran into several problems during their efforts to produce the mirrors, the measurement and polishing being particularly troublesome. Early mirrors required 3,000 hours of grinding, almost four times the estimate. The company was stretched with the manpower it had, projects including the two GAMBIT programs, the NASA Lunar Orbiter and the program soon to be known as HEXAGON, in addition to a special classified project. A change to a fused silica material for the aspheric mirror substrate eased the problem.

The first GAMBIT-3 (KH-8-1) lifted off on a Titan IIIB on July 29, 1963, only four weeks late on a date set three years before. It worked as planned but with somewhat disappointing results, short of the design goal but an improvement on the GAMBIT-1. Now it was merely a matter of holding on to existing GAMBIT-1 flights until the -3 proved it could replace them. Now, the proliferation of high-resolution photography overwhelmed the resources of the interpreters and for a time it produced a log-jam of backlogged photographs waiting for analysis and interpretation.

On June 30, 1967, the decision was made to cancel five planned GAMBIT-1 flights and go over to the GAMBIT-3 system, whose performance was still less than that expected. But Kodak were coming along with the new substitute materials for the mirrors and the new high-speed emulsion on the ultra-thin film was introduced on the 14th GAMBIT-3 flight, launched on June 5, 1968. Over the next 13 flights it outdid all expectations. But there was a Block II version already on the stocks.

Limited by the single-bucket design of the basic KH-8, McNamara had been briefed about a possible two-bucket derivative in January 1965, the logic of which prevailed so that by late the following year work was already under way for the new, heavier, GAMBIT, which would utilize the Titan 23B and its bigger lift capacity.

The Titan 23B adopted the extended length first and second stages of the new Titan IIIC (designed to have two strap-on boosters for the core stage) and replaced the Transtage upper stage, specifically developed for Titan, carried on the IIIA with the Agena D for the KH-8 Block II. There would be no strap-on boosters for the 23B but the longer first and

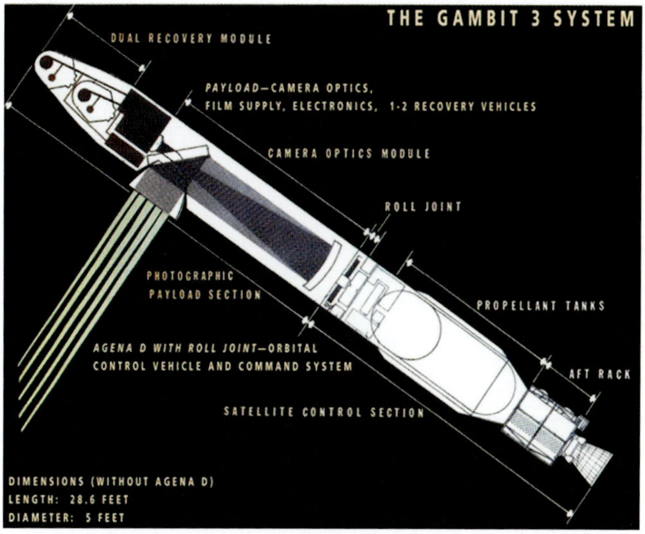

ABOVE A significant feature of the GAMBIT series of KH-7/KH-8 satellites was its roll joint, which allowed the section forward of the Agena to roll back and forth for optimum viewing angles while the main body of the Agena D remained in a fixed attitude, much like a rotating hand pivots at the wrist. *(NRO)*

BELOW The Block 2 version of the KH-8, second in a series of generation updates, incorporating two recovery vehicles. *(Giuseppe de Chiara)*

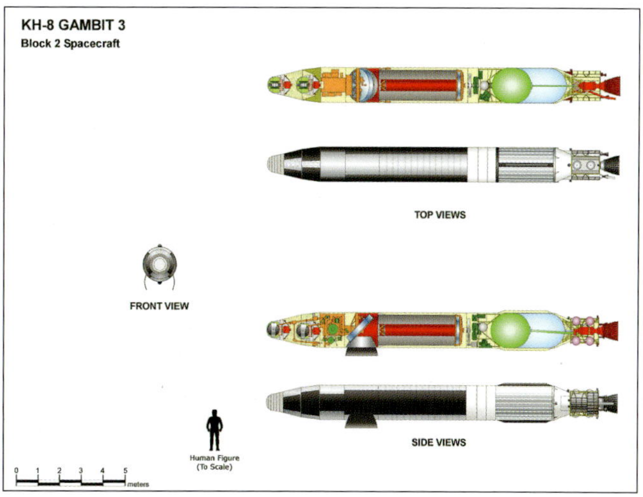

RIGHT This GAMBIT photograph shows the Soviet N-1 launch vehicle on its launch pad at Baikonur, positive proof that the Russians were in a race to the Moon. *(NRO)*

BELOW On display at the USAF Museum in Dayton, Ohio, a GAMBIT spy satellite displays its overall size and configuration. *(USAF Museum)*

second stages carried more propellant, burned longer and lifted more weight. The first launch (with KH-8-23) occurred on August 23, 1969, and it was a success.

The Block II version of the KH-8 carried a camera with a focal length of 175.6 inches (4.46 m), a single-strip system with the image from the ground reflected by a steerable flat mirror to a concave primary mirror with a diameter of 48 inches (1.21 m). The light path passed through an opening in the flat mirror to a Ross corrector, designed by a London-based firm. Three other cameras were contained within the Astro-Position Terrain Camera (APTC) package, incorporating a terrain frame camera with a focal length of 2.95 inches (75 mm) and two stellar cameras with a focal length of 3.5 inches (90 mm).

The use of stellar index cameras and terrain cameras grew out of the KH-5 ARGON program and the later KH-4 systems and demonstrated the maturing technology, plus the continuing need for mapping images and stellar reference alignments for accuracy on the photographs. The stellar cameras were positioned to face opposing directions for photographing star fields and the terrain frame camera took photographs of the ground in the direction of the vehicle's roll position to provide attitude determination.

Successive improvements during the KH-8 program provided improved film, moving from the 3404 type which had a resolving power of 50–100 lines/mm on to the type 1414, a high-definition film, and SO-217, a fine-grain high-definition type. Some satellites carried film incorporating silver-halide crystals with an exceptionally high standard of uniformity and size. The size of the crystals decreased from 1,550Å with the SO-315 film to 1,200Å in SO-312 film, and to 900Å in SO-409.

During GAMBIT-3 operations it became possible to fly an orbit with a periapsis as low as 86 miles (138 km) at which height from the ground the main camera photographed a swathe 3.9 miles (6.3 km) wide on a 8.811-inch- (22.38 cm) wide portion of moving film through the slit aperture. With the 3404 type

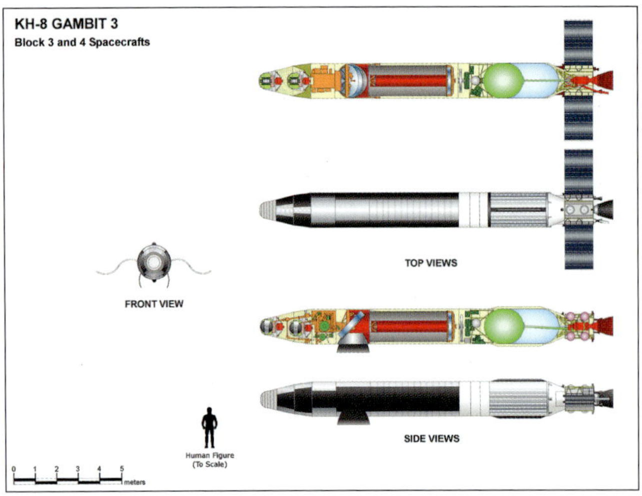

LEFT The Block 3 and 4 GAMBIT-3 series with added solar arrays. *(Giuseppe de Chiara)*

RIGHT A KH-7 single-bucket spy satellite splendidly preserved at the USAF Museum reveals the details of its attachment and of its optical section adjacent to the roll joint. The Agena D is not displayed. *(USAF Museum)*

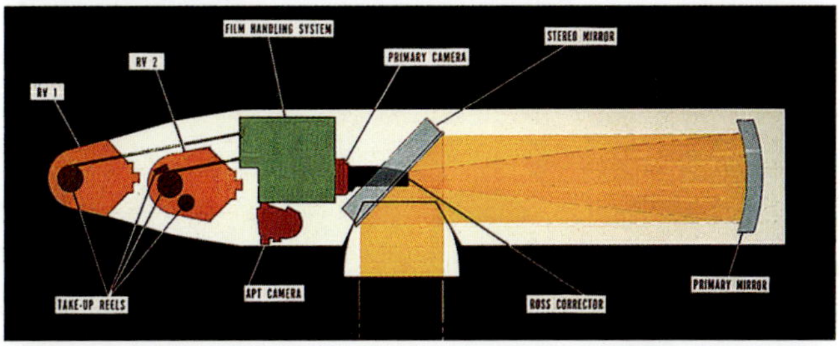

CENTER The optical path for the GAMBIT-3 system and the film transport path to the two recovery capsules. *(NRO)*

film, it would have been possible to discriminate two objects only 1–2 feet (0.28–0.56 m) apart. But utilizing Kodak's 3409 film with a performance of 320–630 lines pairs/mm it would have been possible to resolve objects only 2–4 inches (5–10 cm) across. This is the theoretical limit of an Earth-observing system from minimum orbit.

After 14 KH-8 Block II flights, on December 21, 1972, the Block III was introduced, utilizing a more powerful launch vehicle which had been introduced with the 32nd GAMBIT-3, launched August 12, 1971 – the Titan 24B. This launcher had the greatly extended Titan first stage that had been developed for the Titan IIIM, a rocket intended to launch the Manned Orbiting Laboratory and its DORIAN optical system, cancelled in June 1969. There were 23 flights with the Titan 24B, the last on April 17, 1984, closing the GAMBIT program after seven Block IV launches. In all there had been 54 GAMBIT-3s over a period of almost 20 years, during which the development of the spy satellite had been taken to its ultimate technical performance.

But the GAMBIT had not operated alone, for while it conducted high-resolution images of very specific targets, the intelligence community was working in parallel with a second, wide-area surveillance satellite, much bigger and with much greater orbital life: HEXAGON, or KH-9.

CENTER The aft section of the Agena upper stage with primary propulsion system. *(USAF Museum)*

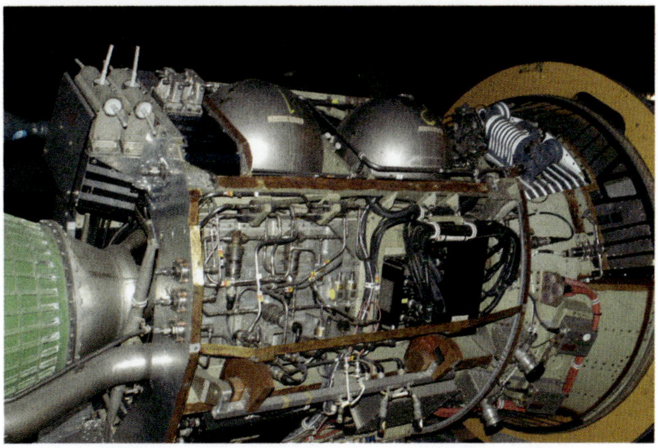

RIGHT A detailed view of the Agena engine shows the pressurant tanks and the support structures. *(USAF Museum)*

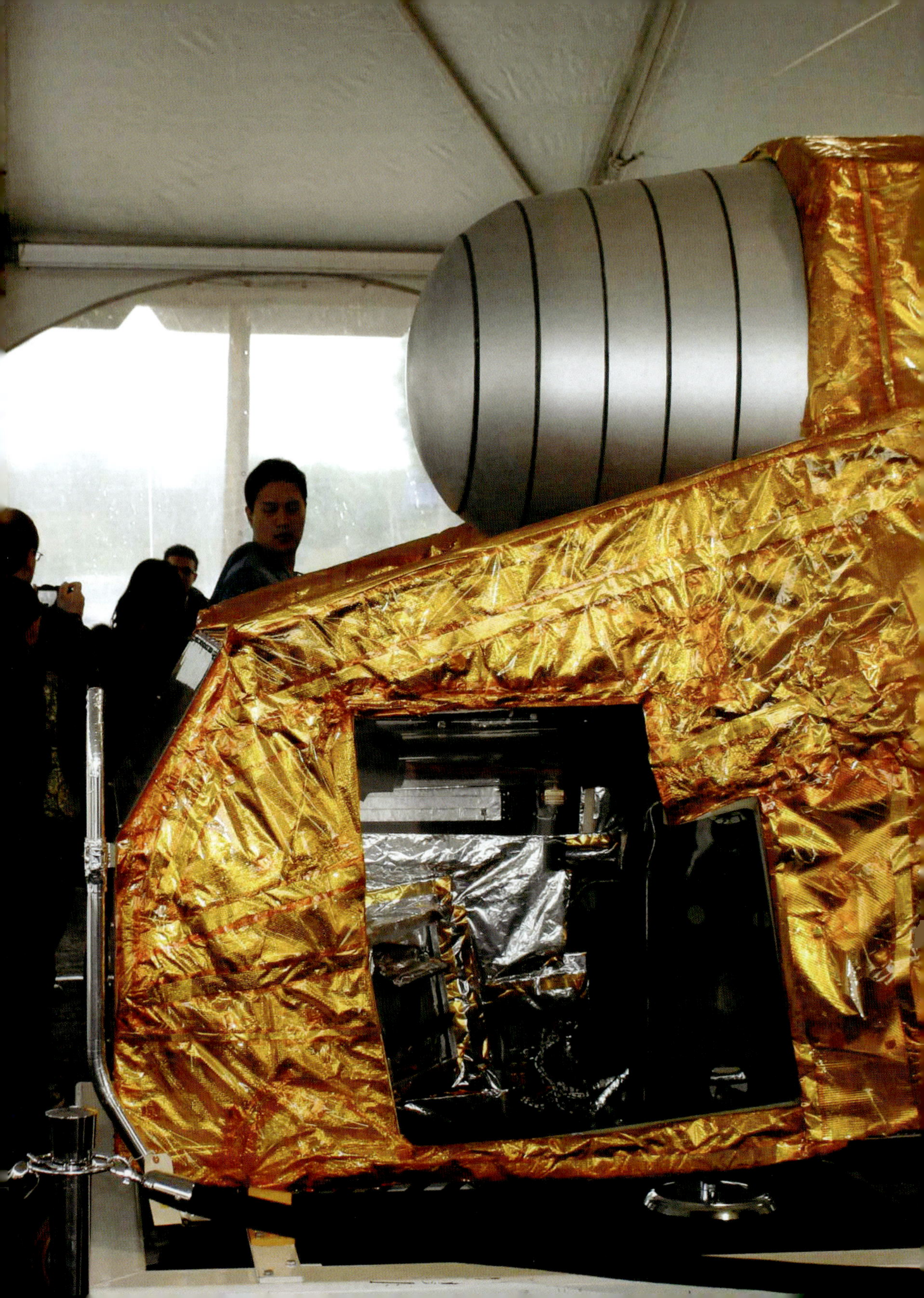

Chapter Seven

Hexagon (KH-9)

The origin of the last of America's bucket-carrying photo-reconnaissance satellites emerged from the Fulcrum program started at Itek in January 1964. This program is mentioned in Chapter 4 along with the S-2 where the CORONA program was considered as an interim to more advanced successors, none of which emerged as intended while CORONA missions gained the confidence of the intelligence community.

OPPOSITE The Mapping Camera attached to the front of the forward section, on view at the National Air and Space Museum. *(Dwayne Day)*

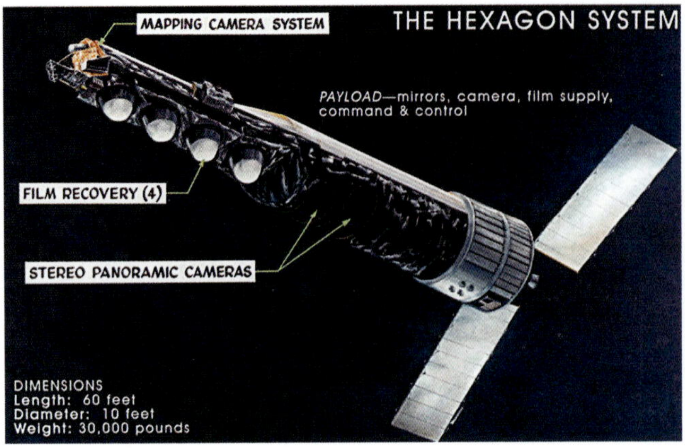

ABOVE Prior to HEXAGON, spy satellites had conducted different roles with different programs and a variety of different optical systems. The KH-9 would combine mapping, area surveillance and high-resolution stereo imaging in one vehicle, with five separate film buckets. *(NRO)*

On November 18, 1963, the West Coast Special Projects Directorate of the NRO contracted with Itek for feasibility studies on a new broad-area search system, which led to the S-2, while the CIA Itek study started Fulcrum. Itek proposed Titan II for Fulcrum built on a pair of rotating 60-inch (152 cm) focal-length cameras transporting a 7-inch (17.8 cm) film in an arrangement similar to KH-4B (J-3), producing images across a ground swathe 360 miles (580 km) wide with a resolution of 2–4 feet (0.6–1.2 m). Carrying 65,000 feet (19,812 m) of film, Fulcrum would be able to photograph 10 million square miles (25.9 million km^2).

Itek's S-2 design was simpler than Fulcrum; with both pointing and panoramic capability it would have a resolution of 3–4 feet (0.91–1.2 m) for the former and 5–8 feet (1.5–2.4 m) for the latter. It would fly on an Atlas-Agena with an enlarged GAMBIT-type system. Both projects were funded and developed through a myriad of claims and counter-claims for the virtues and vicissitudes of each system. In July 1964 a new directive was issued for a definitive requirement for a search system with the area coverage of CORONA and the resolution of GAMBIT.

In February 1965 Itek abruptly pulled out of Fulcrum, their withdrawal believed to have been when the NRO promised them the contract for the S-2 if they withdrew from the CIA-sponsored Fulcrum. But it was Perkin-Elmer that got the contract to continue with Fulcrum and Eastman Kodak got the S-2! The feud between the CIA and the NRO continued and grew increasingly bitter.

In August 1965 a deal was worked out whereby the CIA would be responsible for developing sensors and all related technology for what was now known as HEXAGON, while the NRO would develop the platforms and the vehicle to contain the payload functions, each organ setting up project offices on April 30, 1966. It was during 1968 that significant input derived from requirements for verification of protocols under a series of negotiations then getting under way would culminate in the Strategic Arms Limitation Talks (SALT).

Agreements on the limitation of expansion in the strategic nuclear weapon arsenals and their

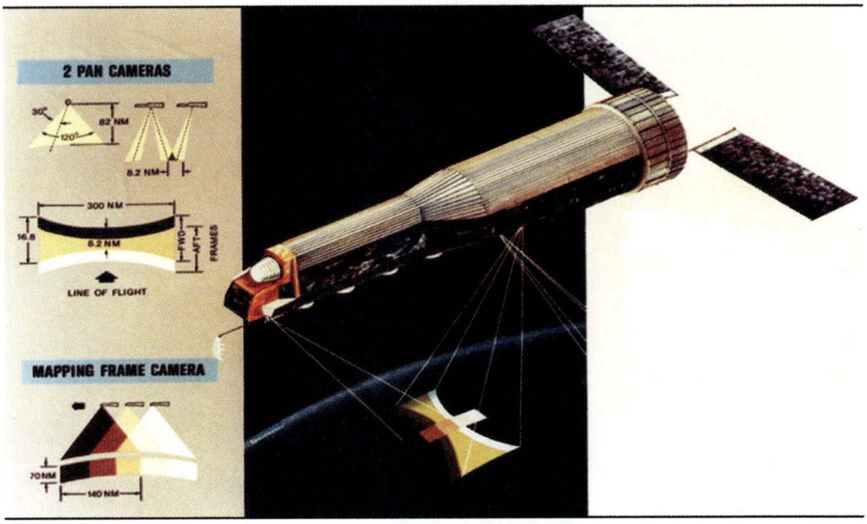

RIGHT The essential function of the KH-9 was to provide two stereo cameras and a terrain-mapping system. *(NRO)*

delivery systems were becoming a concern. The USSR had made major gains in both the number of strategic missiles in their arsenals and in the delivery systems. Without spy satellites none of these agreements would have been possible and now the KH-9 was the first of its kind to be developed in the knowledge that it would have to monitor treaties that would have been impossible without the work of its predecessors such as CORONA and GAMBIT.

Progressive development of launch vehicle capabilities also opened the opportunity for bigger and longer-lived reconnaissance and surveillance satellites that could police those agreements. Successive evolutions of the Titan rocket into an increasingly powerful launch vehicle made possible the use of a variant of the Titan IIIC with two very powerful strap-on boosters, specifically configured for the launch of the HEXAGON spy satellite.

Titan IIIC had been developed on the orders of the Director of Defense Research and Engineering in May 1961 for a wide range of heavyweight military payloads. It had a further extension to the length of the core stage (as described above for Titan 24B) for an extended burn duration. At launch only the two strap-on boosters would fire, producing a lift-off thrust of 10,408 kN (2.34 million lb), more than five times the thrust of the Titan II core stage. For the first time in a Titan launch sequence, the core stage would ignite at altitude after the two solids burned out, the second stage taking over from the first as it too fell away.

The lift capacity of the Titan IIID was 29,000 pounds (13,150 kg) to a low-altitude polar orbit and the KH-9 would be the first photo-reconnaissance satellite not to adopt the Agena stage. Instead, the Satellite Vehicle (SV) itself would be injected into orbit by the second stage of the Titan rocket. A flight control system would stabilize the SV for the duration of its mission from attitude data, attitude-rate change information, commands issued by the flight control computer and by a radio-guidance system communicating through ground stations.

The mission function of HEXAGON was to provide global search and surveillance missions with stereo, panoramic photographic coverage utilizing two cameras and to provide the necessary equipment to perform mapping

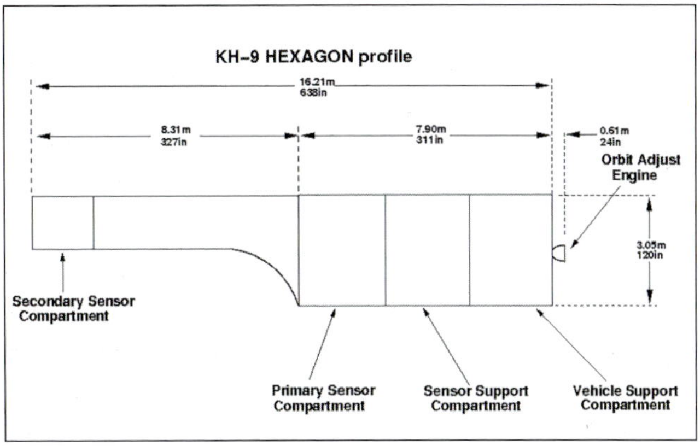

ABOVE **No longer utilizing the Agena stage, HEXAGON would employ a completely different structural arrangement, with its own optical section and control module.** *(Lockheed)*

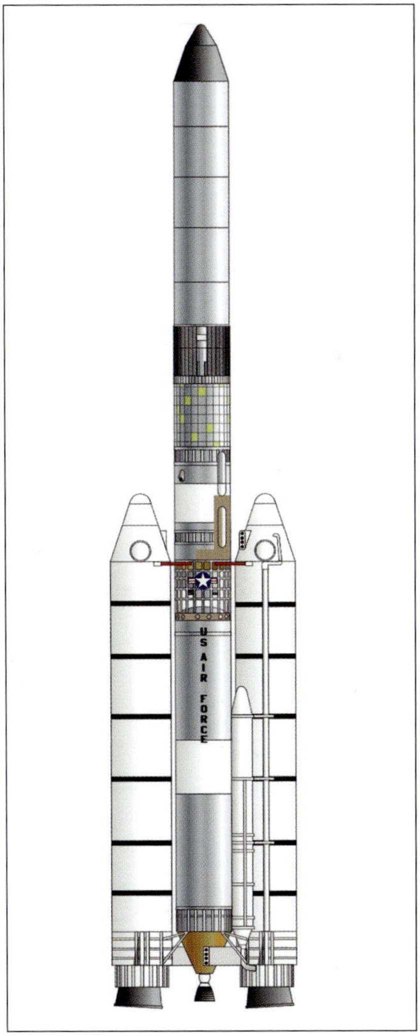

LEFT **The Titan III derivative used for KH-9 would double the payload lifting capacity compared to the biggest CORONA satellite and provide flexible orbital insertion parameters.** *(Giuseppe de Chiara)*

ABOVE **A view of the KH-9 tilted during transfer at the Lockheed manufacturing facility, giving scale to the enormous satellite.** *(Lockheed)*

BELOW **The HEXAGON with deployable solar arrays and a four-bucket primary film recovery system.** *(Giuseppe de Chiara)*

and geodesic surveys. This latter role would be conducted on missions 1205 to 1216. Film from the primary search and surveillance missions would be returned to Earth in four large re-entry vehicles (RVs) based on the GE Mk 8 warhead. Film from the Mapping Camera (MC) would be returned from a Mk 5 re-entry vehicle located on the nose of the SV.

At launch the complete satellite vehicle had a length of 58.7 feet (17.9 m) and a diameter of 10 feet (3 m) with a total mass of 27,000 pounds (12,250 kg) of which 2,800 pounds (1,270 kg) was a large payload shroud encapsulating almost the entire length of the SV, jettisoned during ascent when the ascending stack had exited the atmosphere and aerodynamic loads were sufficiently low.

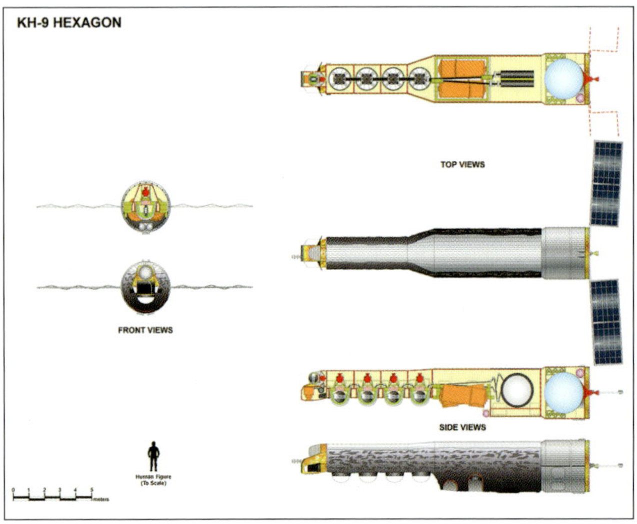

The assembly consisted of aft, mid and forward sections and was of semi-monocoque construction. Te booster adapter contained the separation joint connection to the SV attached to the forward section of the second stage of the Titan. It carried a mild detonating fuse to sever a circumferential beryllium strip after reaching orbit.

The aft section was 6.5 feet (2 m) long and 10 feet (3 m) in diameter. It consisted of an equipment module, the separation assembly and the Orbit Adjust Module (OAM) and the Reaction Control Module (RCM). This took the place of the attitude control and propulsion systems previously part of the Agena D stage on earlier satellites. It comprised a corrugated, reinforced aluminum skin bolted to an aluminum internal frame that also carried the propulsion units and the solar arrays. The aft section was the interface between the SV and connected it to the ground supply of electrical power, battery coolant, fluids and gases prior to launch. The adapter assembly had a height of about 1.5 feet (0.45 m) and 70 square inches (452 cm^2) of venting to release atmospheric pressure.

The OAM/RCM section housed the propellant system for the hydrazine attitude control thrusters as well as the independent lifeboat system – a carryover from KH-7/KH-8 satellites – which provided attitude control and position fixing in the event of a failure in the primary system. The solar array modules were stowed within this section during encapsulation and did not extend beyond the physical diameter of the stacked vehicle. The equipment section had 12 removable corrugation-reinforced aluminum skin panels bolted to the internal aluminum tubular structure that supported honeycomb panels. They were set in a radial configuration around the exterior of the satellite. Each panel covered a single circumferential bay stressed to carry a maximum 500 pounds (227 kg) of equipment in which guidance, command control, and power command equipment was located. Each could be installed or removed at any time.

Crucial for the effective application of the new camera systems, the Attitude Control System (ACS) was responsible for providing

RIGHT The arrangement of the Mapping Camera and the fifth satellite recovery vehicle provided a self-contained "payload" attached to the forward section of HEXAGON and gave mappers a significant increase in capability. *(NRO)*

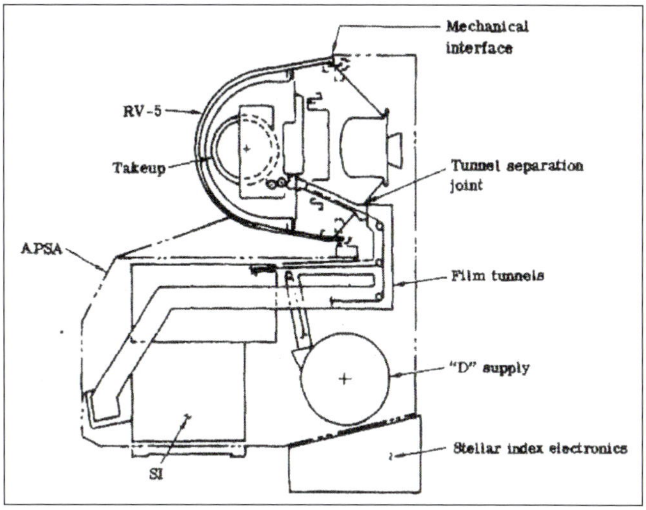

Earth-orientated attitude references and rate sensing. Information from the ACS would control Reaction Control System (RCS) thruster firings to control and maintain required attitude positions. Consisting of a three-axis, rate gyro-integrator system it processed updates in pitch and roll with a horizon sensor, and in yaw by gyrocompassing.

Errors produced by either system were combined in the flight control electronics and modulated by pseudo-rate circuits in each axis, thus generating further firings if necessary with an adjusted impulse bit control to match the demanding requirements of accuracy and timely adjustment. Each element within the system was redundant and cross-reference was provided between the primary and back-up systems so that specific sub-elements within each subsystem could be selected and matched with non-failed sub-elements in another system – a crude form of self-repair.

The ability for electronics and avionics systems to repair themselves through fail-safe/fail-operational design was pursued by engineers throughout the late 1960s and pervaded thoughts of sending spacecraft to the distant parts of the solar system. It formed part of early planning for NASA's Grand Tour of the outer planets, which resulted in the two Voyager missions to Jupiter, Saturn, Uranus and Neptune. For that program it proved too elusive but in the black world of military satellites it was the "Holy Grail" sought by computer scientists and systems design engineers.

Control requirements during active use of the search and surveillance cameras on HEXAGON demanded an attitude accuracy of 0.7° in pitch and roll and 0.64° in yaw, with a rate accuracy of 0.014°/second in pitch and yaw and 0.021°/second in roll. Because the attitude excursions were crucial to satisfactory operation of the primary cameras, the settling time was 0.2 seconds for stereo imaging and 6 seconds for mono photography. In non-horizontal mission mode, attitude accuracy was required to be 1° in roll and yaw and 3° in pitch, with rates accuracy on 0.15°/second in all three axes.

The OAS and RCS systems also had responsibility for maintaining the orbit, nulling dispersions at separation from the Titan second stage, adjusting for perigee and drag-reduction (where the tenuous outer atmosphere was distorting the orbit) and for de-orbiting the SV at the end of its mission. The extreme secrecy of the satellite and its equipment required that it be de-orbited over an area where the remains from fiery re-entry could be sent to the bottom of a very deep ocean.

The propulsion system used catalytic

BELOW Another view of the Mapping Camera and its film recovery vehicle, appropriate areas wrapped in gold foil for thermal control. *(Dwayne Day)*

RIGHT The first manufactured Orbit Adjustment Module/ Reaction Control Module at Lockheed, an integrated system taking over responsibility for orbital changes and attitude control previously the function of the Agena stage. *(Lockheed)*

FAR RIGHT The dedicated Reaction Control Module with propellant tank inside its structural frame forming the aft section of the KH-9. *(NRO)*

decomposition of a hydrazine monopropellant pressure-fed from a propellant tank, the thrust of the OAS engine declining from 1.112 kN (250 lb) to 0.445 kN (100 lb), with RCS thrusters declining from 26.7 N to 8.9 N (2 lb). The ACS controlled firing of the eight RCS thrusters while a quad-redundant valve controlled the flow to the OAS engine, which was mounted facing aft at the centre of the aft section.

The OAS propellant tank would vary with the mission but typically could be a spherical chamber with a diameter of 62 inches (157 cm) loaded with 4,000 pounds (1,815 kg) of propellant. Isolated by pyrotechnic valves, high-pressure nitrogen gas was carried in two separate tanks, initially 34 pounds (15.4 kg), increasing to 68 pounds (31 kg) from the 11th KH-9. Velocity increments of 2–400 feet/second (0.6–122 m/sec) could be achieved.

BELOW Another view of the aft section, on the end of which an adapter will be fitted for the Titan launch vehicle. *(NRO)*

The four 22-inch- (56 cm) diameter RCS hydrazine propellant tanks carried 450–550 pounds (204–249 kg) of propellant, depending on the mission. The KH-9 carried a completely separate set of eight paired thrusters for redundancy, with either ring being fed from the four tanks, each pair of thrusters commanded by primary or redundant valve drivers controlled by the ACS electronics. Propellant management was possible with a cross-feed between the OAS and the RCS tanks.

Primary means of maintaining power on the KH-9 comprised two folding solar array wings, each extending 17 feet (5.2 m), comprising 22 panels with an area of 177 square feet (16.44 m^2) of photo-voltaic cells, one each side of the aft section, and only deployed on orbit. Energy storage for night-side power came from rechargeable nickel-cadmium batteries with unregulated power distribution at 24–33 V dc. There were four parallel segments with an array, charger and battery in each to minimize power collapse from a single failure. Fusing was applied to critical circuits. The system could provide 11 kW hours/day of power over a beta (solar) angle of -8° to +60° by pivoting the solar array about the roll axis. This level of power provision permitted up to 52 minutes for each day of search and surveillance or mapping activity.

The telemetry and tracking provisions were

considerably more advanced than for the Agena B missions and provided a flow of real-time data at 128 kbps for engineering and analysis and 64 kbps for orbit operations. Tape recorders provided bulk temperature data at periodic intervals while 1,500 separate data points were instrumented, some reporting at 500 samples/second.

For controlling functions and programming operations so that the KH-9 could operate autonomously when out of radio contact with the ground, the Extended Command System supported 64 real-time and 626 stored commands to be addressed with a memory capacity of 1,152 commands, with up to 96 secure command activities possible. This increased to 192 secure commands from KH-9-15 to the end of the 20-flight program. These forward commands allowed the vehicle to store both primary and secondary missions and to control critical functions on board. Another manifestation of semi-autonomy.

A Minimal Command System was installed on each KH-9 from the outset, providing 28 real-time and 66 stored program commands with a memory capacity of 56 commands of which 10 were secure. The MCS also provided lifeboat functions for the recovery of the SRV should the main systems fail, controlling and sequencing all the required actions necessary to orientate the main bus, command retro-fire and sequence the bucket for descent.

The Lifeboat II (as it was called for the KH-9) could control the separation and re-entry of two SRVs with emergency operating commands transmitted at 375 MHz. Attitude control for the SRV would be provided by Earth-field magnetometers, rate gyros and a cold gas thruster system using Freon-14. Power for this system came from a type-40 battery and 25% of the solar arrays on the main power supply. Switching circuits moved critical functions from the main supply to the lifeboat bus itself for operation.

The mid-section of the KH-9 had a length of 15.4 feet (5.9 m) and contained the stereo

ABOVE The forward section of the KH-9 cantilevered from the optical bay provided the support structure for the film transport mechanism, the Mapping Camera on the front and the four primary film recovery capsules. *(Dwayne Day)*

BELOW The mid area of the forward section to which the separate return vehicles were attached, arranged so that failure of any one bucket system would not compromise the others. *(Dwayne Day)*

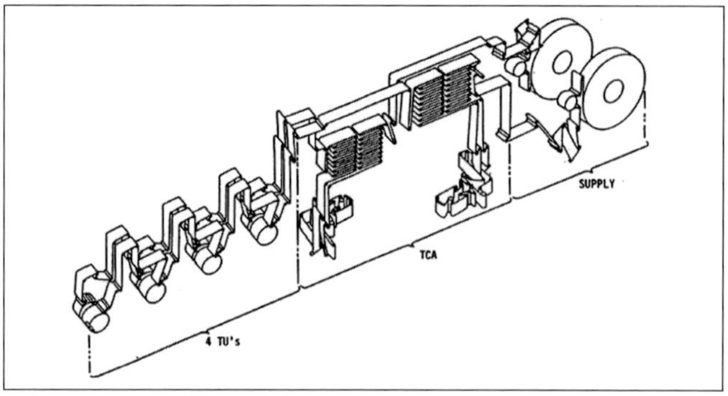

LEFT The film transport mechanism for the two parallel delivery spools was necessarily more complex than the two-bucket satellite configuration of the CORONA and GAMBIT designs, with added difficulties in maintaining film tension and temperatures. *(NRO)*

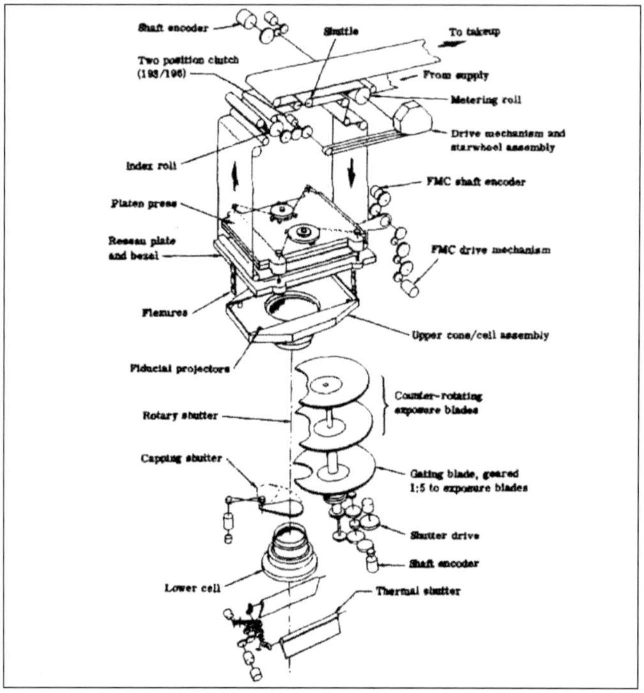

LEFT The terrain camera pointed down on orbit and targeted an area of 9 inches x 18 inches (23 cm x 46 cm). This mechanical layout shows the transport and platen press located above the image plane that advanced the 9.5 inches (24 cm) film into the exposure station and clamped the film to the flat rear surface of the lens (reseau plate) during exposure. *(NRO)*

BELOW LEFT The forward motion compensation (FMC) device was mounted to the base plate and drove the bezel in the direction of flight at the selected rate to prevent blurring of the exposed image. *(NRO)*

BELOW The terrain film transport was attached to the base structure by four mounting posts that allowed the platen press and pressure plate, mounted to the upper cone and cell assembly, to operate the necessary excursions for film clamping. *(NRO)*

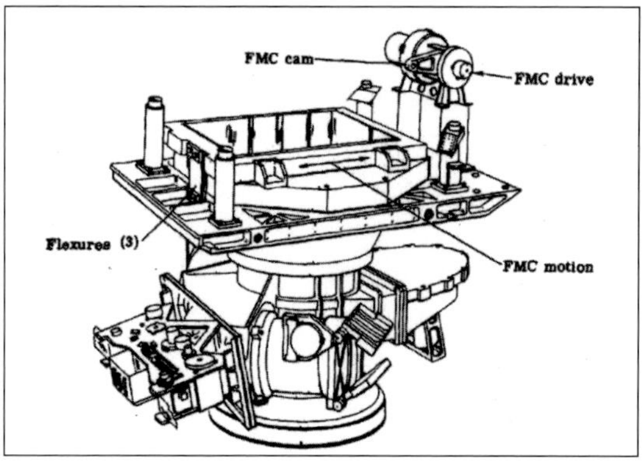

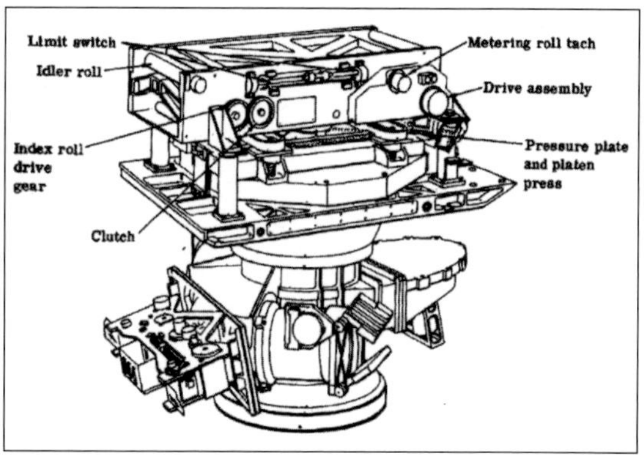

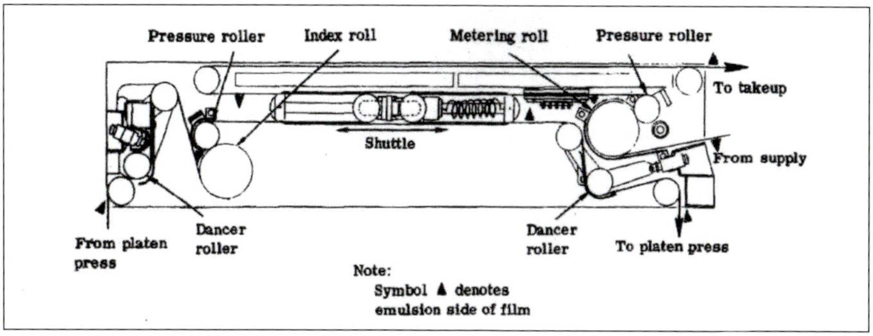

LEFT The terrain transport film flow shows that film was pulled off the supply and fed into the take-up route at a continuous rate determined by the particular framing rate required. The transport was a mechanism that provided this function. The metering roller turned continuously at a rate determined by the selected framing rate. The index roller turned at 4/3 the angular rate of the metering roller for 3/4 of the duration of the selected framing cycle. *(NRO)*

panoramic cameras, their optical systems, support structure, mirrors and all the associated control mechanisms for their operation, together with a film feed mechanism for transporting the exposed film to the SRVs. The four SRVs were housed in a linear arrangement on the long axis of the tapering forward section, which had a length of 22.5 feet (6.8 m). The Mapping Camera and its dedicated film SRV were in the extreme forward end of this section.

The Perkin-Elmer search and surveillance system consisted of two separate and independent panoramic cameras, each controlled individually. They provided target resolution of at least 2.7 feet (0.82 m) at the nadir of a standard operational orbit with a contrast level of 2:1 when the Sun angles were at greater than 30° and when using SO-208 film. The optics had a focal length of 60 inches (152 cm) with an f/3 folded Wright system, essentially a modified Schmidt telescope. The aperture diameter of 20 inches (51 cm) was defined by the aspheric corrector plate that corrected the spherical aberration of the Wright layout.

The image passed through this plate to a 45° mirror to reflect the light on to a concave primary mirror with a diameter of 36 inches (91 cm) which directed the light through an opening in the flat mirror and through a four-element lens on to a film platen. The system produced a field angle of ±2°. The slit width had a range of 0.08–1.3 inches (0.2–3.3 cm). Film was of type 1414 SO-208 and could also be SO-130 infrared and SO-255 for natural colour at a strip width of 6.6 inches (17.7 cm).

Film quantity could vary according to the mission requirement but was typically 155,000 feet (47,245 m) for each camera with a mixed load of SO-315 and color, for a total weight of 2,000 pounds (907 kg). The film stack had a

BELOW LEFT The film recovery capsules situated under the forward section, one of which has its cover removed showing the internal arrangement. *(Dwayne Day)*

BELOW The Satellite Recovery Vehicle (SRV) was a small satellite in its own right, deployed after release to a pre-programmed set of autonomous actions for stability, de-orbiting and recovery. *(Dwayne Day)*

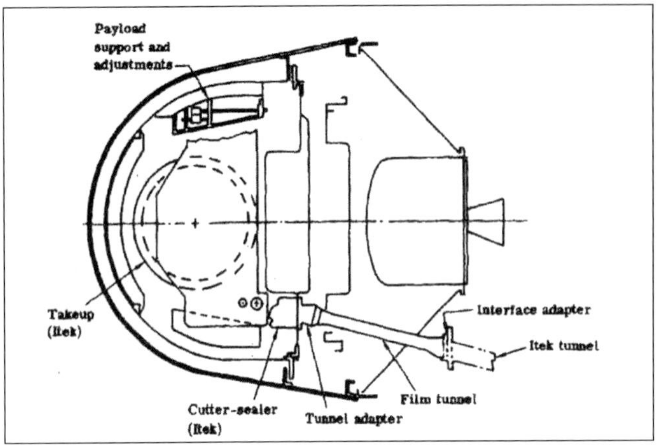

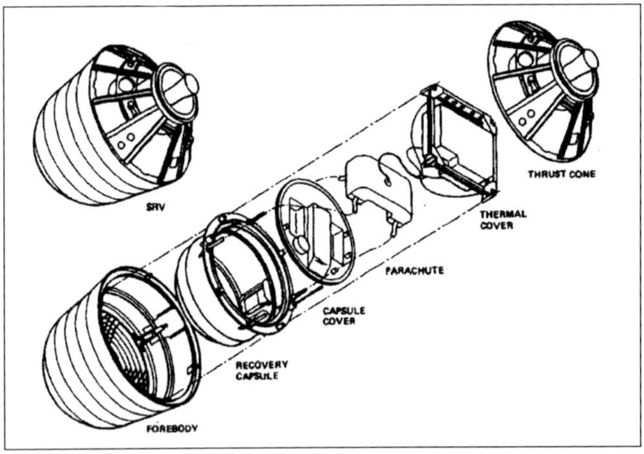

TOP **A simplified cutaway of the Mk V re-entry vehicle showing film transport spool and take-up drum.** *(NRO)*

ABOVE **A sectional breakdown of the satellite recovery vehicle showing the separate detachable elements.** *(NRO)*

diameter of 68 inches (173 cm) for scan modes of 30°, 60°, 90° and 120°, with the center of the scan at 0°, ±15°, ±30° and ±45°, with a maximum attainable scan angle of 60° and a stereo convergence angle of 20°.

The frame format at a maximum 120° scan was 6 inches x 125 inches (15.2 cm x 317.5 cm) with the film moving at a maximum speed of 200 inches/second (508 cm/sec) at the focal plane. The image motion compensation range was 0.018 rad/sec to 0.054 rad/sec for Vx/H (the orbital angular rate in-track) and ±0.0033 rad/sec for Vy/H (the angular rate cross-track).

The two film supply stacks, or drums, were offset in alignment with each other across the width of the mid-section and staggered vertically. These aligned respectively with the forward-viewing camera on the port side and the aft-looking camera on the starboard side. Multiple loop reels carried the film under tension to the two-camera assembly further along in the mid-section and on to the articulators after exposure to individual take-up spools for each SRV. The controlling electronics were situated in the lower part of the mid-section as viewed with the long axis in the direction of orbital travel.

Manufactured by Douglas, the Mk 8 SRV had a diameter of 57.5 inches (146 cm), a height of 85 inches (216 cm) from the base of the heat shield to the tip of the retro-rocket nozzle and a maximum loaded weight of 1,695 pounds (769 kg). The method of use was for the film transport mechanism to thread through the SRV at the extreme forward end of the forward section of the KH-9 and, when it was full, to be ejected at a separation velocity of 3 feet/second (91 cm/sec).

A hot gas generator would spin up the SRV to 10 radians/second before ignition of the retro-rocket, producing a thrust of 7.22 kN (1,623 lb). After burnout the SRV spin rate was slowed to 1.4 radians/second for stability during re-entry. Barometric switches triggered release of the drogue and main parachutes in a sequence starting at a height of 50,000 feet (15,240 m), which, by 15,000 feet (4,572 m) would have reduced the descent rate to 1,200–1,650 feet/minute (366–503 m/min).

If the SRV separation sequence malfunctioned and the descent trajectory was calculated to be excessively long, the heat shield would be ejected and the bucket allowed to burn up in the atmosphere so that it would not fall into inquisitive or unfriendly hands. If the recovery forces missed an air-snatch the capsule would splash down and float, but a salt-water plug would cause it to sink if it was not recovered from the sea within 48–60 hours after splashdown.

The Mapping Camera and its associated systems was supported by the Auxiliary Payload Structure Assembly (APSA), which was attached as a separate unit to the forward section of the SV and contained the Mk 5 RV as an integral element. In all, 20 HEXAGON Mapping Camera systems were built and 12 were flown, beginning with the fifth flight of the KH-9 on March 9, 1973. The last four were also devoid of an MC system.

The requirement placed on the system was for mapping coverage of 50 million square miles (171.7 million km²) of denied territory and global coverage of the rest of the world at the rate of 10 million square miles (34.3 million km²) per year. This was for the preparation of maps with enough accuracy to provide land, sea and air forces with sufficient reference to carry out combat operations or targeting at any point on the Earth's surface. Much of this information was of vital importance to the CIA.

Coverage of the surface was accomplished with a swathe 80.5 miles (129.5 km) wide with triple overlap photography at minimum orbital altitude of 80.5 miles (129.5 km) or quadruple overlap from a periapsis of 115 miles (185 km).

The vertically mounted 12-inch (30.5 cm) focal length f/6 terrain camera provided a 74° in-track and 40° cross-track field angle necessary to compile the 1:50,000 scale map requirements. The 10-inch (25.4 cm) focal length f/2 stellar cameras provided the short exposure and point-to-point separation required for obtaining the angle from star photographs. The Mapping Camera system had a weight of 692 pounds (314 kg), of which the main instrument accounted for 339 pounds (154 kg).

The f/6 terrain lens had a focal length of 12 inches (30.5 cm) with an 80° field of view on a 9 inch x 18 inch (23 cm x 45.7cm) format, had an overall length of 24.4 inches (62 cm) and contained eight powered elements together with the window, filter and reseau plate. The stellar camera would determine the angular position of the Mapping Camera at the moment of the exposure and for that they were required to acquire two stars. During operations it was found that 10 of the 20 stars with known positions were needed for accurate alignment of pitch, roll and yaw and this required sensitivity to stars of sixth magnitude or brighter.

The initial lens for the stellar camera was considered to be a Wild f/8 Falconair with a 9.76-inch (248 mm) focal length and a 25° field of view, but Itek replaced this with one it made itself, but attached to a Falconair mount. The

ABOVE The separate re-entry vehicle and film bucket with heat shield and gold-coated thermal insulation. *(USAF Museum)*

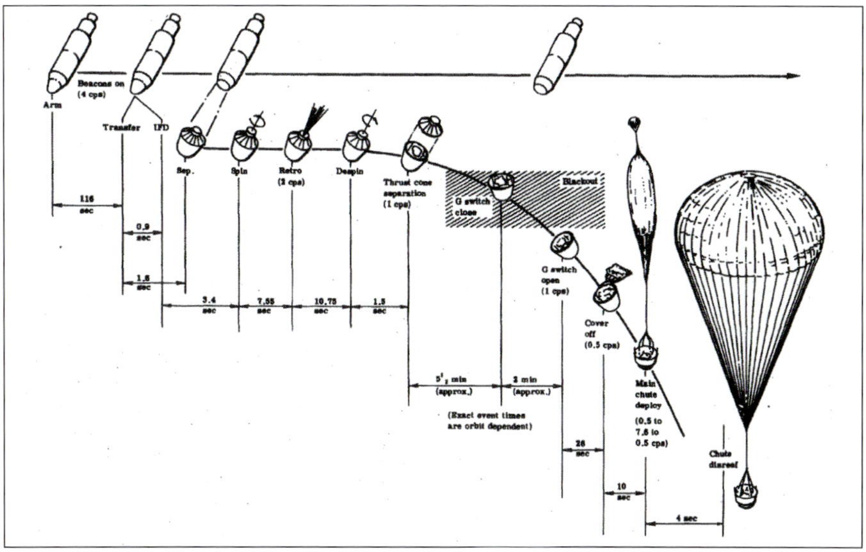

LEFT Although depicting a single bucket re-entry, this chart from the KH-9 technical manual shows the process by which each of the four Mk V SRVs would be returned from a KH-9. *(NRO)*

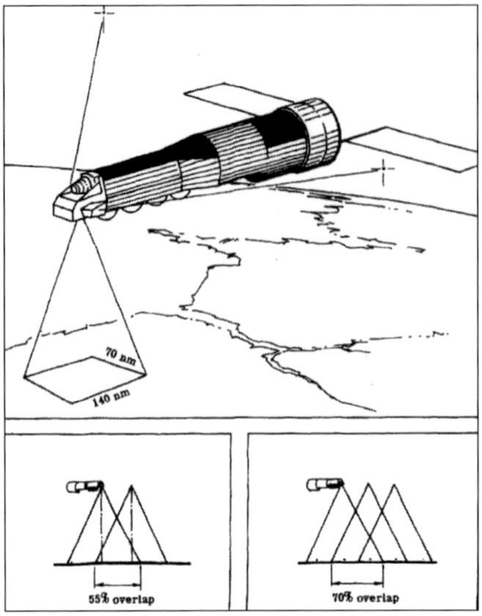

RIGHT Mapping camera operations from a nominal altitude of 106 miles (170.5 km) with bilap (bottom left) or trilap (bottom right) photography. *(NRO)*

stellar camera installed was 13.8 inches (35 cm) in length with a diameter of 5.5 inches (13 cm) and weighed 19.3 pounds (8.75 kg). The barrel mounting was in beryllium, which has a thermal expansion similar to the optical elements and would thus pose no strain on the device.

The Mapping Camera structure was a rigid mount accommodating the main camera, the stellar camera and the terrain lens. It was required to maintain an overall error to 0.8 micrometer between any two photographic frames during a 60-day mission. To maintain the base arc angle at 2.6 arc-sec the mated structural assemblies were accurate to an unprecedented degree, especially for the stellar and terrain lenses. To achieve this, design engineers placed the MC at the center of the structure with a magnesium base-plate attached at the upper end providing the interface between the camera and the APSA, via three kinematic mounts isolating the camera itself from any deformations.

The Mk 5 RV for the Mapping Camera film weighed 390 pounds (177 kg) with a full load of film weighing 70 pounds (32 kg). Wide dispersion limit boundaries were set for the footprint of the Mk 5 RV returning to Earth, specifying 230 miles (390 km) in-track or ± 29 miles (47 km) cross-track. In reality, almost all RVs came down within 4.4 miles (7 km) uprange of the predicted impact point.

The Mk 5 had a three-stage parachute system: a 5.25-foot- (1.6 m) diameter ribbon drogue; a 30-foot- (9 m) diameter ring-slot main canopy reefed; and a main canopy disreefed, with a heavy line for capture by the JC-130 retrieval aircraft. Two recovery beacons were in the RV and two batteries provided 14.8–17.0 V dc. A salt-water valve would cause the RV to sink after 69–107 hours but after the tenth flight this time was reduced to 40 (±5) hours.

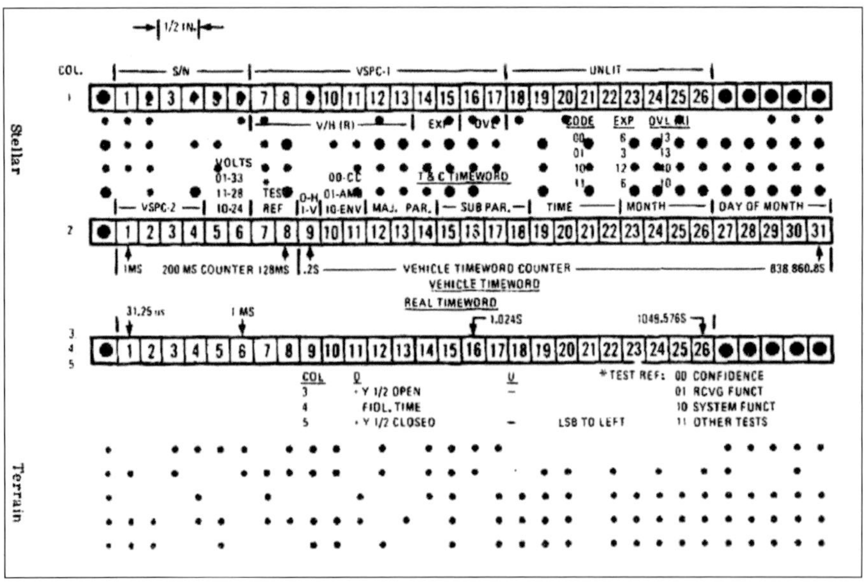

RIGHT Terrain-camera data blocks with readout overlay superimposed. Four projectors in the lens housing imaged fiducial marks at the corners of the format at the moment of exposure. These marks precisely located the moving terrain image with respect to the calibrated reference time of the optics. The time at which the fiducials flashed was recorded in binary code on the data block at one edge of the format. *(NRO)*

RIGHT The stellar-film transport employed the same film advance approach as that used in the terrain-film transport system, albeit with a different mechanism. The metering and index rollers were 2 inches (5 cm) in diameter, and with 1.72 revolutions per frame they advanced the film 10.8 inches (27.4 cm) with a frame interval of 7.0–8.0 seconds. *(NRO)*

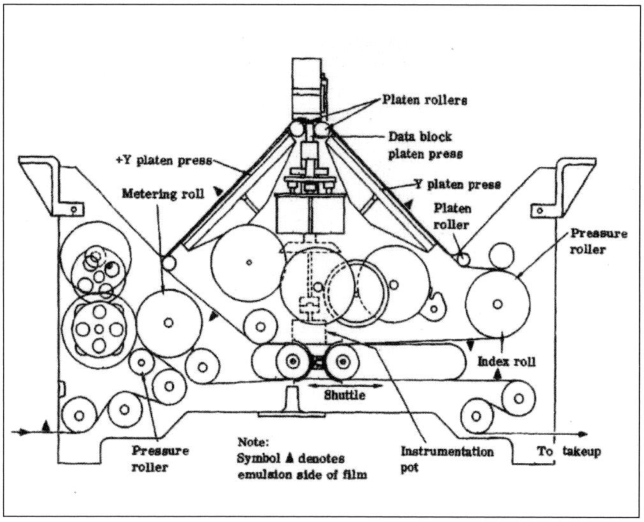

Flight operations

A typical launch began with ignition of the two strap-on solid propellant boosters, the main liquid propellant first stage of the Titan IIID igniting 1 minute 54 seconds into flight followed by booster separation 12 seconds later. The main first stage continued to burn for a total duration of 2 minutes 28 seconds, followed by separation and ignition of the second stage, which fired for 3 minutes 18 seconds, the KH-9 separating 12 seconds later. The solar arrays were deployed on the first orbit and payload operations would normally begin on the fifth orbit, followed by orbit refinement and adjustment every two to four days. All control functions were managed through the Air Force satellite control facilities.

The first flight of the KH-9 began with the launch of vehicle 1201 on June 15, 1971. It remained operational until August 6, and throughout the life of the system the on-orbit duration would increase significantly. The second launch followed with 1202 on January 20, 1972, a year that saw three flights of the KH-9. HEXAGON flights numbered three in 1973, two in 1974, two in 1975 and one in each of the next five years. There were no KH-9 flights in 1981 but one in each of the following three years.

On June 20, 1983, vehicle 1218 was the first KH-9 to fly on Titan 34D, a derivative of the Titan IIIC which had a still further enlarged first stage and bigger and more powerful solid propellant boosters, raising the weight-lifting capacity further. This was useful, as the overall weight of the KH-9 increased with various modifications and improvements.

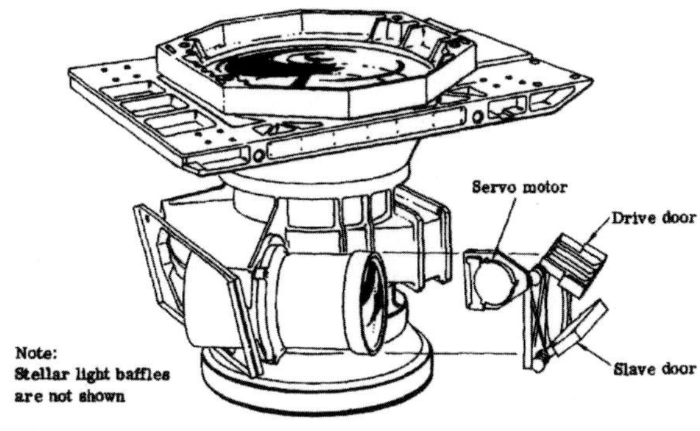

Stellar shutter arrangement

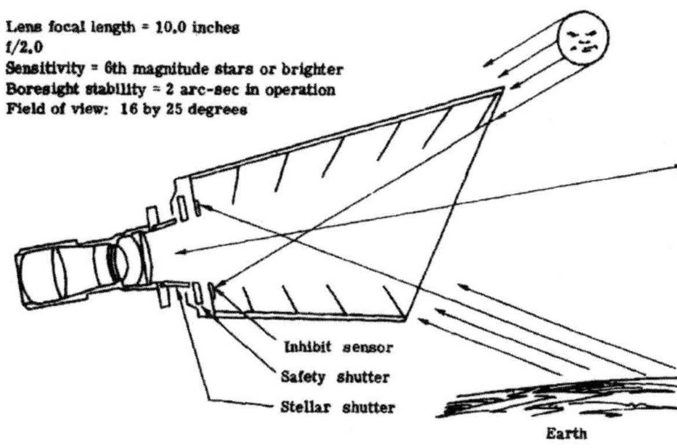

Stellar baffle configuration

RIGHT The configuration of the stellar shuttle (top) and the stellar baffle arrangement. *(NRO)*

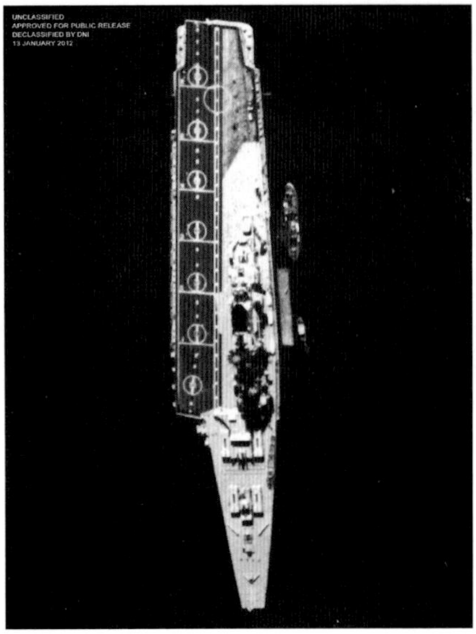

RIGHT A Kiev-class carrier photographed in the Black Sea in 1980 from the KH-9 panoramic camera. *(NRO)*

FAR RIGHT A KH-9 shot of the Kubinka airfield on April 6, 1979, magnified 150 times and showing individual aircraft types. *(NRO)*

Throughout the program, piggyback electronic ferret satellites had flown on 1203, 1207, 1208, 1209 and the eight flights from 1212 to 1219, boosted to higher orbits where they tracked Soviet radars, recorded missile tests and gathered radio communications. Two flights, 1210 and 1212, also carried science subsatellites, and Doppler beacons had been carried on 1205–1207 for measuring the density of the atmosphere at high altitudes.

The last launch, on April 18, 1984, was the only flight to fail when 1220 was lost in a catastrophic accident shortly after lift-off, an inglorious end to a magnificent record of unprecedented success. While the resolution of the Mapping Camera had at first been only 30 feet (9 m), it improved with development through the program and photo-interpreters were getting photographs with a resolution of 20 feet (6 m) by the end. But outright resolution was not the goal – the 29,000 photographs returned to Earth covered 38 million square miles (98.6 million km^2), exceeding the goal when the KH-9 program was approved.

The KH-9 was the ultimate bucket air-recovery system launched to date, incorporating the two functions of high-resolution area surveillance and wide-area mapping, and the system was unique in achieving that. The Defense Mapping Agency, formed on January 1, 1972, took over many of the functions of several other defense and US government departments and its products were almost exclusively reliant on HEXAGON. Mission numbers 1201 through 1204 provided main camera imaging while missions 1205–1216 provided Mapping Camera products, the last three successful flights reverting to the area surveillance cameras.

But that was not the complete story of the KH-9. In January 1972, with the US Air Force committed to flying a large number of military payloads on the NASA Shuttle, Lockheed and Perkin-Elmer were asked to conduct studies into the reuse of HEXAGON satellites either by the on-orbit replacement of expendables, on-orbit maintenance, or capture and return to Earth for refurbishment. A very wide range of possibilities were evaluated with the desirability of using the Shuttle, which had only just that month been approved by President Nixon; in the preceding two years the Department of Defense had backed NASA's development of the Shuttle as a replacement for existing launch vehicles, although the Air Force was concerned about this untried system.

As it turned out, the Shuttle was delayed, not achieving its first orbital mission before April 1981, but the following year a number of astronauts were cleared for briefings on the HEXAGON and NASA was involved in examining the possibility of using the Shuttle

to send up the last two KH-9 vehicles on this reusable launcher. The costs were too high and the idea was dropped, the logic of going that route with a system on its way to retirement being problematic.

But long before the demise of HEXAGON it was being accompanied in orbit by an infinitely more capable system, one that had also been associated with the Shuttle from its very inception. Meanwhile, the future direction of the photo-reconnaissance program may well have taken a very different turn.

ABOVE LEFT A view of Moscow taken with the KH-9 mapping camera on April 6, 1979, showing the downtown and suburban areas in great detail. *(NRO)*

ABOVE A Typhoon-class ballistic missile submarine at Severodvinsk in the White Sea viewed by a KH-9 on October 10, 1982. *(NRO)*

LEFT A KH-9 is immortalized at the USAF Museum, Dayton, Ohio, as it is transported to its display hangar. *(USAF Museum)*

MANNED ORBITING LA
UNITED STATES AIR
FLIGHT CRE

Chapter Eight

Manned Orbiting Laboratory/ DORIAN (KH-10)

The ability of humans to look down on the Earth from space and see objects and activity difficult to determine in a photograph became apparent during the four Mercury orbital flights between February 1962 and May 1963. It came as a great surprise to many that astronauts could apparently discriminate structures on the ground with a clarity previously unimagined.

OPPOSITE The badge selected for Manned Orbital Laboratory (MOL) astronauts. Though they never got to ride Gemini and live in its pressurized work space, photographing targets of national interest, the MOL program was for some a stepping stone to Shuttle flights with NASA. *(USAF)*

From the initial CORONA to the MOL/DORIAN proposal, spy satellites went through several generic evolutions depicted here. From left: KH-8 GAMBIT-3; Manned Orbiting Laboratory/DORIAN; KH-4B CORONA. *(Ian Moores)*

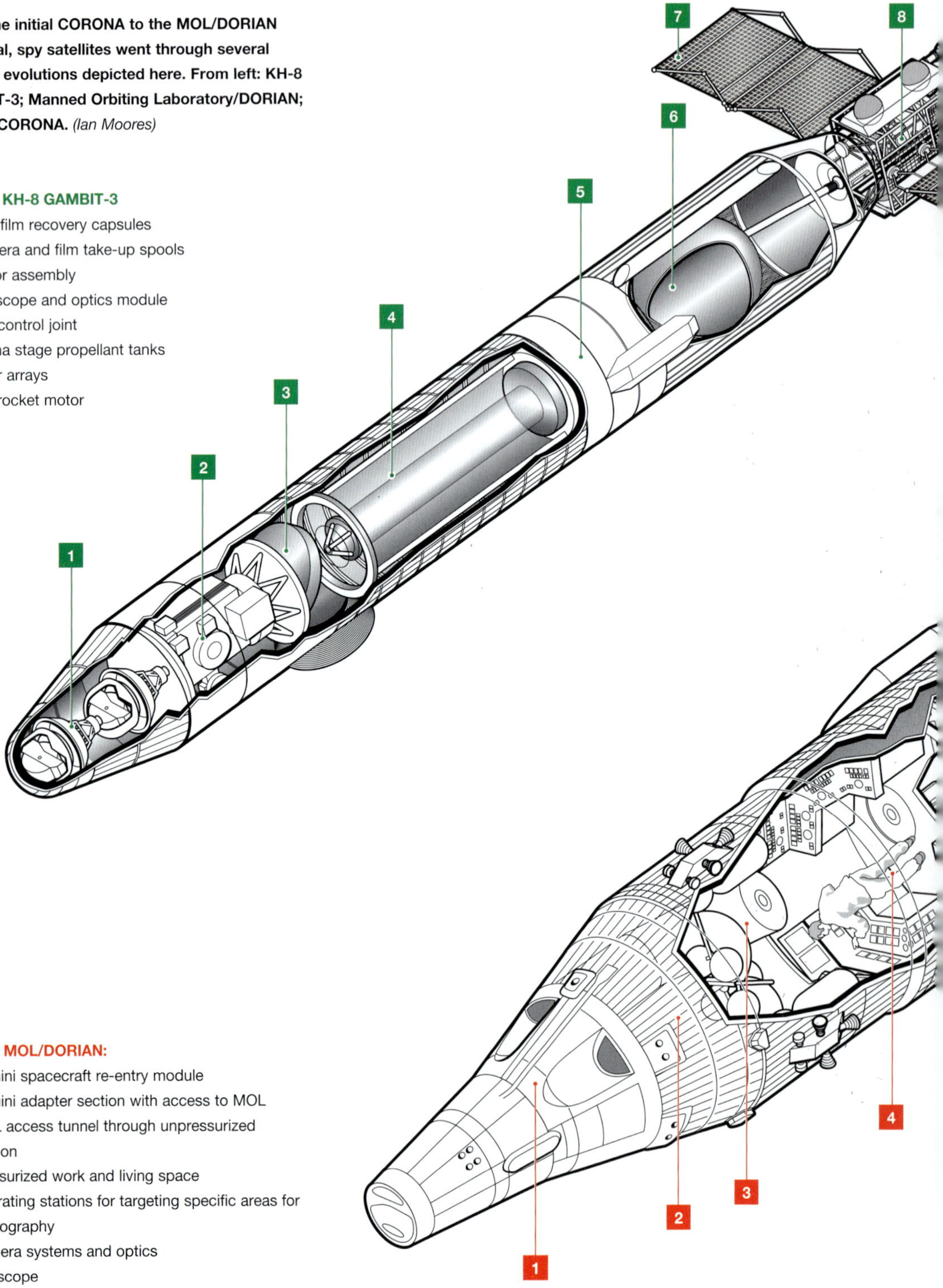

Key for KH-8 GAMBIT-3

1 Two film recovery capsules
2 Camera and film take-up spools
3 Mirror assembly
4 Telescope and optics module
5 Roll control joint
6 Agena stage propellant tanks
7 Solar arrays
8 Bell rocket motor

Key for MOL/DORIAN:

1 Gemini spacecraft re-entry module
2 Gemini adapter section with access to MOL
3 MOL access tunnel through unpressurized section
4 Pressurized work and living space
5 Operating stations for targeting specific areas for photography
6 Camera systems and optics
7 Telescope

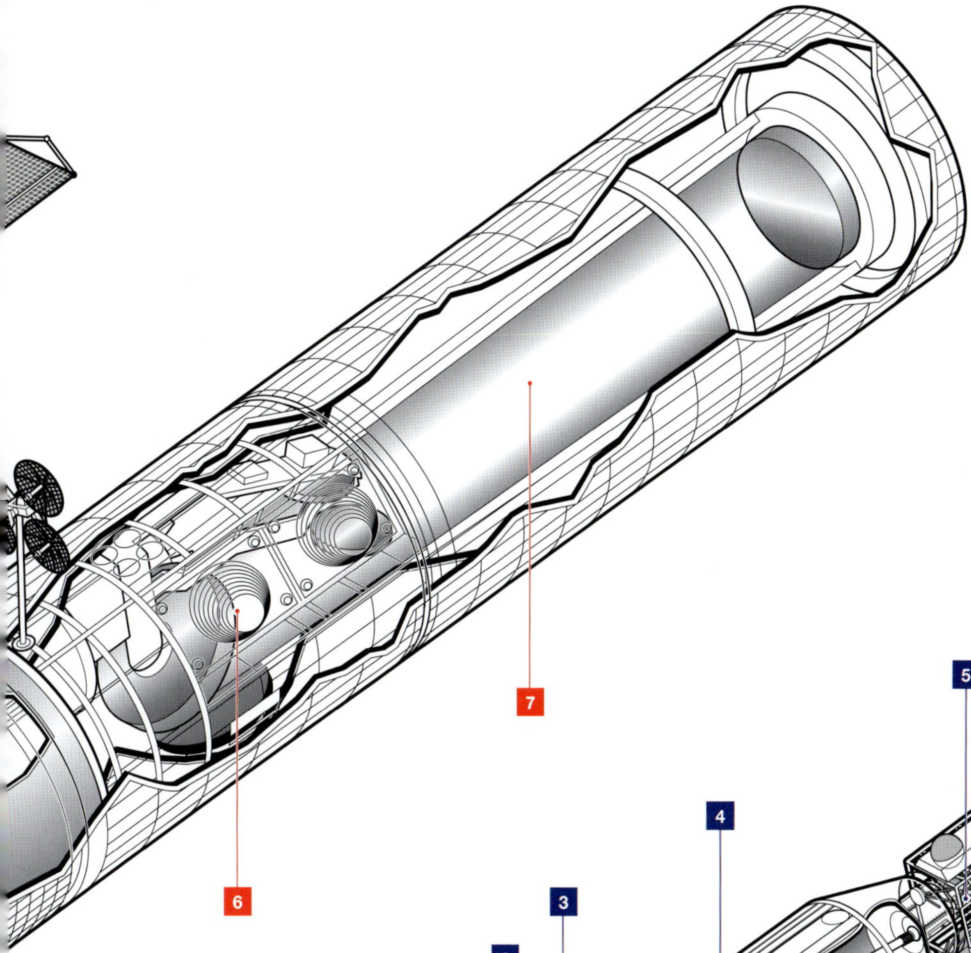

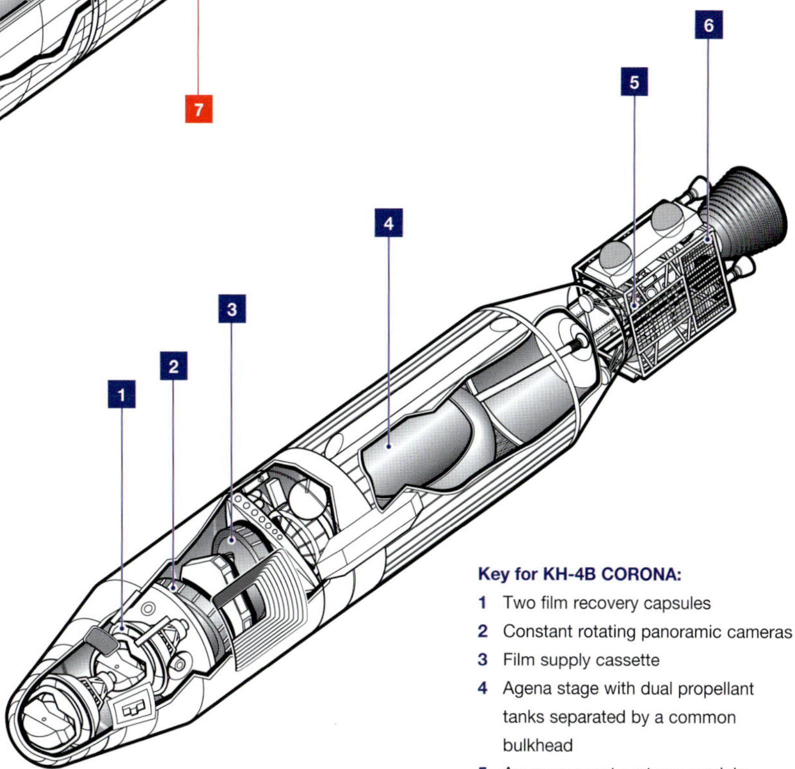

Key for KH-4B CORONA:

1 Two film recovery capsules

2 Constant rotating panoramic cameras

3 Film supply cassette

4 Agena stage with dual propellant tanks separated by a common bulkhead

5 Agena support systems module

6 Bell rocket motor

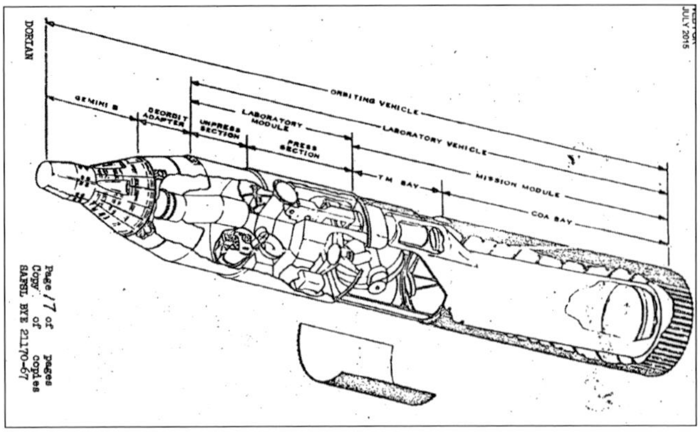

ABOVE The basic arrangement of a Manned Orbiting Laboratory adopted an Air Force Gemini B procured from the existing production line for NASA two-man spacecraft and used it as a crew vehicle for a pressurized laboratory. *(NRO)*

Some believed the astronauts were hallucinating, and could not square the apparent gap between the early CORONA images in black and white photographs and verbal reports from Mercury pilots. Could the human eye interpreting reflected light in a cerebral process really see more than a camera? It became so much a focus of study that specific tasks were set for the last Mercury mission in May 1963 to give its pilot, Gordon Cooper, the chance to make a special study of visual acuity and photographic tasks.

BELOW Optional ingress paths to the pressurized laboratory included a spacewalking (EVA) route through the conventional hatch in the Gemini spacecraft to a hatch in the laboratory, and a tunnel through the Gemini heat shield to the pressurized interior of the module. *(NRO)*

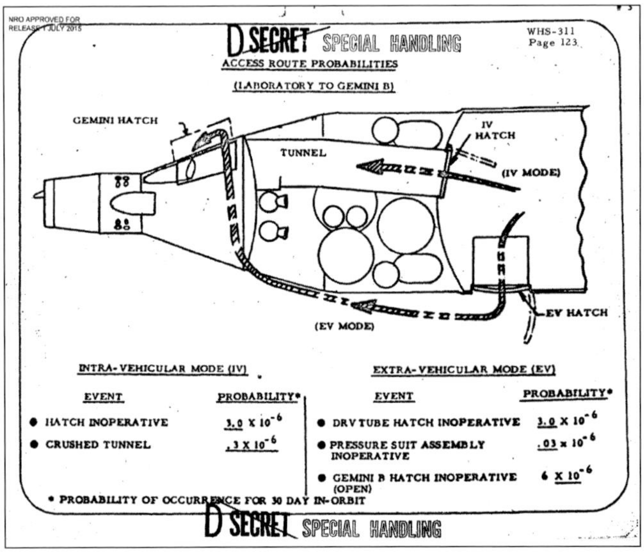

The Air Force, levered from direct participation in human space flight by the decision of President Eisenhower to wrap up all civilian space exploration into a new agency derived from NACA, gave NASA the dominant role. The fact that observations from space might come to involve astronauts was deeply ingrained in Air Force thinking. In fact it originated in a plan drawn up by the Scientific Advisory Board in early 1958 calling for an orbital command post where total surveillance of the planet could take place and where military operations could be monitored.

This was the pre-electronic age and people were believed crucial to any advanced military activity, so in March 1959 the Air Force began a long-range plan for its activities in space. From this emerged what the report referred to as a "manned orbital laboratory," several years before the adoption of this name for a funded project, where new weapons could be tested and operations such as rendezvous and docking could be evaluated. On February 19, 1960, industry was asked to bid on concept designs and 12 responded.

Known as the Military Test Pilot Station (MTPS), the winning bidders were General Electric, Lockheed, McDonnell Aircraft and General Dynamics. Throughout the following year designs were developed, but the Air Force became aware that any orbiting facility would need an efficient ferry vehicle capable of rendezvous and docking, which so far nobody had attempted, and on into 1962 the studies progressed while the Air Force's Dyna-Soar space-plane was accelerated in the expectation that this would provide those services.

However, at the end of 1961, with a mandate from the president to send men to the Moon, NASA authorized development of a two-man version of Mercury, the Gemini spacecraft, which the Air Force eyed as a potential short-term solution before Dyna-Soar was ready. In March 1962 plans were submitted for what was now named the Military Orbital Development System (MODS) and proposals were presented for five Air Force ("Blue") Gemini B missions in 1965. It was believed that Gemini B would be a proving ground for the Air Force and prepare it for a military space station.

With a plethora of military space programs

on the table, the fiscally frugal Robert McNamara urged caution and pruned programs that appeared to parallel NASA's activities, which were evolving faster than anything the Air Force was planning. While pushing ahead with Apollo, with a decision on a military space program only slowly evolving, by 1964 NASA was significantly outspending the Air Force on space activities and was openly planning to use Apollo hardware to build its own space station alongside the Moon missions.

It turned out that NASA's plans would evaporate as quickly as they appeared, when the civilian space budget fell into decline from 1965 and the military space budget began to grow quickly. Nevertheless, NASA named its own planned station the Manned Orbital Research Laboratory (MORL) and the tussle between the two agencies went all the way up to President Johnson, who asked McNamara to make recommendations about options including ideas from NASA about their own plans for a station.

It was this high-level attention during 1963 that reinvigorated MODS, which by the end of the year had been renamed Orbital Space Station (OSS). For a while it appeared that the Air Force may be given overall charge of Gemini and a manned space station but while McNamara wrestled with options the argument for both Dyna-Soar and a Blue Gemini program faced the reality that neither were suited well to the Air Force's plans for military space activities.

In December 1963 McNamara announced his decision: cancellation of the Dyna-Soar spaceplane (already relegated to a test project as the X-20), and development of a space station for the Air Force known as the Manned Military Orbiting Laboratory (it was President Johnson who took out the word "Military"). The idea that MOL would rapidly become the vessel into which all the aspirations of the space-intelligence community would pour was not the intention when the Air Force received permission, but it soon fell in line when that was eventually to become its most attractive function.

An exceptionally wide range of possibilities arose with MOL, including the proposal for a forward-looking radar operating in the

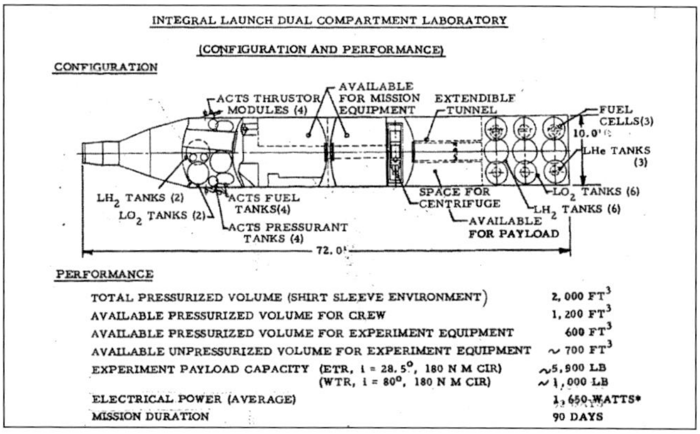

ABOVE **Numerous optional ways of utilizing a pressurized laboratory were examined during the development phase of the MOL, including a pressurized research module where the crew could live and work. Note the inflatable tunnel concept considered as a way of moving from Gemini to the laboratory.** *(NRO)*

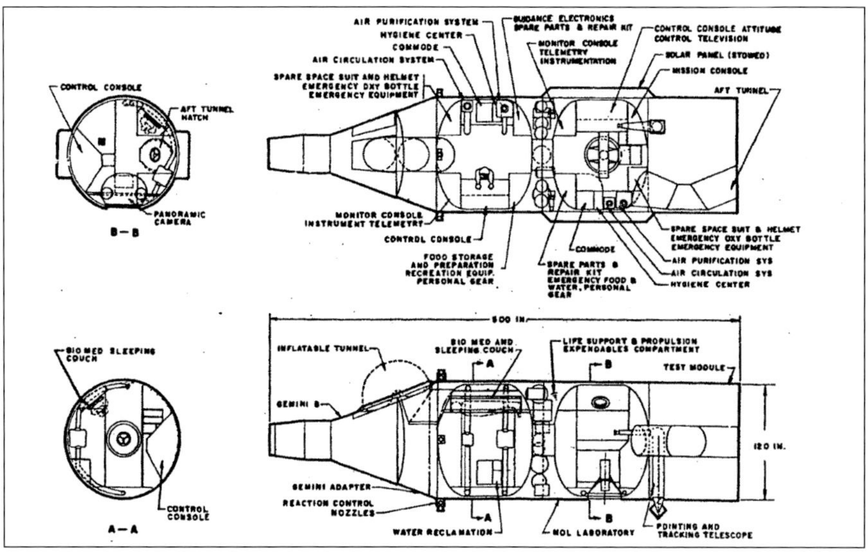

LEFT **A dual configuration MOL concept in which fuel cells would be used to provide electrical power and a wide range of experiments would be incorporated.** *(NRO)*

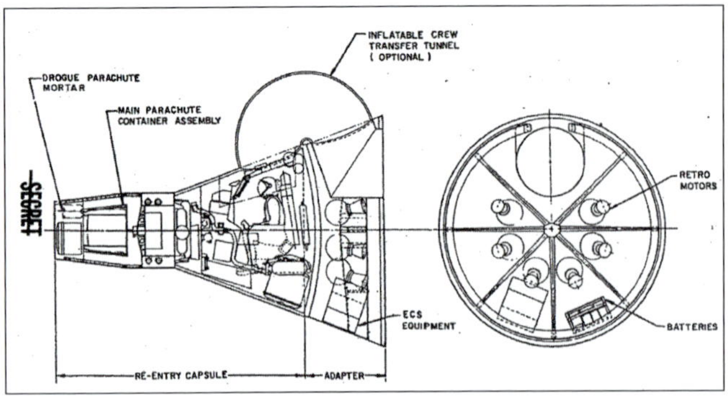

LEFT The Gemini spacecraft, seen here supporting an inflatable airlock for egress to the laboratory, with additional retro-rockets in the equipment section. *(NRO)*

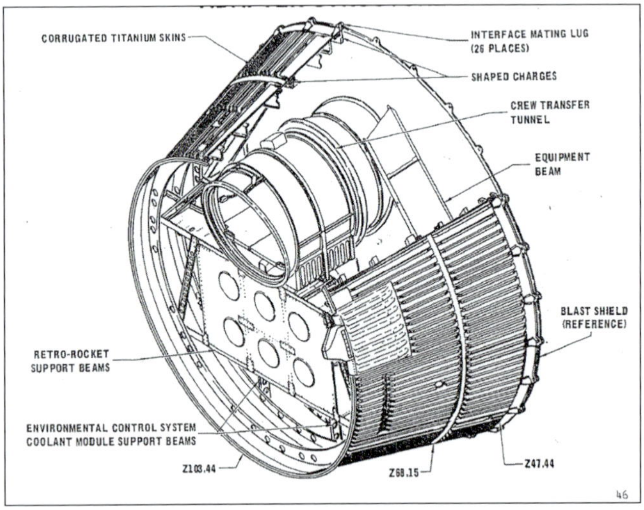

ABOVE Gemini spacecraft manufacturer McDonnell conducted several engineering studies for Gemini B, including a rework of the equipment section to carry a tunnel through the aft heat shield into the MOL. *(McDonnell)*

LEFT A mock-up of the proposed Gemini B retro-module and adapter section. *(NRO)*

300–10,000 MHz frequency range for detecting ship-size targets on the surface of the ocean. Another application put forward was the use of a continuous running low-light level TV image of the surface on the night side of the Earth, using the lights of ships, their wakes and reflected Moonlight to observe and locate the movement of vessels at sea. There was also a proposal to use a Gemini spacecraft in one-man mode equipped with a powerful telescope in the space where the second seat would be located. With this, it was believed the astronaut could conduct an initial survey of areas of interest and pass it across to the MOL or to the intelligence community and their CORONA satellites.

As late as June 1964 the MOL program was being defined as an experimental laboratory for investigating the role of humans in orbit from the military perspective, utilizing a pressurized living space, the Gemini B spacecraft and the Titan III/Transtage launcher. Initially the basic requirement was for a 30-day mission in a shirt-sleeve environment, launched from Cape Canaveral and operating from a low Earth orbit with no greater inclination than 36°, meaning its ground track would be contained within those degrees of latitude north and south of the equator.

The use of Gemini B to rendezvous, dock and to deliver the crew required upgrades to its consumables to double the design lifetime of the NASA vehicle. This would not be the case if an Apollo spacecraft was used instead. Launched on a Saturn IB, a modified Apollo spacecraft could support missions lasting up to 120 days and lift all the experiments for several separate MOL missions on one flight. This consideration was studied by North American Aviation. The ability to have the Apollo reside at a manned orbiting facility in a dormant condition would in fact be utilized during NASA's Skylab missions of 1973–74.

By early 1965 several enhanced program

proposals were being considered, including the mating of two MOL modules end to end, one providing crew habitation and the other carrying an unmanned section with high resolution optical equipment – spy cameras. Electrical power could come from fuel cells (uitilized in the Gemini and Apollo spacecraft) or from solar panels. By this time the shift in emphasis from a general-purpose research laboratory to a large photo-reconnaissance capability, and the integration with MOL of the KH-10 DORIAN system, was already under way.

It was here that clear guidelines were issued for the "white" MOL program, with public disclosure of general research and evaluation of humans in space, and the "black" program with the KH-10 incorporated. In several ways it was déjà vu; CORONA buried within the publicly visible cloak of Discoverer was a precedent, as well as the GAMBIT saga. Special directives were issued about those lines of demarcation.

By May 20, 1965, the switch in priorities from MOL being a general research laboratory to a manned photo-reconnaissance platform was enshrined within a memorandum to Greer at the NRO confirming that its exclusive priority was to carry the KH-10. At this date the program was funded to include a single unmanned launch followed by six manned missions, the first in late 1968 and the last in early 1970. These dates would slip and by the end of 1967 the first of three manned flights was scheduled for August 1971 followed by the first of two unmanned flights in September 1972.

By 1965 a new set of rationales pervaded the requirements list. In addition to all the usual needs was the appearance of a high-resolution system for conducting an assessment of damage sustained by the enemy after a nuclear exchange, to determine which targets remained intact and where to strike next, and also to conduct a total damage assessment from warheads falling on the US and its allies. In this context a mix of manned and unmanned systems served well.

It is worth reminding ourselves that at this date approval had been given for the KH-9 HEXAGON area surveillance and mapping system and that parallel development of the manned KH-10 DORIAN system introduced its own problems. The bigger debate over manned versus unmanned space systems in general was heating up, at a time when great strides were being made in electronics and solid-state technology such that the presence of a human in the loop was less necessary than had been the case even five years earlier. And it was a matter getting attention at the top.

On June 30, 1965, Donald F. Hornig, Special Assistant for Science and Technology, sent a memorandum to Defense Secretary Robert McNamara emphasising the uncertainty about the nature of humans in space within the photo-reconnaissance program. When MOL was a general-purpose research station, humans were part of its *raison d'être* but now it was competing with the more certain technology of an unmanned system versus the as yet unknown value of a manned system.

Hornig did not dismiss the manned MOL but made it known to McNamara that there was no certainty that a manned system would work as well as boasted in presentation briefings. In this he sowed the seeds of doubt that would, eventually, cause McNamara to cancel it. Nevertheless, a study panel was set up to report on the matter by the end of 1965.

One aspect here which appears not to have got the attention of anyone at the time is the instability that a human presence has on an orbiting structure, which responds like a trampoline to astronauts moving around and pushing against the interior. In fairness, this was not to become apparent until larger manned space vehicles with precise position control systems measuring

BELOW When the KH-10 DORIAN camera system was adopted for the MOL the mission module contained the optics with a swinging stereoscopic mirror looking down within a structure 35.6 feet (10.85 m) long using Invar and beryllium for strength, stiffness and low levels of thermal expansion. *(NRO)*

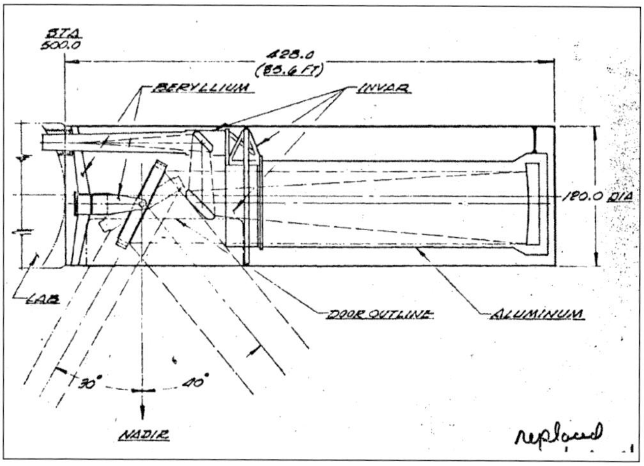

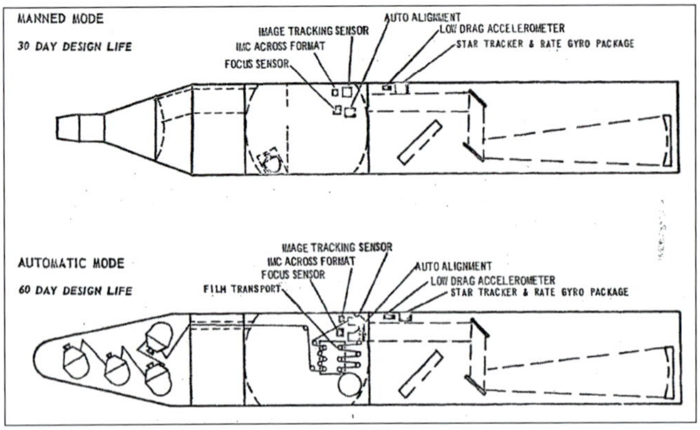

ABOVE Optional schemes were considered for manned and unmanned modes of operation using the same optics but the latter equipped with satellite recovery vehicles. *(NRO)*

BELOW An early concept for the MOL with solar-cell arrays, eventually deleted in favor of fuel cells. *(NRO)*

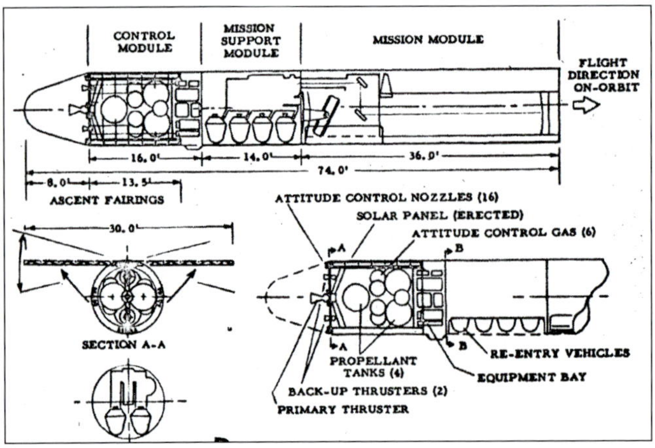

every minor attitude excursion recorded such disturbances; even the Apollo spacecraft's attitude control system responded in a way which made a nonsense of having astronauts inside a finely tuned optical system demanding an accurate and stable fine-pointing platform.

Despite gathering uncertainties about its functionality as a manned vehicle, President Johnson approved MOL on August 25, 1965, and the first eight of a planned corps of 20 MOL astronauts was selected on November 12. At this date MOL would launch in late 1968 followed by five crewed visits starting a year later. The second set of astronauts were selected in May 1966, when five more names were added, the third and final group being announced in June 1967. Several of these men would later fly the NASA Shuttle and one, General James A. Abrahamson, would head the NASA human space flight program during the mid-1980s.

By 1966 the essential design characteristics of the MOL had been decided, and while options were preserved for flying it as an unmanned system the baseline was for a station crewed by pairs of astronauts riding up in a Gemini B spacecraft. The Gemini spacecraft would be situated on top of the cylindrical laboratory and the crew would fly up with their station already assembled on the ground. Gone were the early proposals for solar cells, the entire MOL looking like an elongated cylinder devoid of external protuberances save for communications antennae.

Gemini B would be essentially the same as a NASA Gemini, except for a circular cut-out in the aft heat shield that would incorporate a hatch, suitably coated with heat-shield material which would, when opened on orbit, allow crew access to the pressurized compartment of MOL via a short transfer tunnel through the interior of the Gemini Equipment Module.

The Laboratory Module directly behind the Gemini B Equipment Module had a length of 19 feet (5.8 m), a diameter of 10 feet (3 m) and a

LEFT Not dissimilar to a rearrangement of modules characteristic of the KH-9 HEXAGON, optional layouts for unmanned versions of the MOL would have borrowed design and technology from that program. *(NRO)*

pressurized volume of 1,000 cubic feet (28.3 m^3) where the two-man crew would live and work. Approximately 1,000 pounds (454 kg) of systems essential for the man-tended MOL could be removed to make space for equipment to support a 60-day mission in unmanned mode. A support module would take the place of the Gemini B in the absence of the need for a crew, which would provide Data Return Vehicles (DRVs) returning to Earth with film, much as with the KH-9.

The DORIAN telescope itself had an effective clear aperture of 60 inches (152.4 cm) with an optical diameter of 72 inches (183 cm), and took the form of a folded Newtonian reflector with a Ross corrector to compensate for aberration and with a 1.08° field of view. It was contained within the unpressurized Mission Module, which had a length of 35.6 feet (10.85 m) and a diameter of 10 feet (3 m). The MM was fabricated in two sections, the forward section being 14 feet (4.26 m) in length and housing much of the support equipment. Much of the outer shell was fabricated from beryllium for reasons of thermal control, with Invar on structural elements for stiffening.

A lens barrel provided the optical alignment, controlled the thermal environment and served as the mounting structure for the aspheric mirror, the Newtonian and Ross (45°) folding mirrors and the corrector lens assembly. The camera located in the Laboratory Module was a frame-type, the platen equipped with image motion compensation for reducing degradation at the frame edge due to relative motion in the exposure. The image would be circular, 9.4 inches (23.9 cm) in diameter, with relevant data points within the format of each frame.

The primary and tracking mirrors for DORIAN were of "egg-crate" construction. The primary had a diameter of 71.5 inches (181.6 cm) with a fused silica faceplate of 0.9 inches (2.3 cm) thickness and a back plate 0.5 inches (1.27 cm) thick, sandwiched between which was a honeycomb core 0.22 inches (0.56 cm) thick with each cell 3 inches (7.6 cm) across. The primary mirror weighed 1,020 pounds (463 kg) and the mirror surface had an optical tolerance of one wavelength.

The photographic system itself would have provided a static-lens film resolution equal to or greater than 114 lines/mm at the film plane as

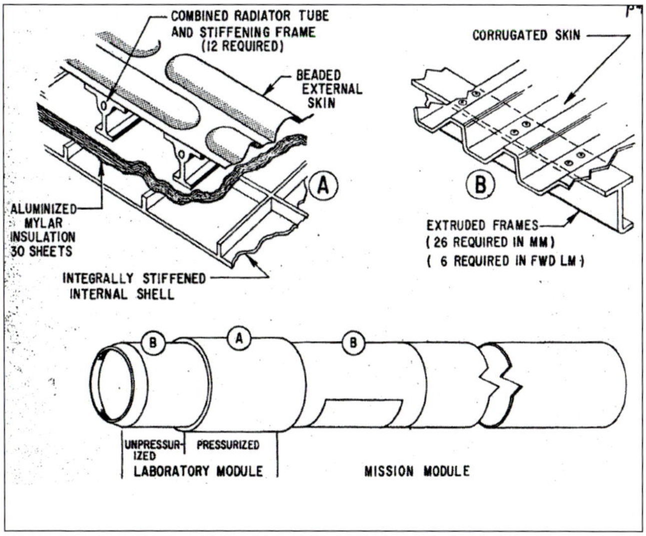

ABOVE **Structural design of the MOL had to accommodate a pressurized compartment as well as a large optical mission module, and considerable attention was given to its layout, materials and engineering.** *(NRO)*

LEFT **A structural test article is prepared for analysis at Lockheed.** *(NRO)*

a 2:1 apparent scene contrast and illumination when using film type 3404 and an exposure index of 6.0. It would be capable of north-bound and south-bound photography from an altitude of 80.5 miles (129.5 km) to 265 miles (426 km). MOL would have had 13,570 feet (4,136 m) of film with a width of 9 inches (23 cm), sufficient for 7,500 stereo pairs.

The Attitude Control and Translation System (ACTS) was responsible for pointing and attitude stabilization and for orbital changes. It consisted of four quads of four 112 N thrusters and four of 444.8 N thrust. They used nitrogen tetroxide and unsymmetrical dimethyl hydrazine propellants, supporting pointing requirements of 0.5° in all axes and a 0.004°/second rate

RIGHT One aspect of the MOL's design was how to provide crewmembers with the ability to move around and transfer to another vehicle in space for inspection. The Astronaut Maneuvering Unit (AMU) was developed by the US Air Force and was to have been tried out during the Gemini IX-A mission in 1966. Difficulties with the pilot's life-support system prevented this taking place. *(USAF)*

change tolerance. The 30-day baseline MOL configuration would carry 2,000 pounds (907 kg) of hypergolic propellants in eight tanks.

As said, solar arrays had been rejected as too large and cumbersome for the power requirements of the MOL. Instead, fuel cells would be provided for the electrical production system and these were of the Apollo type, the technology being taken directly from that program. There were to be three 1,000-hour modules with an average power output of 2 kW or 4.5 kW at peak demand providing a 28 V direct current. Two cryogenic hydrogen and two cryogenic oxygen tanks, as with the Apollo Service Module, would ensure a 30-day life with a 16-day reserve.

Data was to be handled through two identical airborne digital computers, an auxiliary memory unit, a keyboard and display unit, two printers and a subsystem controller. The level of electronic support represented a quantum leap from systems on the cutting edge only a few years earlier. Each digital computer had a 512 K memory (at 16,000 words) with a storage capacity of two million data bits and a transfer rate of 600,000 bits/minute to the computer. Either one of the two computers could handle all on-board requirements. Wideband data would be transmitted at 20 mbps with telemetry on 64 kbps or stored at 1,024 kbps.

The oxygen/helium atmosphere would be at a constant pressure of 34.475 kPa (5 lb/in^2), of which 24.1 kPa (3.5 lb/in^2) would be oxygen, with supercritical oxygen stored as a backup. A molecular sieve would control carbon dioxide levels to no more than 5 mm Hg. The atmosphere revitalization system would provide for full re-pressurization within five minutes. Thermal control would be through inner wall heaters, heat exchangers and cold plates with external radiators to discharge excess heat. MOL would carry 1,330 pounds (603 kg) of helium and cryogenic hydrogen and oxygen.

MOL would be launched by Titan IIIM, and this defined the diameter of the station itself. The rocket would have a total lift-off thrust of 13,344 kN from the seven-segment solids and use a firing sequence similar to that of the Titan IIID used for HEXAGON. It had a payload lift capability of 32,800 pounds (14,880 kg) to low Earth orbit. The baseline weight of the Gemini B spacecraft was 6,100 pounds (2,767 kg), the Laboratory Module had a weight of 14,100 pounds (6,395 kg) and the Mission Module weighed 8,400 pounds (3,810 kg), a total mass at launch of 28,600 pounds (12,972 kg).

Safety in space flight was always a priority but the dangers inherent were brought home when three NASA astronauts – Virgil "Gus" Grissom, Edward White and Roger Chaffee – died in their oxygen-filled Apollo spacecraft during a pad rehearsal on January 27, 1967. Four days later two Air Force airmen – William Bartley and Richard Harmon – also succumbed to a pure oxygen fire in a test chamber at Brooks Air Force Base, Texas. A thorough analysis was made of potential fire risks in the MOL program as NASA got back on track.

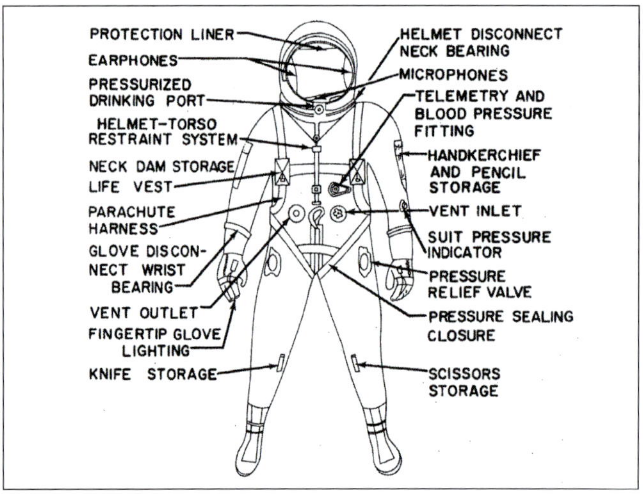

BELOW A space suit specifically designed for the MOL astronauts was planned, differing from NASA suits of the time only in detail. *(NRO)*

Over time, since the KH-10 became the dominant reason for MOL, the low-inclination launches that were appropriate for an Earth-orbiting research laboratory became totally inappropriate for photo-reconnaissance. It was then that the launch site shifted from Cape Canaveral to Vandenberg Air Force Base, where flights into polar or Sun-synchronous orbit were possible. On March 12, 1966, work began on Space Launch Complex-6 (SLC-6, or "slick six" as it was called) to launch the Titan IIIM and its MOL/Gemini payload.

In a test of the reworked Gemini spacecraft demonstrating the plausibility of returning through the atmosphere with a circular hatch in the aft shield, on November 3, 1966, the US Air Force launched mission OPS 0855 carrying back into space on a Titan IIIC the second unmanned Gemini spacecraft previously flown by NASA in January 1965 on a test flight. Gemini was separated for re-entry prior to the terminal stage putting two satellites and several experiments into orbit and safely splashed down intact.

MOL labored on through cost increases and delays as the inevitable technical problems cut into schedules and projected launch dates. Competing with the KH-9 HEXAGON since 1964, the Manned Orbiting Laboratory/DORIAN system was a highly valued asset and while its precise technical specification is still classified, it would have exceeded anything to date.

MOL was cancelled in June 1969, still at least two years away from the first manned launch. In the end it had been the escalating costs of the Vietnam War and the realization that unmanned systems could do just as well for much less money that boxed it in and brought its demise. Paradoxically, the latter argument still exists in the civilian space programs of NASA.

ABOVE LEFT Titan IIIC launched on November 3, 1966, as part of heat shield tests, carrying the Gemini 2 spacecraft previously flown by NASA and a mock-up of the MOL. *(USAF)*

ABOVE Space Launch Complex 6 (SLC-6) was built to carry MOL and its astronauts into space as the first Air Force man-in-space program since losing out to NASA with its MISS program in 1958 and the cancellation of Dyna-Soar/X-20 in 1963. MOL itself was cancelled in 1969 and SLC-6 was adapted for Air Force Shuttle flights until that role too was cancelled in 1986. *(USAF)*

BELOW The definitive MOL laboratory, with fuel-cell electrical power production and a 30-day manned life. *(Giuseppe de Chiara)*

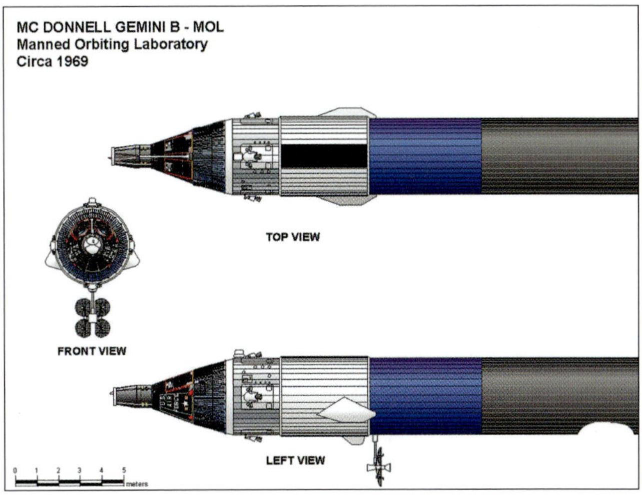

Chapter Nine

KENNEN/ CRYSTAL (KH-11)

The desirability of photo-reconnaissance satellites capable of transmitting to ground stations real-time pictures of denied areas goes right back to the earliest days of spy satellites and to the original concept. The limitations of technology prevented that occurring until a suitable infrastructure existed for transmitting high-resolution imagery, for receiving it at secure centers irrespective of the location of the satellite in its orbit and of handling the vast quantity of data generated. Until that became possible, wet-film imagery returned in buckets from KH-1 to KH-9 dominated satellite photo-reconnaissance.

OPPOSITE Although the SDAS satellites were designed to fly in the Shuttle, most were launched on Titan IIIB-Agena rockets. *(USAF)*

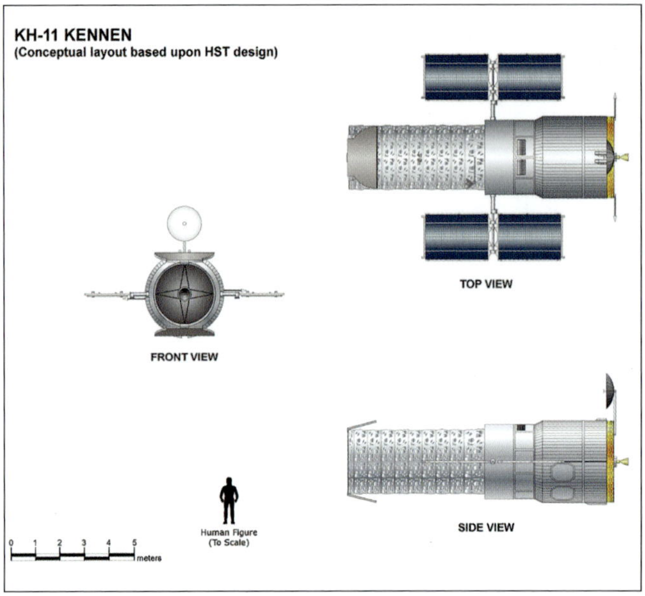

ABOVE **The KH-11 KENNEN (or CRYSTAL) spy satellite is highly classified and there are no images available for publication, but its general configuration may look close to this exterior profile three-view illustration.** *(Giuseppe de Chiara)*

BELOW **The interior layout of the KH-11 is based on a folded Cassegrain reflector with secondary steerable mirrors. The KH-11 is designed to operate in packs, covering a large portion of the Earth's surface on a frequent basis.** *(Giuseppe de Chiara)*

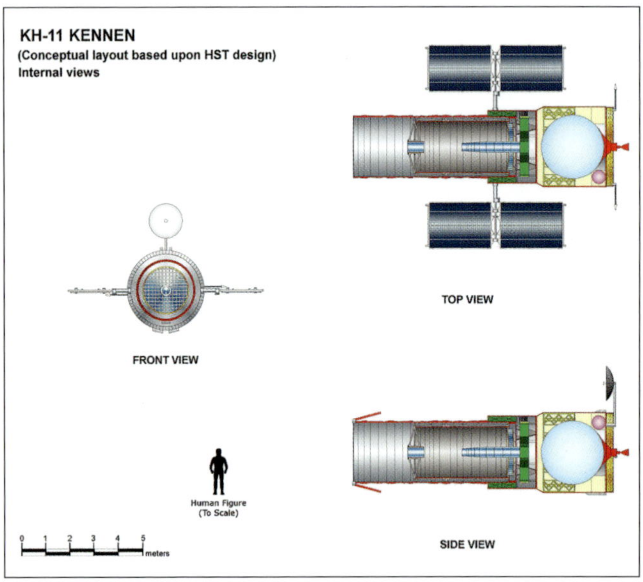

Paradoxically, it was NASA that showed the way and took a converted weather satellite, built by General Electric, and had that company modify it into the world's first dedicated remote sensing satellite. Called Landsat 1 it was launched on July 23, 1972, the first in a progressively more capable series of Earth-observing satellites which spawned generations of parallel systems around the world. But the technology inherent in the Landsat series opened the door on electro-optical systems for intelligence gathering. By the late 1960s, the opportunity arose to build a highly capable system to replace the KH-9.

Generally identified under the name KENNEN, the KH-11 was designed as an electro-optical telescope system capable of very high-resolution imaging, captured on tape and transmitted to the ground over appropriate stations. Initially the KH-11 employed a primary mirror with a diameter of 7.7 feet (2.34 m) but this was increased to 7.9 feet (2.4 m) in later spacecraft, exactly the same as the Hubble Space Telescope, which bears many similarities to the KENNEN series. Under ideal conditions the KH-11 would have a resolution of approximately 6 inches (15 cm).

Powered by large solar arrays deployed on orbit with batteries for eclipse coverage and additional requirements, the KH-11 was built by Lockheed for launch aboard the Titan, which had a payload capability of 27,100 pounds (12,300 kg). The overall weight of the KH-11 increased through successive block upgrades, reaching a mass of 43,220 pounds (19,600 kg) and necessitating a shift to the Delta IV-Heavy launcher. The KH-11 had a length of 64 feet (19.5 m) and a diameter of about 10 feet (3 m).

The operational plan for deployment of the KH-11 was different from the KH-9 in that primary and back-up satellites would operate in each of two orbital planes, covering the same areas in early morning and in afternoon hours at the same locations. The pattern of the orbits is such that each satellite repeats the exact same ground track every four days. With a constellation of four satellites the globe would be covered in a matter of days and the satellites, with modest orbit-change capability, could be moved to operate in different paths. All this was made possible because the usability of the optical system was slaved to the life of the satellite itself, breaking the lock on usefulness restricted to the number of return vehicles.

When mature, the KH-11 system had four working satellites in two orbital planes, in orbits known as "East" and "West," which are separated by an average 49° of longitude, while the secondary satellites are displaced 20° east of the former (East) and 10° west of the latter (West) primary satellites. The alignment of the constellations allows optimum use of shadow length to determine angular dimensions of objects on the ground. The nature of the orbital parameters provides a useful and repetitive sequence of images to show the temporal nature of targets as well as chronological observation of activities spaced only a few days apart.

The optical elements of the KH-11 are classified but they do incorporate steerable secondary mirrors and a shorter focal length for a wider field of view. The link between the KH-11 and the Hubble Space Telescope is very strong, although the technology for the satellite itself varies somewhat for dedicated and functional reasons defined by their respective missions. Nevertheless, the NRO conducted valuable research into a computer-controlled mirror polishing technology that was applied to the mirrors on KH-11 and to the Hubble Space Telescope.

The first KH-11 was launched on December 19, 1976, to a 141 mile x 331 mile (247 km x 533 km) orbit inclined 96.9°. It remained in space until January 28, 1979, by which time the second had been launched on June 14, 1978. The first six KH-11s launched successfully but the seventh on August 28, 1985, failed due to a malfunction in the Titan, which destroyed the complete stack. The Block 2 KH-11 was adapted to carry infrared imaging capability, first launched in December 1984, and it was one of these that was lost in the accident. But the real development came with the Improved CRYSTAL first launched in November 1992.

By this time the KH-11 had become universally referred to as CRYSTAL, the new name standing for "Improved Metric CRYSTAL System" (IMCS) which provided a significant range of enhanced capabilities, including an added mapping value from enhancements to marks on the film to enhanced optics. There was also a very significant improvement in

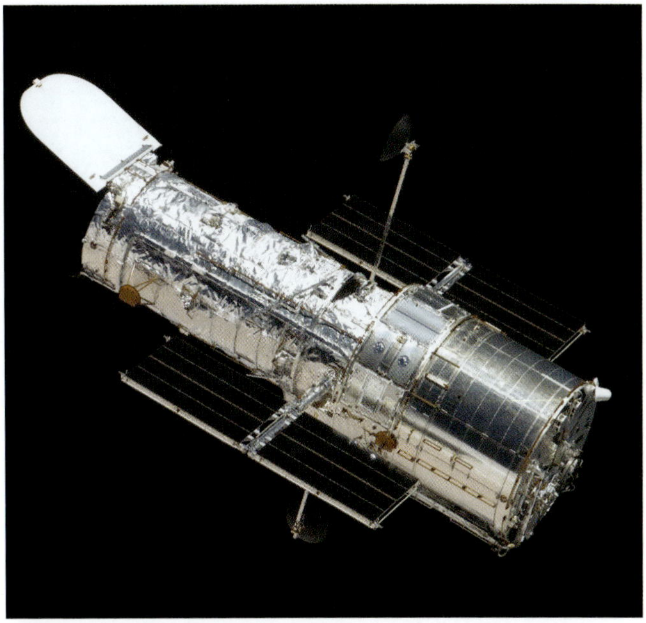

ABOVE The Hubble Space Telescope shares many technology aspects with the KH-11, including the diameter of its main mirror, but its optics are somewhat different as Hubble is an astronomical observatory whereas the KH-11 operates more like a refracting telescope. *(NASA)*

BELOW A typical KH-11 constellation, this geometry being the orbital configuration in September 2013. *(Optimum)*

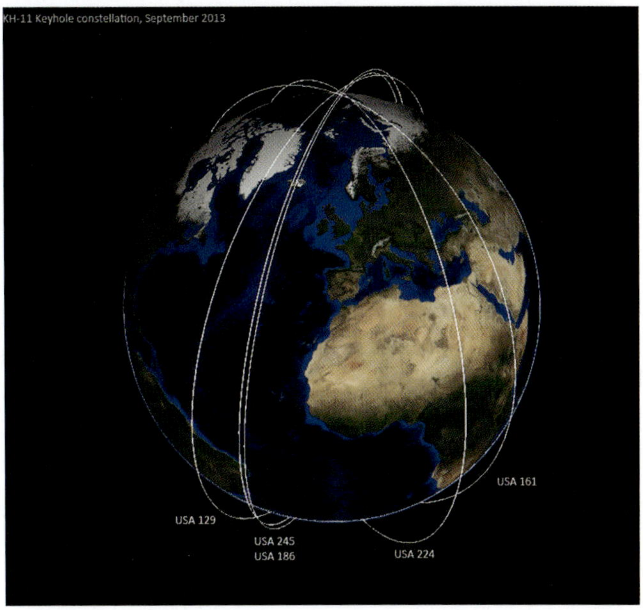

RIGHT The Defense Support Program (DSP) has been a routine accompaniment to the KH-11 as it is used to relay data and communications as well as receive telemetry from these advanced optical systems. *(NASA)*

BELOW A KH-11 photo of the Zhawar Kili Al Badr terrorist camp in Afghanistan, symbolic of the shift away from superpower confrontation to the wide range of threats from organized gangs of disruptive, violent and fanatical warriors who challenge the very fabric of organized society. *(NRO)*

the data transmission rate and in the relay capabilities with the Satellite Data System (SDS). Some sources refer to the Improved CRYSTAL as the Block 3 version, four of which were launched beginning in November 1992 and ending with the Block 4 variant, three of which were launched, in 2005, 2011 and 2013. In all 16 KH-11s were launched over a period of almost 37 years.

Later versions had a larger primary mirror, up to 10.2 feet (3.1 m) in diameter, while changes to the Cassegrain reflector telescope allowed it

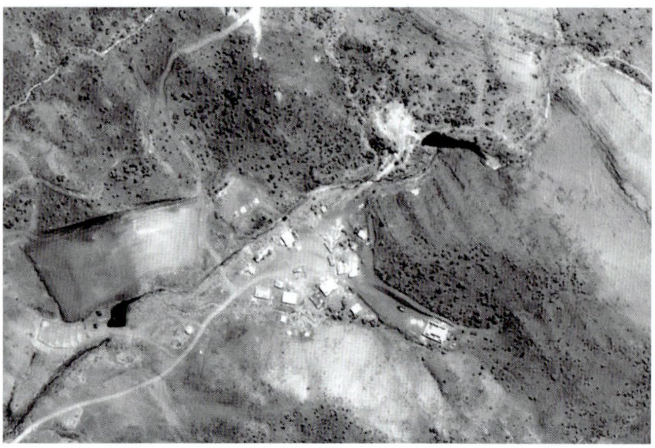

to be movable for optimal alignment with offset targets. Equipped with IMCS, the Improved CRYSTAL carried additional orbit maneuvering propellant and had a design life of eight years. Numerous technical advances were incorporated and each flight vehicle had various modifications and performance-enhancing capabilities.

The successor to KH-11 and its derivatives evolved through a circuitous and painful readjustment of priorities and requirements. Toward the end of the 1990s it was decided to replace the KENNEN with a new electro-optical system defined under the Future Imaging Architecture (FIA) program, a contract won by Boeing in 1999 to the astonishment of Lockheed Martin (renamed following its merger with Martin in 1995), which had enjoyed an exclusive hold on spy satellites since CORONA. Technical and design problems kept the program behind schedule, and, with costs escalating, by 2005 the FIA had been cancelled. With the expectation that the last KH-11 would be launched in 2005, an additional two KENNEN satellites were ordered from Lockheed Martin, and these were launched in 2011 and 2013 as described above.

Data from the KH-11 was transmitted to the ground via Satellite Data System (SDS) satellites (QUASAR) placed in highly elliptical orbits of 310 miles x 24,360 miles (500 km x 39,200 km) at an orbital inclination of 57°. These are known as Molniya orbits after the Soviet communication satellites which used Keplerian orbital mechanics to spend most of their orbital time over the northern hemisphere and polar latitudes. This is especially useful for serving as relay links for Sun-synchronous satellites in low orbits. SDS satellites weighed about 1,390 pounds (630 kg) and consisted of a cylindrical "bus" with a payload of communications antennae on a de-spun upper section. Each satellite produced around 980 W of power and supported 12 communications channels. The first was launched from Vandenberg AFB by Titan 3B-Agena D on June 2, 1976, and the last (SDS-7) on February 12, 1987.

A second-generation series was designed specifically for launch by the NASA Shuttle. The first three of these, with a 15-foot (4.5 m) diameter dish antennae to make maximum use of the Obiter cargo bay, were launched in

August 1989, November 1990 and December 1992. The fourth was lifted to orbit by Titan IV in July 1996. The SDS-2 satellites have additional antennae for uplink communications and for telemetry and command functions and the structure of the spacecraft itself has heritage legacy from the Leasat satellites designed and built by Hughes, which also produced the first-generation SDS and advanced SDS-2 series.

With flights commencing in January 1998 and continuing to the present, some SDS-2 satellites occupy geosynchronous orbits while others continue to go into Molniya orbits. These are launched by Atlas and Delta rockets, the most recent in May 2014 bringing to 12 the total number of second-generation SDSs launched so far. The operation of KH-11 would have been heavily restricted without these relay satellites and they have tasks and relay functions outside the somewhat narrow realm of support for electro-optical and radar imaging satellites.

From the early 1970s the space programs of the civilian and military/intelligence-gathering sectors changed dramatically. With NASA budgets down considerably due to the end of investment in development and manufacturing for Apollo hardware, the reusable Space Shuttle was generally accepted as a replacement for expendable rockets. To garner support for its new program, NASA sized the Shuttle Orbiter to allow large military payloads to launch on this manned system and for that the abandoned SLC-6 launch complex at Vandenberg AFB was to be adapted for flights of the Shuttle to polar and Sun-synchronous orbits.

While the specific plans for launching military payloads on the Shuttle remain classified, the type of orbits sought by the military for incorporation within the Shuttle specification define the roles. By giving the Shuttle a West Coast launch capability, the Air Force anticipated the launch of electro-optical reconnaissance satellites to polar orbit, with the requirement for the Orbiter to return to Earth before a single orbit had been completed, landing back at Edwards Air Force Base, California. To achieve this, the Shuttle had to be capable of flying 1,500 miles (2,400 km) to left or right of the ground track.

This cross-range capability was necessary because in the 90 minutes to make one orbit of the Earth the planet rotates 1/18th of a full revolution, or 2,400 km. If returning to Earth directly in the plane of the ground track it would land in the Pacific Ocean. By making a turn during re-entry in the atmosphere and gradually flying back over land, the Orbiter could put down at Edwards. By making only a single orbit of the Earth a photo-reconnaissance satellite could be placed in orbit and the Shuttle returned before the Russians could track its position. Moreover, stealthy satellites could also be placed in this

LEFT A radar imaging satellite from the NRO's Future Imaging Architecture program, launched by the National Reconnaissance Office on December 14, 2006, went awry and entered the wrong orbit. Shown here is an SM-3 missile launched from the USS *Lake Erie* on February 21, 2008, which intercepted the vehicle and destroyed it. *(USN)*

BELOW Vice Chairman of the Joint Chiefs of Staff US Marine General James E. Cartwright (left) and Deputy Defense Secretary Gordon R. England follow the progress of the Standard Missile-3 launched in pursuit of the errant satellite. *(USN)*

ABOVE **Indicative of the size and mass of the KH-11 system, one of the last satellites of this class to fly was launched by Delta IV-Heavy on January 20, 2011. This line of launch vehicles began with the Thor that launched the CORONA series from 1959 onwards.** *(ULA)*

orbit and rapid deployment was a key feature of several military payloads.

But the KH-11 did not operate alone, at first sharing operating time with the KH-9 and then with a new generation of imaging synthetic aperture radar satellites in a development program begun in 1976 and authorized seven years later. They were first developed under the code name INDIGO, which changed to LACROSSE and is now known as ONYX. Capable of visually identifying objects night and day, they have an advantage over the electro-optical systems in that they are not precluded from observations by night or by cloud.

The first ONYX was launched by Shuttle *Atlantis* from Florida on December 2, 1988. It operated for more than eight years and was intentionally brought to destructive re-entry in July 1997. The second ONYX went up from Vandenberg on a Titan IV in March 1991 and was followed by the third in October 1997. A fourth followed in August 2000 and a fifth in April 2005.

These satellites were operated in tandem, at respective orbital inclinations of 57° and 68° at orbital altitudes around 404 miles (650 km). Radar requires lots of electrical power and the solar arrays of this class are almost 148 feet (45 m) across and produce 10–20 kW. Each satellite has a mass in the range 31,000–35,280 pounds (914,500–16,000 kg). With a resolution of 3–5 feet (0.9–1.5 m) they were crucial in supporting bomb-damage assessment during the first Iraq war of 1992 and in a wide range of reconnaissance and surveillance tasks driven by the war on terror in the years since then. As the Cold War transitioned to a war against rogue states, radar-imaging satellites were a vital ingredient in obtaining information about groups of organized terrorists and corrupt pseudo-military organizations.

Following the ONYX series were the TOPAZ satellites, long in development and four years behind schedule. They emerged from the failed FIA program of the 1990s and comprised the radar element of that initiative, which remained with Boeing. Operating in orbital altitudes of around 683 miles (1,100 km), the first was launched by Atlas V in September 2010, followed by the second on a Delta IVM in April 2012, the third in December 2013 on an Atlas V and the fourth by a Delta IVM in February 2016.

There is at least one other derivative of the KH-11 program, the MISTY series of two stealth satellites launched in February 1990 by the Shuttle *Atlantis* and in May 1999 by Titan 4B. These are very large electro-optical satellites weighing 43,220 pounds (19,600 kg) with stealth characteristics that significantly reduce its optical signature. They are coated in Vantablack, a material made of carbon nanotubes absorbing 99.965% of visible light. If able to avoid detection by ground-based optical instruments

BELOW **The signals intelligence obtained by dedicated satellites overlays that obtained from optical and radar-imaging satellites. This coverage by the VORTEX system and the earlier CHALET satellites allowed full global coverage, each satellite possessing an umbrella-shaped signals collecting dish, deployed on orbit, with a diameter of 125 feet (38 m).** *(David Baker)*

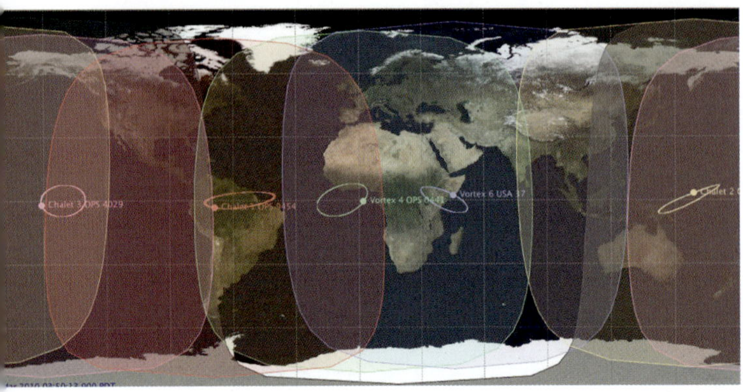

BELOW **MISTY is a variant of the KH-11 and has been launched by Shuttle and by Titan 4B. This stealthy satellite is probably coated with a Vantablack light-absorbing material and is capable of evading detection by conventional means.** *(David Baker)*

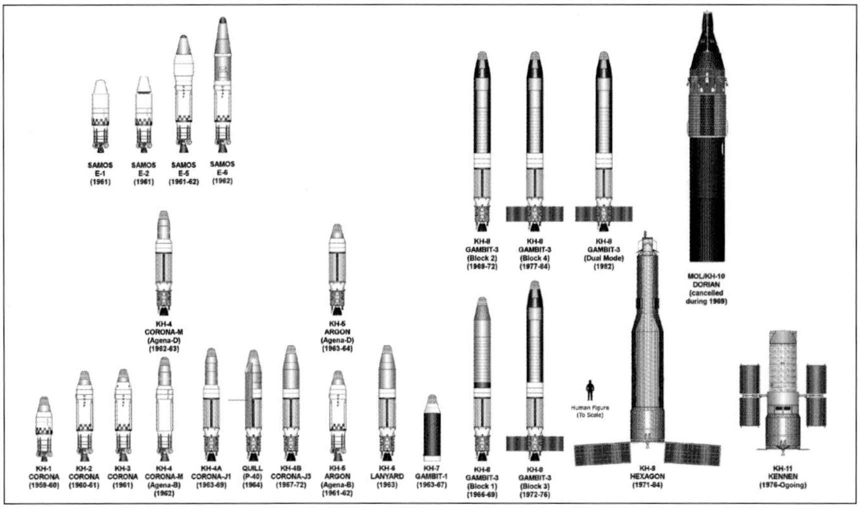

LEFT **Since 1959 spy-satellite flights have charted an ever-expanding range of capabilities and a widening level of sophistication, a roadmap of technologies in satellite design, optical engineering, space operations and performance.** *(Giuseppe de Chiara)*

satellites such as these could operate with impunity and, undetected, overfly denied areas on an unpredictable basis. They would also be very difficult to attack with killer satellites.

Outside government, and in parallel with uncertainties regarding the availability of replacement systems, the commercial world of satellite imagery has made great strides and the available resolution is almost equal to that from the best classified spy satellites. But there is more to photo-intelligence than resolution, and the specific capabilities and targeting schedules required by the intelligence community are very different to those of the commercial world, where satellites are orbited for their support of business activities in the hydrocarbon, environmental and national town and rural planning communities.

When the first of NASA's Landsat remote-sensing satellites was launched in the 1970s, government restrictions prevented US satellites from carrying cameras capable of a resolution better than 164 feet (50 m). The images broadcast by digital transmission to ground stations were available freely to anyone, anywhere. Their imaging products were of outstanding value in the developing countries where accurate surveys and inventorying of natural resources by conventional means was unavailable. But the fear from the US State Department was that high-resolution images could be used by terrorist organizations and rogue governments to plan and execute conflict.

This situation lasted only until the French Spot Image company, set up in the mid-1980s, provided commercial imagery down to 16 feet (5 m). Eventually, under great international pressure, the Americans rescinded this legal limit and opened the door to the current plethora of commercial high-resolution satellites, many emanating from companies in the US. Small, cheap and extremely powerful, they opened an opportunity for the military and the photo-intelligence world to utilize photo-reconnaissance more fully.

In the wake of the FIA fiasco there were considered to be three separate levels of intelligence imagery: high-resolution images obtained by electro-optical telescopes; medium-level resolution; and low-resolution coverage. The medium-resolution category was met under its Broad Area Satellite Imagery Collection program, which involved government satellites capable of resolution down to 9 inches (25 cm), while the low-resolution category would be met by procuring images at market prices from private companies. The logic of this evaporated when the commercial companies assured the government access to the defined requirement under medium-resolution, and plans for dedicated NRO satellites for that category were cancelled.

In March 2009, President Obama approved a new generation of improved reconnaissance satellites to replace the KH-11 and its derivatives. But that is another story.

Appendix 1

The intelligence community

Most countries have intelligence organizations to safeguard their citizens, to combat national crime, to root out and destroy terrorism and to serve as guardians of national law. The British have MI5 (formed in 1909) and the Americans have the FBI (Federal Bureau of Investigation, founded in 1908). Participation in foreign wars, however, led to a need for intelligence gathering outside the boundaries of host countries. In Britain, MI6 (the Secret Intelligence Service) was formed along with MI5, at the time to provide His Majesty's Government with intelligence information about foreign powers, their capabilities, intentions and actions.

The United States was very late forming a national foreign intelligence service. With a policy of non-intervention, and later isolation from world affairs, it was US entry into the First World War during 1917 that brought matters to the fore. But if the political elite in Washington DC lacked the foresight of many other countries, the armed services were not found wanting.

The oldest member of the US intelligence community is the Office of Naval Intelligence (ONI). Formed on March 23, 1882, by then Secretary of the Navy, William H. Hunt, it was tasked with obtaining information about foreign powers insofar as they affected plans for naval action, should that be required. First employed during the war with Spain in 1898 – paradoxically also involving Cuba – in which conflict Winston Churchill was a participant, it also extended its role to rooting out spies and saboteurs.

The US Army had less reason to engage in foreign intelligence: by definition and task it was not likely to confront foreign powers on a routine basis, unlike the Navy, which existed to protect US interests on the high seas and would routinely be called upon to operate in and among ships registered to foreign powers. The Army relied to some extent on the "intelligence" from the Department of State, which acquired information through its embassies around the world.

It should be remembered, however, that George Washington had been keen on acquiring intelligence information about the British during the War of Independence, but after his term as president this fell away and left the Army woefully ill-informed, which resulted in an embarrassing lack of preparedness during the war with Mexico declared in 1846. It was left to individual generals to set up their own personalized networks of spies and informants – hardly suitable clay for shaping a professional intelligence service! Even during the Civil War, Confederates and Union troops alike were limited in what they could achieve.

When the ONI was set up the Army organized its own mode of intelligence gathering, by forming a topographic mapping unit to serve the needs of local commanders in

BELOW The US intelligence community comprises 16 agencies under the auspices of the Office of the Director of National Intelligence. *(ODNI)*

the war with Spain – hardly suitable for strategic planning. While some organized intelligence groups were set up by the Army during the First World War, they were little more than reporting agents serving the tactical needs of field commanders. Not until June 1917, three months after America entered the conflict, was a Code and Cipher Bureau set up. By the 1930s, both the ONI and the Army Signals Intelligence Service had field stations across the Pacific Ocean collecting communications traffic from Japanese sources.

Since the First World War the Army had control of US military aviation, leaving the Navy and the Marine Corps to organize their own air combat and support units. Ground and air units obtained intelligence from individual reconnaissance units vital to the prosecution of military campaigns and in direct support of tactical ambitions. US military intelligence during the Second World War was an extension of what had evolved in the previous decade, lacking breadth and depth, but after 1945 US Army intelligence was consumed by a transformation which prepared the way for spy satellites.

Throughout the two world wars, from 1914 to 1945, British intelligence operations straddled the globe as the world's most advanced and sophisticated organization of its type – not only to directly support Allied military operations but also to empower active guerrilla units and partisans across Nazi-occupied Europe from the Pyrenees to the tip of Norway and from Sweden to the Mediterranean coast. Their covert operations greatly impressed the Americans and in 1942 William Stephenson, the senior British intelligence officer in America, advised President Roosevelt to combine the separate intelligence organizations into an active unit. On June 13 the Office of Strategic Services (OSS) was formed, which some regard as the forerunner to the CIA.

The outstanding achievements of the US Army Air Forces toward the end of the war encouraged a determination to separate air operations from the Army and this was achieved through an Act of Congress which set up the Department of Defense (DoD) to combine the interests of all four US armed services, including the Army, the Navy, the Marine Corps and the (yet to be separated) United States Air Force (USAF). General Leslie R. Groves had completed

BELOW US President Obama and Vice President Biden wait with Hillary Clinton and national security officials as intelligence information allows the senior leadership to follow the pursuit of terrorist leader Osama Bin Laden to his hideaway. Without an integrated net of intelligence information such pursuits would be impossible. *(White House)*

LEFT **Headquartered in Chantilly, Virginia, the National Reconnaissance Office was specifically formed to manage, develop and operate US intelligence-gathering satellites.** *(NRO)*

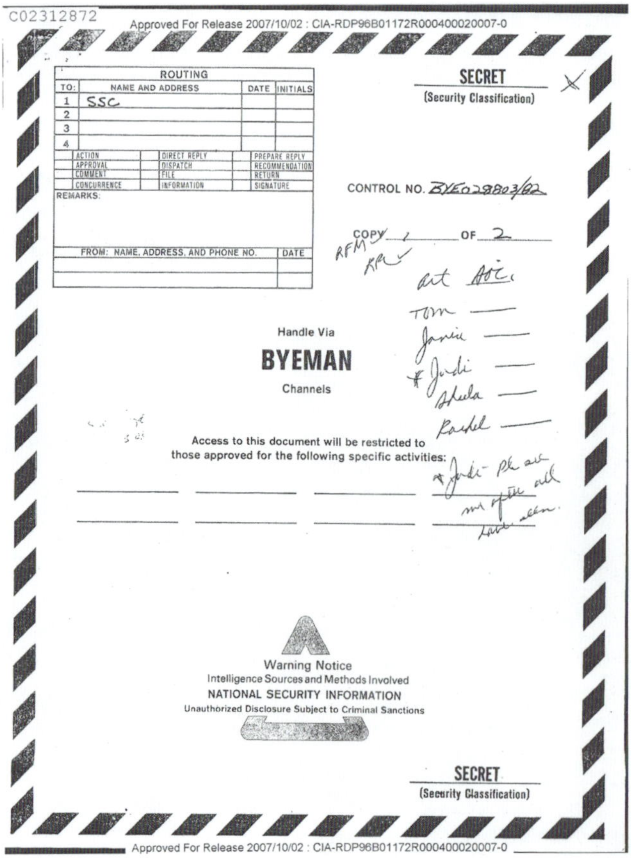

C02312872 Approved For Release 2007/10/02 : CIA-RDP96B01172R000400020007-0

ROUTING

TO:	NAME AND ADDRESS	DATE	INITIALS
1	SSC		
2			
3			
4			

ACTION	DIRECT REPLY	PREPARE REPLY
APPROVAL	DISPATCH	RECOMMENDATION
COMMENT	FILE	RETURN
CONCURRENCE	INFORMATION	SIGNATURE

REMARKS:

FROM: NAME, ADDRESS, AND PHONE NO.	DATE

SECRET
(Security Classification)

CONTROL NO. BYE029803/82

COPY 1 OF 2

Handle Via
BYEMAN
Channels

Access to this document will be restricted to those approved for the following specific activities:

Warning Notice
Intelligence Sources and Methods Involved
NATIONAL SECURITY INFORMATION
Unauthorized Disclosure Subject to Criminal Sanctions

SECRET
(Security Classification)

Approved For Release 2007/10/02 : CIA-RDP96B01172R000400020007-0

the new Pentagon building close to Washington DC in 1942 and went on to head the Manhattan Project developing the atomic bomb, both manifestations of a new resolve never again to retreat into a damaging period of isolation.

The National Security Act of July 26, 1947, which established the DoD (initially known as the National Military Establishment) and the USAF also set up the Central Intelligence Agency (CIA) and the National Security Council (NSC), the latter a tacit acknowledgement that the Department of State was incapable of handling foreign policy in an increasingly tense political environment with America confronting the Soviet Union.

Both the CIA and the NSC would be crucial in the development of advanced technological assets for intelligence gathering. The breadth of capability and the comprehensive mandate possessed by the CIA was a direct result of the British influence that served as its model, as well as the direct use of British MI6 personnel to help set it up. Never again would America be as vulnerable as it had been in the past, tragically epitomized by the pre-emptive attack on Pearl Harbor on December 7, 1941.

As intelligence gathering took on a new role and a more robust purpose, resilient and with a broad mandate, it armed itself with tools and instruments fit for the new technological age of nuclear weapons and Cold War confrontation. Intelligence operations had to be proactive, not reactive as they had been in the past. For that to be achieved, land, sea and air assets were recruited for the purpose of gathering comprehensive intelligence about every country on Earth, focusing particularly on unfriendly nations and those with a stated objective to

LEFT **The BYEMAN system controlled access to Keyhole programs and was a secure network of "need-to-know" access which securely locked out prying eyes and those without authority to access Top Secret and higher data.** *(NRO)*

confront the United States and its allies.

As recounted in Chapter 2, development of aerial reconnaissance stimulated deployment of Soviet air defense systems which quickly neutralized the advantage held by the U-2 spy-plane in overflying the Soviet Union and communist China, leaving American intelligence officials in need of a radical new method for obtaining direct information about defense programs potentially threatening to US interests. Although unprecedented, the decision in 1954 to put spy cameras in space was both radical and bold; nobody had placed an artificial satellite in space and the technology concept itself was challenged by some who believed that the decision had been made prematurely.

Before the development of spy satellites, however, another organization was set up to handle signals intelligence collected by other intelligence organs and to operate as an equivalent to the GCHQ (Government Communications Head Quarters) in the UK. GCHQ is the successor to operations in code-breaking and signals intelligence conducted during World War Two at Bletchley Park, England. The UK is a key player in the collection of signals intelligence and a recent major expansion has considerably increased the scale and scope of its activities, as well as the personnel employed, at Menwith Hill in Yorkshire – the largest data-gathering facility outside the US.

A key feeder for data and information into the NSA and the CIA is the National Reconnaissance Office (NRO), set up on August 25, 1960, on the orders of President Dwight D. Eisenhower. With headquarters in Fairfax County, Virginia, it was mandated to design and manufacture reconnaissance satellites and to provide images, but more especially signals intelligence, to the rest of the intelligence community. It was set up due to failings with the early CORONA and SAMOS spy satellite programs and to stand independently of the vested interests which benefitted from their products, to help get the technical management and development of these programs back on track and to manage their operation. The very existence of the NRO was not made public until September 1992.

The next major intelligence organization relevant to spy satellite activity is the Defense Intelligence Agency (DIA) which came into being on October 1, 1961, and which reports directly to the Secretary of Defense rather than through the regular chain of command. It is, in essence, the Pentagon's separate intelligence organization, but it is influential in that it alone contributes about a quarter of the President's Daily Report. Because it is a largely independent organ of the DoD, the DIA has a level of freedom to acquire information unaccountable through the usual channels, and satellite data is probably less important to its activities.

ABOVE The Defense Intelligence Agency provides a wide range of expertise and has been involved in a broad variety of assets, fed through spy satellite networks as well as involving other space-based capabilities, aircraft and naval vessels. *(DIA)*

After the CIA, the NSA, the NRO and the DIA, the most recent addition to the top tier of US intelligence-gathering organizations is the National Geospatial-intelligence Agency (NGA). Set up on October 1, 1996, it was originally named the National Imagery and Mapping Agency (NIMA), comprising several pre-existing organizations responsible for mapping and measurement of precise geospatial position-fixing. Satellite images are an important part of NGA activities but to a lesser degree than with the other security-related organizations. Located at Fort Belvoir, Springfield, Virginia, the NGA has recently moved into new headquarters for some of its 16,000 employees.

All these intelligence and national security organizations either manage or employ spy satellites and their products in the interests of

RIGHT The Memorial Wall at the Defense Intelligence Agency HQ at Joint Base, Anacostia-Bolling, Washington, DC, remembers those who have given their lives for the security of the United States and its allies. *(DIA)*

BELOW The National Geospatial and Mapping Agency is situated at Fort Belvoir, Springfield, Virginia, and has been a prolific user of mapping images from US satellites over several decades. *(NIMA)*

the United States and its allies. Collectively, they absorb a vast amount of resources and are expensive to run. Key spy satellite-related organizations consisting of the CIA, the NSA, the NRO and the NGA cost the American taxpayer considerably more than twice the annual budget of NASA – the National Aeronautics and Space Administration. And that total is, in turn, about one-half the total amount of money spent each year on intelligence for defence or national security.

More than 25% of the money spent on these capabilities goes to contractors outside the government, but the controls over access and the ability to maintain secrecy compliant with their mandates requires a special vetting and control system which began many decades ago. About 850,000 US citizens have access to top-secret information, barely one in 400 of the total population, yet even this number calls for special vetting and monitoring to avoid leaks and misuse of information.

Taking its name from a person who works underground – a *byeman* – when it was set up in 1961 to run the US spy satellite programs, the NRO adopted the Byeman Control System (BCS), configured a year earlier by the CIA. More commonly known simply as Byeman, it was phased out in 2005 and replaced with the Talent-Keyhole Control System (TKCS). That name was derived by combining classifications for highly sensitive photographs obtained from overflights of Soviet territory by manned aircraft set up in 1956 (Talent), and for information obtained from reconnaissance satellites from 1960 (Keyhole). The Byeman system protected the development of the satellites while the Talent and Keyhole systems controlled access to the data they produced, the latter folding into the former after 2005.

There are, of course, many more organizations connected to national intelligence in the US, but 16 – including those mentioned above – are bound into a federation known as the United States Intelligence Community. While this may appear repetitive in role, duplicating the activities of individual intelligence organs, in fact it collates and assesses national defense and security intelligence for independent recommendation, a filter in some respects, used by several government and national security leaders for a wide range of information. It also epitomizes the depth and breadth of information obtained by satellites tasked with providing the user community with unique assets obtained by what used to be known in official documents as "national technical means."

Appendix 2

Types of intelligence

There are several levels of intelligence that spy satellites serve in various proportions and in different categories of importance. Some of it is purely military, some is purely political, and a lot of it supports overall assessments of a nation's capability for domestic and foreign interventions and actions. Across a variety of intelligence-gathering functions, two crucial aspects must lock together to complete a full-spectrum analysis: spatial and temporal data collection and interpretation for dissemination to approved recipients.

Spatial intelligence covers a broad awareness of what is happening across the full geographic expanse of a country – a single-shot analysis of what exists across a very wide area. Temporal intelligence provides a measurement of long-term changes occurring at specific places within the regional distribution of national activity. Each requires a specific capability and, where spy satellites are used, two completely different types of asset in very different types of orbit.

In supporting foreign intelligence purposes regarding economic activity, spatial intelligence, for instance, may measure the total area given over to crop production or livestock farming, thus providing a measure of investment of national wealth in food production. Temporal intelligence in the same identical category would provide detailed information about the changes over time to the allocation of land to those particular activities. This information is crucial to assessment of how a country's econometrics is changing over time.

For military purposes, spatial intelligence could include a snapshot of where all the armed services have land bases, naval bases, depots, airfields, command centers, camps, munitions dumps etc. Temporal intelligence would add depth to that breadth of information by providing knowledge on how those assets are evolving over time, either increasing or decreasing at various places. Thus "information" providing analysis leads to "knowledge" about a country and its structures and its assets as they evolve.

But there is more to it than that. The general requirement determines the type of coverage required. For instance, it might be necessary to observe very large areas to gain spatial awareness of what is situated where. This calls for wide-angle observation, usually imagery, but the rate at which the observed targets within this large area change over time – its temporal dimension – determines how frequently the area must be viewed. That, in turn, dictates the priority of target assignment to any given wide-angle satellite coverage, a function known as surveillance.

If, within the large area previously observed, there are specific targets which are of special interest, a narrow-angle view helps focus attention in the image down upon the point of interest, concentrating the light-gathering capabilities of the telescope upon a smaller field of view (fov) – see Appendix 3. And the frequency with which activity at the target point

BELOW
Headquartered at Fort Meade, Maryland, the National Security Agency majors on electronic eavesdropping and signals intelligence, providing information to, and supporting, all US armed services as well as civilian agencies such as Homeland Security. *(NSA)*

ABOVE **The Utah Data Center at Bluffdale, Utah, is the national storage agency for extremely large volumes of data, some of which is gathered by satellite systems. It is largely run by the NSA but also serves as a pillar of the Comprehensive National Cybersecurity Initiative.** *(UDC)*

is expected to change drives the revisit rate of the imaging instrument to establish a temporal dimension to the changes observed.

Strategic intelligence covers a wide range of issues including not only the military capabilities of a country but also the economics and the political power-shifts that occur over time. In this way agencies require both spatial and temporal analysis to provide a complete and coherent picture of a country's assets, wealth, capabilities and economic performance over time.

Tactical intelligence supports short-term actions or activities that may be for surveillance, for proaction or for reaction. Surveillance for tactical purposes can maintain watch on a specific target to support planned pre-emptive military activities. Intelligence for tactical proactive purposes may support existing, continuing military action to assess its impact etc. Reactive tactical requirements observe a target (or location) to watch for changes that are pre-determined to trigger a prepared response.

Satellite intelligence gathering is usually one of several elements within a matrix of information and data. The analyst tasked with determining, or looking for, the location of a fixed set of parameters will assume that the vast assemblage of "unknown" information takes the form of a cube with three axes and six sides. Two of the three axes equate to the geodetic location (*x* and *y*) of the observed events (fixed but changing elements with a two-dimensional frame of reference), targets (specific objects of interest) or activities (fluidic motion of events) within the cube. The third axis is time (*t*).

The integration of the three axes within the cube allows "knowns" to be placed within the void of "unknowns," gradually placing an increasing number of the latter in an attempt to locate hidden "known-unknowns." This is best understood by analogy to, for instance, a breath of wind that moves a flag on its pole. The pole and the flag are "knowns" but the wind (being invisible) is the "known-unknown." In fact, if these undetectable but apparent elements or forces change the nature of the "knowns" (such as if the wind tears loose the flag or brings down the pole), then they become "critical known-unknowns." In every intelligence matrix the game is to highlight the "known-unknowns" to reveal the cause of the effect, or the inducement in the action for which there will be a reaction.

But there is another level to which the enemy or adversary seeks complete invisibility – the existence of "unknown-unknowns," which are those elements that the adversary will always attempt to hide deep within the matrix of "knowns" observed by his enemy. These can be crucial if left undetected and unsuspected (the very definition of "unknown-unknowns") and by shifting from analogy to real-world example the implications are apparent.

During the early 1970s, when the Strategic Arms Limitation Talks were under way, the Russians agreed to a verification method whereby US "national technical means" (spy satellites) would be used to take pictures of the open lids of underground silos containing Soviet

ICBMs as part of their nuclear arsenal. This was to ensure (to verify) that the Russians were not cheating on the number of missiles they had deployed – satellites would take pictures of the open silos and count the missiles.

But the SALT agreement also sought to limit the offensive strike power of individual Soviet missiles and, here too, the open-door policy seemed to allow the American spy satellites to ensure that the silos got no bigger, which implied that the size of the missiles would be constrained by the diameter of the silo. This was because the missile had to be much smaller in diameter than the silo itself to allow sufficient room for the rocket exhaust to escape up the sides of the silo as the missile ascended, cleared the ground and went on its way. Each side signed up to the agreement and each side would abide by the letter of the agreement.

However, after the agreement had been signed, the Russians changed the way they launched a bigger and more powerful ICBM by adopting the cold-launch concept employed by submarine-launched ballistic missiles (SLBMs). Instead of igniting the missile at the base of the tube to propel it out of the submarine (hot launch), SLBMs are ejected by pressurized gas like a cork from a champagne bottle, the rocket motor only igniting after the missile clears the surface.

Quite unexpected, as an "unknown-unknown," the Russians switched from hot-launch silos to the cold launch method. This meant a standard silo could accommodate a much bigger missile with more warheads in its aerodynamic shroud, contrary to the intention of the agreement, but perfectly within the letter of the attached protocols. In reply to protests, the Russians said they never sign intentions, only agreements. While some in the West condemned the Soviets as "cheats," others quietly rubbed their intellectual bruises and admitted they had been out-smarted.

This application of "lessons learned" has been repeated numerous times as the matrix of the "observable" invisible creates voids in which the coordinates of "knowns" and "unknowns" are frequently left floating in undefined locations. The balance between assumptions and belief is a very fine line made almost invisible by a belief in the technological superiority of "national technical means" and the inadequate preparedness over-confidence hauls along as excess baggage.

Intelligence gathering is about balancing "knowns," "unknowns" and "unknown-unknowns" and the spy satellites play a very big role in achieving that desired equilibrium which combines optical, radar and signals intelligence within an integrated and three-dimensional model of the real world. Another example illustrates this. Since the early days of the Cold War the USSR had been relying on grain imports to feed its people, and since the Khrushchev years (1953) there had been a program to boost meat production through imported feed grain.

One interest the CIA had was to use spy satellites to build a record of domestic grain production through spatial analysis set against their imports and to calculate, through temporal observation, the margin between imports used

BELOW A Zenit photograph of Washington, DC, taken by Russia's first-generation series of spy satellites, serving to remind spooks that the watchers are themselves being watched and that reconnaissance and surveillance is not the exclusive preserve of the United States. *(David Baker)*

to improve the range of foodstuffs available and food required for subsistence. Each year spy satellites would measure crop yield and provide a much more accurate picture to the State Department of annual production levels than was available through Russian figures.

This data was placed within the matrix of bargaining ploys used to apply pressure to the USSR over a wide range of bargaining interests so as to fold to US advantage interactions with Soviet politicians about subjects assessed as critical to Western interests. Infrared imaging was particularly useful here as it showed the level of health in crops and this too provided data on the grade level of farming standards across the USSR. Strategic intelligence such as this provided an advantage to Western diplomats.

But intelligence information from spy satellites was also of value within the United States, even down to advantages sought by one political party over another at presidential elections where national intelligence information could play to the advantage of one candidate over another. The classic case was the 1960 election where, according to the law, once nominated by their respective parties as the presidential candidate they each received classified security briefings so that they would be in a position to avoid embarrassing statements or promises they would later have to recant if they were successful and won the election.

As explained in Chapter 3, Republican President Dwight D. Eisenhower had a conservative view of economic policy and sought to balance the budget while using every conceivable application of smart-thinking and sound intelligence data to increase the value for each dollar the government spent on national defense. To the average American, far removed from the exalted halls of national intelligence, it appeared that the quiet actions of the president were a sign of apathetic disregard for the real danger from the USSR.

The election of 1960 came at the end of Eisenhower's second term and the public were interested in the actions of the party rather than the man, tainting Vice President Richard M. Nixon, standing for the highest office, with the perceived weakness in his boss. Standing against Nixon, Democrat nominee John F. Kennedy was aware of the frustration felt by hawkish defense chiefs such as General Curtis LeMay, head of Strategic Air Command, when the Eisenhower White House continually

BELOW The US's allies are integrally connected to its surveillance network. In the UK, the Government Communications Headquarters located at Cheltenham is a vital part of the net that stretches across the globe in the fight against aggression, terrorism, criminality and subversion. *(HMG)*

turned down their requests for major increases in ICBMs, manned bombers and exotic hypersonic research projects.

Kennedy played to his audience, ramping up discontent over defense issues and promising defense chiefs, the Air Force in particular, massive expansion of military power and a major increase in the nuclear arsenal. By late 1960 it had become apparent to intelligence officers that the USSR had very few ICBMs deployed while the US was rapidly expanding its weapons capability with more than 1,600 jet bombers capable of dropping nuclear bombs on Russia and rapid growth in ICBM deployment. Eisenhower was unable to declare this position vis-à-vis the USSR, or how he knew it, due to the security classification of the CORONA program. But as presidential nominee, Kennedy received classified briefings on the general situation.

Kennedy was briefed by the CIA on July 23 and on September 19, where he was given secret information about the true position, but there was no corroboration from Top Secret data. At a third intelligence briefing, this time from the Navy, Kennedy learned that projections of an impending disparity in force levels were unfounded and not corroborated by the best US intelligence. Kennedy chose to ignore this information and publicly fuelled alarmist warnings about a runaway "missile-gap," making this a major element in his campaign.

After he became president in January 1961 by a very narrow margin, Kennedy began to wind back expectations of major defense, missile and nuclear force expansion, claiming that intelligence information he had received after taking office showed no gap and that in fact, as the US was ahead of Russia in missile deployments, there would be no need to increase force levels, to the fury and anger of service chiefs. The services never did get their massive overkill, although the quiet policies of the Eisenhower administration would keep the US far ahead of the USSR until the mid-1970s, when the Russians began to close the gap.

This story has a sequel. When confronting Khrushchev over missile deployments to Cuba in October 1962, Kennedy knew the Russians were massively outnumbered and that they would never risk annihilation over a few intermediate-range nuclear weapons on a far-off island. To the general public, who still believed the Russians to pose a strategic threat far beyond the reality of the situation, it was a close-run thing and Kennedy triumphed in a poker game he could not have risked had it not been for spy satellites.

ABOVE Menwith Hill, Yorkshire, England, is one of the largest electronic monitoring stations in the world and has a large number of satellite dishes for connecting with British interests around the globe, as well as supporting the interests of NATO and the Atlantic Alliance, work that frequently incorporates the use of satellite data. *(David Baker)*

LEFT One of the many weather protection domes for satellite dishes at Menwith Hill. *(David Baker)*

Appendix 3

Instrument capabilities

In examining the possibilities opened up by satellite reconnaissance, the Air Force evaluated the steps in development that had, by 1950, brought a revolution in both cameras and operating equipment. The major breakthrough had occurred around 1943 when specialized, highly trained photographic observers were carried along on combat missions to record targets of interest while the main body of the few went about the business of destroying enemy targets. In that year camera technology reached a level of sophistication where the Air Corp observers were redundant and the specialist training camp at Brooke Field, Texas, closed.

By the early 1950s aerial reconnaissance equipment could provide high-quality black and white images on wet film at heights of up to 55,000 feet (16,760 m) in clear daylight or 40,000 feet (12,190 m) on a clear moonlit night. Cameras with automatic exposure controls had focal lengths of from 3 inches (7.6 mm) to 20 feet (6 m) with format sizes from 5 square inches (32.2 cm^2) to nearly 5 square feet (0.464 m^2). The theoretical resolution of the day was around 40 lines per millimeter, but losses through atmospheric aberration reduced that to 10–14 lines per millimeter. The level of automation which had closed down the observer training schools in favor of automated cameras installed within the aircraft itself, provided image motion

BELOW Several thousand objects encircle the globe from 60 years of space activity, a lot of it devoted to matters of national security, intelligence gathering and the support of military forces at home and abroad. Among these pieces of debris may be rogue weapons launched by dysfunctional states. The monitoring of intentions among lawless groups on Earth and the threat from such weapons is a functional part of securing the protection of law-abiding people around the globe. *(John Adams)*

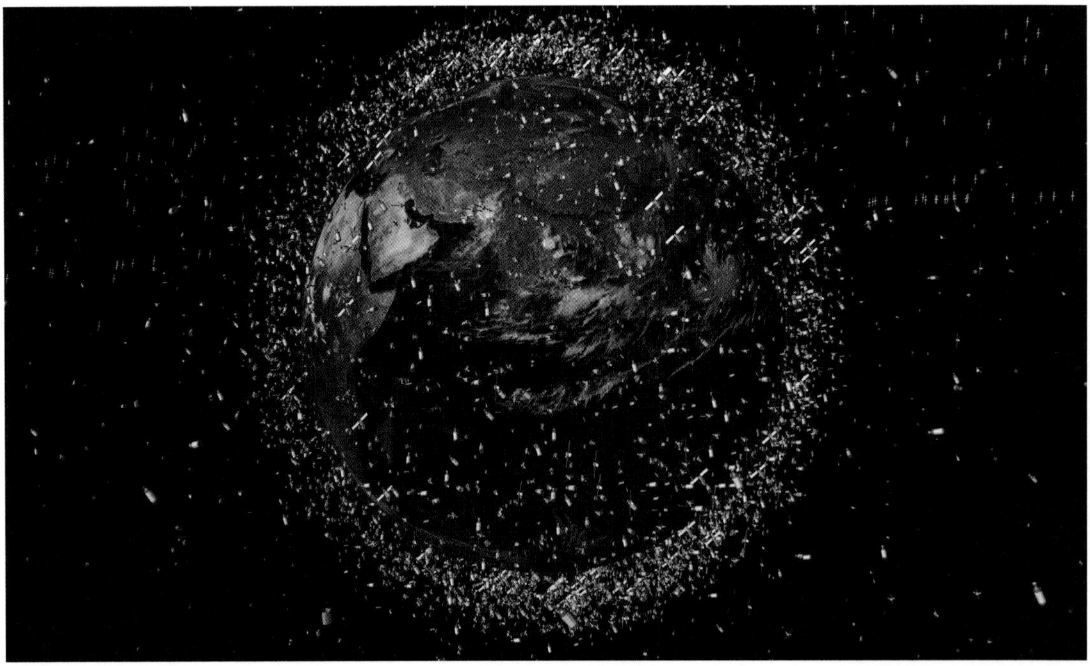

LEFT The badge of the US Intelligence Community is a reminder of an unblinking surveillance, an essential part of a disciplined, peaceful and productive community. *(USIC)*

compensation according to the required setting determined by altitude.

Tasked with examining the possibilities of designing an orbiting photo-reconnaissance satellite, RAND calculated that the motion of a high-flying subsonic photographic aircraft would pass a single identifiable point on the Earth at about 880 feet/second (268 m/sec) while the same spot as viewed from a satellite would appear to move at 23,467 feet/second (7,152 m/sec) – slightly less than the distance travelled by the satellite in its orbit because it is in a higher position relative to the surface of Earth.

The challenges for camera systems selected for satellite work were high and the initial specification for their development was quite conservative. However, because the satellite was so much higher than an aircraft, the slant-angle view was far greater and the optical qualities of the system favored wide-angle shots of large areas. This suited the military, as deep penetration of Soviet airspace took advantage of special camera systems being applied to wide-area surveillance.

In 1948 a demonstration flight was made across the United States from Los Angeles to New York using a "tri-metrogon" system. A continuous strip of images was made from an altitude of 40,000 feet (12,190 m) using one central camera with additional cameras either side for oblique views. By the mid-1950s, the US Air Force was routinely using cameras with a focal length of 6 inches (152 mm) or 12 inches (305 mm) focal length but relatively short lenses to provide wide-area coverage from high altitude. The smaller cameras were designated K-17C, K-22, KA-12 and T-11, while the larger ones included the K-38, KA-1 and KA-2. A wide range of aircraft carried these types, from the giant RB-36 to the RF-104 Starfighter. The Fairchild K-17C produced 9-inch (228 mm) square negatives from a magazine with 390 feet (119 m) of film, 9.5 inches (241 mm) wide.

The camera was highly adaptable and could accommodate lenses of 6 inches (152 mm) f/6.3, 12 inches (305mm) f/5.0, or 24 inches (610 mm) f/6.0 relative aperture. The *relative* aperture is obtained by dividing the focal length by the diameter of the lens' *effective* aperture. It describes the amount of light the lens transmits at various settings of the iris diaphragm. Shutter speeds ranged from 1/50 second to 1/400 second. The camera could take an image every 1.5 seconds. For coverage horizon to horizon, across the line of flight, three tri-metrogon cameras would be mounted in the forward bay of the RB-36 forward of the vertical station.

Also by the mid-1950s, these cameras were rapidly becoming obsolete as the technology, as well as the capability, was undergoing a massive revolution. Panoramic cameras were becoming practicable and these would have a great influence on the attraction of satellite application as well as the expanded capabilities of airborne photo-reconnaissance aircraft. Since March 1949 Perkin-Elmer had been developing a transverse panoramic camera that employed a rotating prism to produce a wide sweep of the terrain.

Designated E-1, this bulky camera carried its film spool in the ceiling of the fuselage, which translated down into a sleeve in the format area. This allowed very great lengths of film to be carried, limited only by the capacity of the aircraft to contain the spool, and by separating camera from film spool it reduced the challenge of stabilizing a combined spool/camera assembly. The E-1 incorporated a 122 mm lens with negatives 18 inches (45.7 cm) wide by several meters in length.

Because of its bulk, the Air Force sought a compact version, developed by Vectron as the E-2, test versions being available by May 1953. This camera was on the critical path to the camera systems used in the first US reconnaissance satellites and as such is worthy of explanation.

The E-2 was designed to provide a

resolution of 20–25 lines per millimeter, while the triple-scanners in the RVB-36 were capable of 20–25 lines, much lower than the standard single-frame cameras. The higher resolution of the E-2 was in part due to the design. One beneficial aspect of its design was that only the focal plane and optics required stabilization. The focal plane is the area perpendicular to the lens axis where the quality of the image is optimum for a given focal length and lens aperture.

The E-2 provided 150° of ground coverage transverse to the line of flight, with graded image compensation, taking it from zero at one horizon to maximum 3,320 mm/second at the nadir and progressively back to zero at the opposite horizon. Moreover, because the camera utilized a focal-plane shutter that incorporated a variable-width slit sweeping across the negative plane, precise exposure control was available for every point on the negative from one horizon to the other.

With a total weight of 1,600 pounds (725 kg), the E-2 was slightly down on the multiple cameras of the same focal length with a bulk only half as great. The camera was more reliable because there were fewer moving parts and, because those moved at slower speeds, it had less shock and vibration. Maximum diameter was about 31 inches (78.7 cm).

The USAF Aerial Reconnaissance Laboratory (ARL) expected to have the E-2 ready for operational testing by 1956 and applied sufficient funds to make that happen. Operationally, it was assessed to provide a coverage of 180° and be capable of resolving objects as small as 4 feet (1.22 m) square from an altitude of about 100,000 feet (30,000 m) with object recognition 16 feet (4.88 m) square. The ARL planned to deploy the camera with 5-foot (1.5 m) resolution that moved through the gate at a constant speed, a process that assisted rapid processing.

The E-2 was but one of several new types of area-surveillance as well as high-resolution mapping cameras developed during the mid to late 1950s for a range of aerial and space-based platforms. Very few people outside the "need-to-know" fraternity were fully cognizant of why these driving imperatives were being encouraged with such effort, and almost all outside that elite fraternity believed them to be aimed at very fast, high-altitude aircraft, some of which were then in development.

A general operational requirement was issued around 1955–56 for an aerial mapping capability far beyond anything which had existed before, or which could be reasonably predicted by leading camera experts of the period. That story is told in Chapter 3, but the extraordinary requirements called for appear to have amazed the very people responsible for drawing up the specification. It was required, said the document, to achieve a "time-phased increase in the amount of detail that can be recorded on film and thus provide an effective substitute for increased focal length, bulk and weight of equipment, and the present production of fantastic quantities of negatives and print…a single small photograph taken from very high altitude will yield, when examined by a microscope, the same amount of information that now is extracted from thousands of aerial photographs." It seems even the authors of the document were impressed by their own request!

Å – Ångström: one ten-billionth of a meter (0.1 nm).

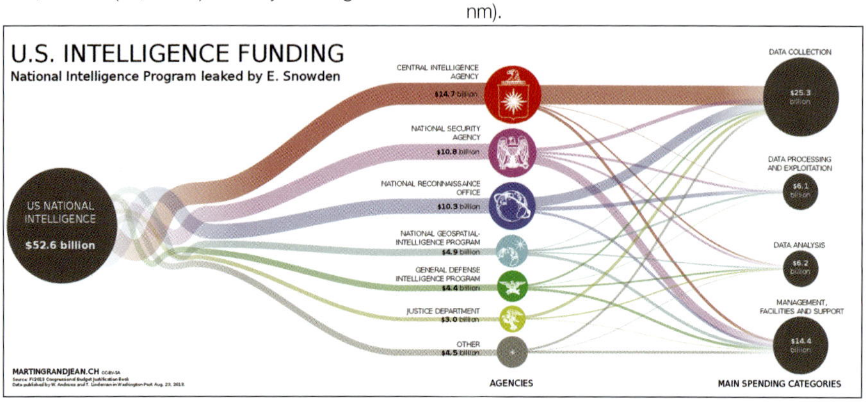

RIGHT **Security is expensive, as shown by this graphic of national intelligence and security expenditure in 2013.** *(The Washington Post)*

Abbreviations

ABM – Anti-ballistic missile.
ACS – Attitude Control System.
ACTS – Attitude Control and Translation System.
AFB – Air Force Base.
AFBMD – Air Force Ballistic Missile Division.
AFSC – Air Force Systems Command.
AMU – Astronaut Maneuvering Unit.
APSA – Auxiliary Payload Structure Assembly.
APTC – Astro-Position Terrain Camera.
ARDC – Air Research and Development Command.
ARL – Aerial Reconnaissance Laboratory.
ARPA – Advanced Research Projects Agency.
ARS – Advanced Reconnaissance System.
BCS – Byeman Control System.
BMD – Ballistic Missile Division.
BMEWS – Ballistic Missile Early Warning System.
CIA – Central Intelligence Agency.
COMAR – Committee on Overhead Reconnaissance.
DDR&E – Directorate of Defense Research and Engineering.
DIA – Defence Intelligence Agency.
DISIC – Dual Improved Stellar Index Camera.
DMSP – Defense Meteorology Satellite Program.
DoD – Department of Defense.
DRV – Data Return Vehicle.
DSP – Defense Support Program.
Δ**V** – Delta-velocity.
ELINT – Electronic intelligence.
ESSA – Environmental Science Services Administration.
FIA – Future Imaging Architecture.
fov – Field of view.
ft – Feet.
G^3 – Advanced GAMBIT.
G&N – Guidance and navigation.
GE – General Electric.
GHz – Gigahertz.
GOR – General Operational Requirement.
GRAB – Galactic Radiation and Background.
Humint – Human intelligence gathering.
ICBM – Intercontinental ballistic missile.
IGY – International Geophysical Year.
IMCS – Improved Metric CRYSTAL System.
IR – Infrared.
IRBM – Intermediate-range ballistic missile.
IRFNA – Inhibiting red fuming nitric acid.
KH – Key Hole.
kN – Kilonewton(s).
LRBM – Long-range ballistic missile.
LTTAT – Long Tank Thrust-Augmented Thor, or Thorad.
Mach – Speed of sound.
MAD – Mutual assured destruction.
MC – Mapping Camera.
MCS – Minimal Command System.
MHz – Megahertz.
MIDAS – Missile Defense Alarm Satellite.
min – Minute(s).
MISS – Man-In-Space-Soonest.
MIT – Massachusetts Institute of Technology.
Mk – Mark.
MM – Mission Module.
MODS – Military Orbital Development System.
MOL – Manned Orbiting Laboratory.
MTPS – Military Test Pilot Station.
NACA – National Advisory Committee for Aeronautics.
NASA – National Aeronautics and Space Administration.
NATO – North Atlantic Treaty Organization.
NGA – National Geospatial-intelligence Agency.
NIE – National Intelligence Estimate.
NIMA – National Imagery and Mapping Agency.
nm – Nautical mile(s).
NOAA – National Oceanic and Atmospheric Administration.
NOSS – Naval Ocean Surveillance System.
NRL – Naval Research Laboratory.
NRO – National Reconnaissance Office.
NSA – National Security Agency.
NSC – National Security Council.
OAM – Orbit Adjust Module.
OCV – Orbital Control Vehicle.
OM – Optics Module.
ONI – Office of Naval Intelligence.
OSCAR – Orbiting Satellite Carrying Amateur Radio.
OSS – Office of Strategic Services.
OTH – Over-the-horizon.
PHOTINT – Photographic intelligence.
PPS – Primary propulsion system.
RAF – Royal Air Force.
RAND – Research and Development.
RCM – Reaction Control Module.
RCS – Reaction Control System.
RFNA – Red fuming nitric acid.
rpm – Revolutions per minute.
RTG – Radioisotope thermo-electric generator.
RV – Re-entry vehicle.
SAC – Strategic Air Command.
SALT – Strategic Arms Limitation Talks.
SAM – Surface-to-air missile.
SDS – Satellite Data System.
sec – Second(s).
SIGINT – Signals intelligence.
Skunk Works – Classified manufacturing facility at Burbank, California.
SLBM – Submarine-launched ballistic missile.
SLC – Space Launch Complex.
SMC – Space and Missile Systems Center.
SMEC – Strategic Missiles Evaluation Committee.
SNAP – Systems for nuclear auxiliary power.
SPS – Secondary propulsion system.
SRV – Satellite Recovery Vehicle.
STL – Space Technology Laboratories.
SV – Satellite Vehicle.
TAT – Thrust-Augmented Thor.
TCP – Technological Capabilities Panel.
Tiros – Television and Infra-Red Observation System.
TKCS – Talent-Keyhole Control System.
TWT – Travelling-wave-tube.
UDMH – Unsymmetrical dimethylhydrazine.
USAF – United States Air Force.
WDD – Western Development Division.

Glossary

acquiesced Accepted or complied.

bulwark Something, often a wall, the provides protection.

clandestine Done in a private or secret way.

cryogenic Of, relating to, or requiring the use of very low temperatures.

curio A small object that is unusual, rare or interesting.

drogue parachute A small parachute used for stabilizing or decelerating something or for pulling a larger parachute out of stowage.

fiscal year A 12-month period used by an organization, government, or business for accounting purposes; a fiscal year does not have to be the same as the standard calendar year.

galvanize To cause people to become excited or concerned about something, often so that they want to do something about it.

half-life The time it takes for half the nuclei in a radioactive substance to spontaneously disintegrate.

humint Short for human intelligence gathering; covert intelligence-gathering by people such as spies.

International Geophysical Year An international program that consisted of geophysical research conducted from July 1957 to December 1958.

jettison To get rid of or drop something, often from a moving ship or aircraft.

reconnaissance Military activity in which soldiers or aircraft are sent to observe and find out information about an enemy.

sortie A mission or attack by a single plane.

vagaries Changes that are difficult to predict or control.

For More Information

Central Intelligence Agency (CIA)
Office of Public Affairs
Washington, DC 20505
(703) 482-0623
Website: www.cia.gov
Facebook: @Central.Intelligence.Agency
Twitter: @CIA
YouTube: Central Intelligence Agency
The CIA was created with the signing, by President Truman, of the National Security Act in 1947. The agency is tasked with providing national security intelligence to top-ranking US government officials.

NASA
300 E. Street SW, Suite 5R30
Washington, DC 20546
(202) 358-0001
Website: www.nasa.gov
NASA is the space agency of the United States. Its vision is to "reach for new heights and reveal the unknown for the benefit of humankind." NASA has been instrumental in US spy satellite programs.

National Air and Space Museum
Independence Ave at 6th St, SW
Washington, DC 20560
(202) 633-2214
Website: airandspace.si.edu
Facebook and Twitter: @airandspace
YouTube: Smithsonian National Air and Space Museum
The Smithsonian's National Air and Space Museum maintains the world's largest collection of aviation and space artifacts. It is the most visited museum in the country, and its exhibits often feature interesting information on US spy satellites.

National Museum of the US Air Force
1100 Spaatz Street
Wright-Patterson AFB, OH 45433
(937) 255-3286
Website: www.nationalmuseum.af.mil
Facebook and Twitter: @AFmuseum
The National Museum of the US Air Force features fascinating exhibits and collections, and offers special programs and educational outreach to teach the public about the history of the United States Air Force. Located at Wright-Patterson Air Force Base, near Dayton, Ohio, it is the oldest and largest military aviation museum in the world.

For Further Reading

Bougie, Matt. *Strategic Inventions of the Cold War*. New York, NY: Cavendish Square Publishing, 2016.

Byers, Ann. *The Legacy of the Cold War.* New York, NY: Cavendish Square Publishing, 2018.

Cobb, Allan B. *How the US Security Agencies Work*. Minneapolis, MN: Core Library, An Imprint of Abdo Publishing, 2015.

Connolly, Kieron. *America's Bloody History from World War II to the Civil Rights Movement*. New York, NY: Enslow Publishing, 2017.

Dienesch, Robert M. *Eyeing the Red Storm: Eisenhower and the First Attempt to Build a Spy Satellite*. Lincoln, NE: University of Nebraska Press, 2016.

Ford, Jeanne Marie. *Code Breakers and Spies of World War I*. New York, NY: Cavendish Square, 2019.

Hamilton, John. *Missiles and Spy Satellites*. Minneapolis, MN: Abdo Publishing, 2019.

Hurt, Avery Elizabeth. *Code Breakers and Spies of the Cold War*. New York, NY: Cavendish Square, 2019.

Langston-George, Rebecca. *Deep-Cover Spies and Double-Crossers of the Cold War*. North Mankato, MN: Compass Point Books, 2017

Lassieur, Allison. *Cyber Spies and Secret Agents of Modern Times*. North Mankato, MN: Compass Point Books, 2017.

Lusted, Marcia Amidon. *World War II Espionage*. Minneapolis, MN: Abdo Publishing, 2016.

Mitchell, Susan K. *The Secret World of Spy Agencies*. Berkeley Heights, NJ: Enslow Publishers, 2012.

Rice, Earle, Jr. *Rockets & Satellites: Surveillance from Space*. New York, NY: Enslow Publishers, 2017.

Samuels, Charlie. *Machines and Weaponry of the Cold War*. New York, NY: Gareth Stevens Publishing, 2013.

Small, Cathleen. *Code Breakers and Spies of World War II*. New York, NY: Cavendish Square, 2019.

Index